Wildwood

Wildwood

COOKING FROM THE SOURCE IN THE PACIFIC NORTHWEST

CORY SCHREIBER

LOCATION PHOTOGRAPHY BY Jerome Hart
FOOD PHOTOGRAPHY BY Richard Jung

TEN SPEED PRESS
Berkeley   Toronto

*— **This book is dedicated to Pamela, Arianna & Graham.***

Upper left title page photo:

The Wachsmuth clan on the Long Beach Peninsula, c. 1923. From left to right: Edith Wachsmuth, Chester Wachsmuth Sr. (Uncle Chet), Meinert Wachsmuth Jr., Louis Charles Wachsmuth (founder of the Oyster Bar), Jack Cottle, Elizabeth Cottle, Richard T. Wachsmuth, and Louis Arthur Wachsmuth (my grandfather).

Lower left title page photo:

Louis Charles Wachsmuth with sons, c. 1939.

Ten Speed Press
P.O. Box 7123
Berkeley, California 94707
www.tenspeed.com

Distributed in Australia by Simon and Schuster Australia, in Canada by Ten Speed Press Canada, in New Zealand by Southern Publishers Group, in South Africa by Real Books, and in the United Kingdom and Europe by Airlift Books.

Design by Nancy Austin

Black-and-white photography © 2000 by Jerome Hart

Food photography © 2000 by Richard Jung

Historical photography from the author's family archive

Recipes from Chapter 11, "James Beard's Passion for Oregon," reprinted with the permission of Scribner, a division of Simon & Schuster, from *Delights and Prejudices* by James Beard. © 1964 James Beard

Library of Congress Cataloging-in-Publication Data
Schreiber, Cory, 1961-
    The Wildwood cookbook: cooking from the source / Cory Schreiber.
         p. cm.
    Includes index.
    ISBN 1-58008-142-8 (cloth)
         1. Cookery--Oregon. I. Title.
 TX715 .S29698 2000
 641.59795--dc21

First printing, 2000

Printed in China

4 5 6 7 8 9 10 – 09 08 07 06 05

CONTENTS

3. Dan & Louis Oyster Bar: Spanning the Century ⟶ 36

4. The Willamette Valley: Spring Vegetables ⟶ 58

5. Sauvie Island: An Agricultural Island with Outlets to the City — 82

6. From the Coast to the Cascades: In Search of the Wild Mushroom — 102

7. Oregon Wine Country: True Flavor from the Soil — 124

8. The Lower Columbia River Region: Game and Fowl Cookery — 142

9. The Willamette Valley: Summer's Bounty of Berries ⟶ 164

10. The Hood River Valley: Orchards in the Shadow of Mount Hood ⟶ 186

11. James Beard's Passion for Oregon:

Favorite Recipes from *Delights & Prejudices* — 210

Wildwood Pantry: Basic Recipes and Techniques — 221

ACKNOWLEDGMENTS

My special thanks are due to many individuals who have assisted, contributed, and helped nurture this book along its path.

Donna Neerhout, who understood the essential quality of the narrative portion of the book. After being familiar with my family for over twenty years, she was able to share the vision of the stories and anecdotes, working with great passion, organization, and tireless perfection.

My mother, LouAnn Schreiber, and father, Roy J. Schreiber Jr., who allowed me to observe the qualities of the Pacific Northwest with endless outings and discoveries in the early years, including letting me work in the family restaurant at age eleven!

Tucker Wachsmuth, the family historian, who shared facts, stories, and photographs to no end.

Sandy Krogh, who professionally tested the recipes in her kitchen and contributed to building a standardized and functional recipe format.

Jerry Hart, for his understanding of the Pacific Northwest landscape and ability to translate those images to the pages of this book. Richard Jung, who allowed me to work with the food in my own way, capturing the finished recipes in their natural form.

Morgan Brownlow, who brought precise details to the preparation and execution of the food.

Phil Wood, Kirsty Melville, Aaron Wehner, and Nancy Austin, the great people at Ten Speed Press, who understood the unique quality of this book and led me through the process of understanding the detailed steps, always visualizing the end result.

Carolyn Miller and Sharon Silva, for lending their editorial expertise to the book.

To all of the staff at Wildwood Restaurant, especially Jennifer Welshhons, who contributed her dessert recipes; Jesse Dodson who shared the bread recipes; and Krista Anderson, Brad Root, and Adam Sappington, who tested and contributed recipes. Also to Hal Finkelstein, Randy Goodman, Mary Peterson, and Steve Walterscheid, who keep things running smoothly.

INTRODUCTION

Pacific Northwest Origins—Cooking from the Source

"No place on earth, with the exception of Paris, has done as much to influence my professional life," wrote James Beard in *Delights & Prejudices*, describing his native Oregon. As a man who experienced much that the world has to offer, Beard recognized the magic of the region from which he came and the endless potential of its indigenous ingredients.

It occurred to me upon my return to Portland in the spring of 1994 that I was like a salmon returning to my native waters. I had covered great distances and experienced many culinary adventures, yet my instincts had brought me full circle, back to where the journey began. It was this sense of renewal that inspired me to open the Wildwood Restaurant soon after my return.

A fifth-generation Oregonian, I've always considered the Pacific Northwest my true home. I am the great-grandson of a well-known Portland restaurateur, so food is my heritage. I remember walking through my father's garden in our rural Oregon home during early childhood; working in my family's oyster beds in Yaquina Bay; and, a few years later, seeing the excitement on a farmer or forager's face as he or she brought wild mushrooms or local vegetables into the kitchen of the Benson Hotel during my apprenticeship there. My early appreciation for the unique flavors and feel of the Northwest has developed into a passion for the land and the riches it has to offer. The caliber and variety of the region's ingredients have helped shape my culinary style, which focuses on simple preparations that preserve the natural flavors of these foods. Even now, my backyard garden is of great value, as it constantly reminds me of how foods are grown and the importance of considering such origins when creating recipes.

Practicing the philosophy of "cooking from the source" opens new dimensions in the kitchen, as it moves the cook one step back in the process to the abundant garden, the saltwater oyster or clam bed, the damp indigenous forest, and all other places where foods are found and produced. Gaining a basic understanding of sources means learning about the seasonal availability of ingredients; the different kinds of soil and their impact on the flavor of fruits and vegetables; the importance of numerous varieties of produce and how their differences inspire endless culinary possibilities; the fishing industry and the politics of wild salmon in the Pacific Northwest; the growing of wine grapes and how our maritime climate affects them—the list is almost endless.

A great meal begins with shopping for the ingredients. The quality of your selections will determine, long before you begin cooking the meal, how the flavors, textures, and overall appeal of a dish will be achieved. Farmer's markets are wonderful resources that allow us to come into direct contact with the people who grow the foods we consume and who provide stewardship of the renewable lands on which they rely. When purchasing high-quality local foods, we begin to see the link between the farmers and the community and the importance of this relationship. When talking to farmers in the marketplace, I find inspiration for the Wildwood menu based on what they tell me about local foods and their availability. This creates a process that continually renews itself and connects us back to the land and the resources it provides.

Within these chapters, I will share with you, the reader, the part of this process that the Wildwood kitchen engages in on a daily basis. Along the way, I will lead you on a culinary tour through the landscape of the Pacific Northwest, from the early beginnings of my family in the small village of Oysterville in the southwest corner of Washington, where my great-great-grandfather was a pioneer in the late 1800s, to spring in the Willamette Valley; from summer produce on Sauvie Island, located just outside of Portland, to mushroom gathering in the damp forest of the coastal mountains. In the hope of bringing the unique qualities of each of these regions into high relief, I have organized the recipes by place rather than by course. The recipes themselves focus on time-honored techniques and pairings that allow the natural beauty and flavors of the ingredients to shine forth. I've also included historic recipes that have withstood the test of time. Among them is an oyster stew that has remained popular at my family's restaurant for close to one hundred years.

History, tradition, and place—these are all themes woven throughout this book, and they have had a profound influence on my life and cooking style. Within these pages are my origins, and I invite you to share in the bounty of the Pacific Northwest with me.

OYSTERVILLE

Oysterville
Ford

1. OYSTERVILLE: EARLY BEGINNINGS

*Christina Wachsmuth Cottle
(Aunt Christina)*

Meinert Wachsmuth Sr.

*I*t was not quite sunrise, but close enough. As the moon took its leave, it tugged the tide and pulled us from our sleep—it was time for clamming with Aunt Christina. With groggy anticipation, my mother, father, brother, sister, and I fumbled to get dressed and set out into the silent morning. Through the dawn, we watched the sea fog hug the Washington coast with a sleepy embrace that would lift by daylight.

Our morning expeditions took us to the ocean side of the Long Beach Peninsula. This sliver of land, located in the southwest corner of Washington state, hosts a procession of small towns, including Ocean Park, Nahcotta, and Oysterville. To the east lies Willapa Bay, which runs north along the peninsula until it meets the ocean at Leadbetter Point.

As a boy of two, armed with a bucket and shovel, I dug into the cold sand with visions of buried treasures left by bands of pirates. Meanwhile, my family hunted for treasures of their own: razor clams for that evening's dinner.

At the age of eighty-five, Aunt Christina was by far the fastest clam digger anyone had ever seen. During low tide, she'd be out in the breaking waves watching for air bubbles, the betrayers of hiding clams. Spotting the bubbles, she'd make a clean scoop in the wet sand. The long, thin blade of her shovel ensured victory over the clams' attempts to dive deeper. As the tide began to rise, she continued her pursuit on drier land, where her shovel moved faster, or the clams a little slower.

My history with Oysterville dates back to 1864, when my great-great-grandfather, Meinert Wachsmuth, arrived from San Francisco on the sailing ship *Sarah Louise*. The township, established in 1854 along Shoalwater Bay, had become a well-known supplier of oysters on the West Coast. By the time Meinert arrived, the community had grown to a population of five hundred and was in full swing, with three hotels, three saloons, boat shops, blacksmith stables, general stores, a tannery, a school, and a church.

Oysterville is the northernmost town on the peninsula. Part of its charm is that it hasn't changed much over the past century. White picket fences surround the older homes, and inside, collections of old bottles stand on crooked windowsills creating a kaleidoscope of color in the summer light. Salal berries, salmon berries, azaleas, and wild coast blackberries line the streets of town. Batches of blueberries and raspberries abound in the summer months behind my cousin Tucker's cabin, offering a morning meal to be picked and eaten with nothing more than a splash of cream and a dusting of sugar. Merchant Street and Clay

Street are only grassy paths now, lazy reminders of the once-bustling thoroughfares that led to the bay.

The locals derived the name Shoalwater Bay from the nautical term shoal, which refers to a shallow place in a body of water. Today, the area is commonly referred to as Willapa Bay among nonnatives, and its saltwater estuary still produces large numbers of commercially grown oysters, mussels, and clams.

For my family, Oysterville is a beloved place that offers a common ground and comforting memories. The only piece of property that I truly own in this world is in this place: a one-thousand-square-foot plot of mud with a bed of hard-shell littleneck clams hiding beneath it. Part of the area's allure is its tranquillity, which seems to cast a calming spell on each of its visitors. Just wander barefoot into the pools of the bay, and you'll immediately feel the warmth of the water. Kneel down in the mud and use your hand to follow the bubble holes like the ones Aunt Christina found so easily with her trusty shovel. The only sound you will hear is the suck of the mud pulling up with a clam when you claim it as your own.

The unique old-fashioned quality of Oysterville inspired me at a young age to appreciate the gathering of food in its natural habitat. Finding, capturing, and bringing home wild salmon, razor clams, wild berries, oysters, or Dungeness crab were daily rituals in my family's history in this area for over one hundred years. These activities were carried out with a tremendous respect for ingredients and the natural habitat from which they came.

On summer evenings in Oysterville, the winds die down, creating a wonderful stillness. The fading light sinks into the bay and the cool air settles in for the night. Imagine yourself sitting by an open fire in Oysterville on a still evening with the distant sound of the Pacific Ocean on the western side of the peninsula and the stillness of Willapa Bay on the eastern side. The evening sun is casting light on the old houses, and you can hear the sound of oysters popping open over the hot coals of an open fire, reminding you that the simple act of eating the mollusks that this township was named after is an act of preserving tradition.

Bags of oyster seed being unloaded at Yaquina Bay, c. 1930.

Panfried Razor Clams with Bread Crumbs, Herbs, and Lemon — SERVES 6 AS AN APPETIZER

2 cups buttermilk

12 razor clams, scrubbed, cleaned, and split

1¹/₂ cups finely ground fresh bread crumbs (about 3 slices thick sourdough or Italian bread, crust removed, ground in a food processor)

1 teaspoon minced fresh flat-leaf parsley

1 teaspoon minced fresh tarragon

1 teaspoon minced fresh chives

¹/₂ teaspoon salt

¹/₄ teaspoon freshly ground black pepper

About 8 tablespoons vegetable oil

1 lemon, halved

Most of the razor clams that you find in stores or fish markets are already shelled, cleaned, and packaged. These clams come from Washington or Alaska and have likely been frozen due to their high perishability. Razor clams by nature are slightly chewy or tough and may need to be tenderized. At Wildwood, we use two methods to tenderize them. One is to place them between two pieces of plastic wrap and pound them lightly with the back of a knife or a meat tenderizer before breading them. The second method, which involves soaking the clams in buttermilk, is used in the following recipe. The buttermilk has an enzyme that assists in tenderizing the clams and also works as the liquid to allow the bread crumbs to adhere to the clams.

Pour the buttermilk into a shallow pan and place the razor clams in the buttermilk to soak for 3 hours.

Remove the clams from the buttermilk and drain for 5 minutes. In a shallow bowl, combine the crumbs, parsley, tarragon, chives, salt, and pepper. Dip a clam into the bread-crumb mixture and coat thoroughly on both sides. Place the clam on a wire rack to allow the coating to set, about 5 minutes. Repeat with the remaining clams.

In a 12-inch skillet, heat 2 tablespoons of the oil over medium heat. Put 3 clams in the skillet. Cook for about 20 seconds, or until they begin to brown, then turn and cook on the other side for 20 seconds, or until the edges of the clams begin to curl up. It is important to cook the clams quickly so that they do not become tough. Place the cooked clams on a serving plate and keep warm in a low oven. Repeat the process with the remaining clams, adding more oil as necessary.

Squeeze fresh lemon juice over the clams and serve immediately.

Clam Cakes with Tarragon, Green Peppers, and Tartar Sauce — SERVES 6 AS AN APPETIZER OR LUNCH ENTRÉE

In Willapa Bay, clams are harvested into wire nets that are then suspended in the bay to help rinse out the sand. I like to keep clams in their native saltwater until I am ready to cook them, then use some of the water to steam the clams open, often adding a few aromatics such as carrots, onions, garlic, celery, bay leaf, and peppercorns.

There are many ways to prepare the littleneck clam. Clam cakes are a classic in many regions of the country. Here is my rendition, which includes tartar sauce for dipping.

To make the tartar sauce: In a medium bowl, combine all of the ingredients and stir to blend. Cover and refrigerate until ready to use. This sauce can be made up to 2 days ahead.

To make the clam cakes: If using clams in their shells, combine the clams and water in a large skillet. Bring to a boil, reduce heat to simmer, then cover. Steam for 3 to 4 minutes, or until the shells open. Discard any clams that do not open. Remove from heat and let the clams cool in their shells. Take the meat out of the shells. Strain the clam juice, reserving 3/4 cup. Coarsely chop the clam meat. This will produce approximately 1 1/4 cups of chopped meat. If using jarred clams, drain well, reserving 3/4 cup of the juice.

In a medium bowl, combine the chopped clams, onion, bell pepper, parsley, and tarragon; set aside.

In a large bowl, combine the all-purpose flour, semolina flour, baking powder, cayenne pepper, and salt. In a medium bowl, whisk together the milk, reserved or bottled clam juice, egg yolks, melted butter, and lemon juice. Stir the liquid ingredients and clam mixture into the dry ingredients to form a batter; set aside.

In a large bowl, beat the egg whites until stiff, glossy peaks form. Fold them into the batter. Let the batter stand for 15 minutes.

In a large nonstick skillet, heat 2 teaspoons of the oil over medium heat. Spoon in about 3 tablespoons of the batter for each clam cake (about 4 per batch). Cook, turning once, until lightly browned on each side, about 3 minutes total. Place the cakes on a plate in a low oven to keep warm. Repeat the process, adding more oil as needed, until all the batter is used. Serve hot with the tartar sauce.

TARTAR SAUCE

1 cup mayonnaise

3 tablespoons finely chopped red onion

1 teaspoon finely minced fresh flat-leaf parsley

1 teaspoon capers, drained and chopped

1 teaspoon chopped cornichon or dill pickle

1 anchovy fillet, chopped

1 teaspoon fresh lemon juice

Salt and cayenne pepper to taste

CLAM CAKES

2 pounds littleneck clams in their shells, scrubbed, or one 12-ounce jar chopped clams with juice

1/2 cup water, if using fresh clams

1 small yellow onion, coarsely grated

1/2 cup chopped green bell pepper

2 teaspoons minced fresh flat-leaf parsley

2 teaspoons minced fresh tarragon

1 cup all-purpose flour

1/4 cup semolina flour

1 tablespoon baking powder

1 teaspoon cayenne pepper

1/2 teaspoon salt

1/2 cup milk

2 large eggs, separated

2 tablespoons unsalted butter, melted

1 teaspoon fresh lemon juice

About 1/4 cup vegetable oil

Wood-Roasted Clams with Saffron, Tomato, Garlic, and Grilled Bread — SERVES 4 AS AN APPETIZER OR LUNCH ENTRÉE

SAFFRON VINAIGRETTE

1/2 cup Chardonnay vinegar or other white wine vinegar

6 to 7 saffron threads

1/3 cup extra-virgin olive oil

1/3 cup vegetable oil

1 teaspoon salt

3/4 teaspoon freshly ground black pepper

4 pounds littleneck clams in their shells, scrubbed

1 cup cherry tomatoes, halved, or 1/2 cup sun-dried tomatoes, coarsely chopped

2 shallots, thinly sliced

1 tablespoon minced garlic

2 tablespoons fresh lemon juice

1/2 cup chopped fresh flat-leaf parsley

Four 1/2-inch-thick slices hard-crusted country bread, toasted and rubbed with garlic, for serving

Cooking over a wood fire frees you from the complexities of the kitchen, with all of its gadgets and devices, and inspires simplicity, allowing you to focus on the natural flavors of the food. In experimenting with open-hearth cooking, whether indoors or outside, remember that temperature and timing are crucial. Plan to burn the wood for 1 to 2 hours beforehand to ensure a hot bed of coals. Alder, cherry, apple, and fir are common woods used in the Pacific Northwest. When the fire is ready, set a metal grate strong enough to support a large pot or skillet in place 8 to 12 inches above the coals. The grate also acts as an excellent grill for large cut pieces of vegetables such as peppers, onions, corn, or squash.

One of my favorite recipes for clams includes saffron, garlic, and tomatoes. Although this recipe is prepared in the wood-burning brick oven at the restaurant, a conventional out-door grill works well, with wood chips added to the coals. The juice from the clams mixes with the oil and vinegar, creating a rich-flavored broth that is an excellent dipping sauce for a crusty piece of bread. Mussels also work well in this recipe. Use the same amount, but reduce the cooking time to 3 to 4 minutes.

To make the vinaigrette: In a medium nonreactive saucepan, combine the vinegar and saffron threads. Bring to a simmer over medium heat. Remove from heat and let cool. Whisk in the oils, salt, and pepper; set aside.

To make the clams: Using mesquite or other wood chips, prepare a very hot grill. (The temperature should be at 600° to 700°, very hot for a quick cooking time.) For added smoky flavor, cover the grill. Put the clams in a 12-inch ovenproof skillet. Add the tomatoes, shallots, and garlic. Pour the vinaigrette over the clams and vegetables. Cover the skillet, place on the grill, and cover the grill. Cook the clams for 5 to 6 minutes. Uncover the grill and skillet and continue to cook the clams until they open, transferring them as they do to a covered container to keep warm. Discard any clams that do not open during the cooking process. Add the lemon juice to the vinaigrette and cook for 30 seconds. Stir in the parsley.

Divide the clams among 4 bowls and pour the hot vinaigrette over them. Serve with the toasted bread.

Potato and Clam Soup with
Sour Cream, Thyme, and Garlic Croutons — SERVES 8

GARLIC CROUTONS

2 tablespoons olive oil

1 clove garlic, minced

2 cups 1/2-inch-cubed country bread

Salt and ground black pepper
   to taste

POTATO AND CLAM SOUP

2 tablespoons butter

2 white onions, chopped

2 leeks (white part only), washed
   and chopped

1 fennel bulb, trimmed and chopped

3 ribs celery, chopped

2 teaspoons salt

1 teaspoon ground
   white pepper

2 cups Sauvignon Blanc wine

6 cups water

3 russet potatoes, peeled and
   chopped

1 tablespoon minced fresh thyme

10 drops red pepper sauce

3 pounds littleneck clams, scrubbed

2 tablespoons fresh lemon juice

Sour cream and minced fresh thyme
   for garnish

Chowder is perhaps the most popular soup preparation for clams. This incorporates some of the standard ingredients into a purée using potato as a thickener. I use water instead of the traditional fish stock, which allows the excess juice from the clams to provide the shellfish flavor and the natural flavors of the vegetables to come through. A dollop of sour cream adds finish to the flavor, and a little chopped cooked bacon mixed with the croutons and thyme makes a tasty garnish.

To make the croutons: Preheat the oven to 350°. In a large skillet, heat the oil over medium heat and sauté the garlic for 3 minutes, or until translucent; do not brown. Add the bread cubes, tossing to coat. Place them on a baking sheet and sprinkle with salt and pepper. Bake in the oven for 10 minutes, or until golden brown. Set aside.

To make the soup: In a large saucepan, melt the butter over medium heat. Add the onions, leeks, fennel, celery, salt, and pepper. Cover, reduce heat to low, and cook the vegetables for 20 minutes, stirring frequently. Mix in the white wine, cover, and cook for 10 minutes. Stir in 5 cups of the water and bring to a boil. Add the potatoes, thyme, and red pepper sauce; reduce heat to a simmer and cook for 20 minutes. Let cool slightly. Purée in a food processor until smooth; set aside.

In a large skillet, combine the clams and the remaining 1 cup of water. Cover and bring to a boil. Reduce heat and steam for 3 to 4 minutes, or until the shells open. Discard any clams that do not open after 8 minutes of cooking. Remove from heat and let the clams cool in their shells. Take the clam meat out of the shells, allowing the clam juice to drip back into the skillet. Strain the clam juice and reserve it.

In a large pot, heat the vegetable purée. Stir in the reserved clam juice, clams, and lemon juice. Season with salt and pepper to taste.

To serve, ladle the chowder into soup bowls. Garnish with the sour cream, thyme, and garlic croutons.

Apple Cider–Cured Smoked Salmon — SERVES 4 AS AN ENTRÉE

At Wildwood, we often use a tandoor, or clay oven, to roast meats, poultry, and fish. The foods are skewered and roasted over mesquite charcoal, infusing them with a light smoke flavor even in the relatively short ten- to fifteen-minute cooking time. The tandoor cools overnight, and in the morning, a bed of coals remains, creating an excellent heat source for smoking. A wire rack is placed over the opening to the oven, which is about two feet above the fire, and salmon is smoked for approximately fifteen minutes.

Before I smoke meats and fish, I often cure them in a liquid brine or a dry cure of salt and sugar. I prefer a liquid brine since it moistens the meat or fish, while the latter absorbs the aromatics from the brine and cures in the liquid. Using apple cider as the liquid produces a slightly sweet smoked salmon that takes on a mahogany tone from the amber juice. This brine can also be used for trout, chicken, or pork.

The smoked salmon recipe that follows has been adapted for an outdoor grill. Large center-cut portions of salmon are ideal for this preparation; if you use smaller pieces, reduce the cooking time accordingly. Serve the salmon with roasted potatoes and sautéed spinach, or cool and flake into a salad or sandwich.

~~~~~~

To make the brine: In a saucepan, combine the brown sugar, salt, and apple juice and bring to a boil. Add the remaining brine ingredients, remove from the heat, and cool. This brine can be made 2 to 3 days in advance and kept in the refrigerator.

Submerge the salmon fillets in the liquid brine for at least 6 hours, or overnight. Remove the salmon from the brine and place, uncovered, on a wire rack set in a sheet pan. Refrigerate the fillets for at least 6 hours, or overnight, to dry them out. (A dry fillet will take on smoke quicker than a moist fillet.)

To smoke the salmon: In an outdoor grill, make a small fire using mesquite charcoal or briquettes. Once the fire has burned down to a hot bed of coals, after about 1 hour, place the soaked wood on the coals. Position the grate 8 to 12 inches above the smoking wood and place the salmon fillets on the grate. Cover the grill and shut any open air vents. After 5 minutes, check the heat of the grill; large fillets will be cooked and smoked through in approximately 30 minutes if the heat is low, about 300° to 350°, while a hotter fire will cook the fillets in 15 to 20 minutes.

Serve the salmon hot off the grill.

APPLE CIDER BRINE

1 cup brown sugar

$^3/_4$ cup salt

4 cups apple cider or juice

2 cinnamon sticks

1 teaspoon fennel seeds

1 teaspoon whole allspice

1 teaspoon black peppercorns

1 bay leaf

1 teaspoon red pepper flakes

6 sprigs thyme or $^1/_2$ teaspoon dried thyme

2 large center-cut salmon fillets (about 1 pound each), skin and pin bones removed

A small bundle of wood chips or chunks, such as alder, pine, cherry, apple, or fir, soaked in water for at least 2 hours, but preferably overnight

Herbed Salmon Baked on Rock Salt, with Red Onion–Caper Vinaigrette — SERVES 8 AS AN ENTRÉE

When a salmon fillet is properly cooked, you'll find that it flakes off of the skin with relative ease. Baking the fish on rock salt tempers and distributes the heat, resulting in moist, evenly cooked flesh. The red onion vinaigrette adds a light, yet pungent flavor to the salmon, or you can serve the salmon with the tartar sauce on page 7. Any leftover fish can be flaked into salads, soups, or made into salmon cakes.

To prepare the vinaigrette: In a small bowl, whisk together the oil, vinegar, and mustard. Stir in the remaining ingredients. Cover and refrigerate until ready to use. The vinaigrette can be made up to 2 days ahead.

To prepare the salmon: Rub the fillet with the minced herbs and fennel seeds. Season with salt and pepper. At this point, the salmon can be covered and refrigerated overnight.

Preheat the oven to 325°. Cover a large jelly-roll or roasting pan with aluminum foil. Pour the rock or kosher salt into the pan, covering its surface. Place the salmon, skin side down, on the salt. Bake in the oven for 35 to 45 minutes, or until opaque on the outside and slightly translucent in the center. This method of cooking allows the salmon to cook through without becoming dry. Remove from the oven, cover loosely with aluminum foil, and let stand for 5 minutes (the salmon will continue to cook).

To serve, use a wide spatula to remove the salmon from the salt. Remove the skin and portion the salmon onto plates. Spoon some of the red onion–caper vinaigrette over each portion and serve.

CHEF'S NOTE: Though the salt on which the salmon is baked will absorb juices from the fish, there's no reason to throw it out. Instead, set it aside for use the next time you prepare this dish, or one similar to it.

RED ONION–CAPER VINAIGRETTE

1 cup olive oil

$1/4$ cup sherry vinegar

1 teaspoon Dijon mustard

1 red onion, thinly sliced

2 teaspoons capers, drained

1 teaspoon chopped fresh basil

1 teaspoon salt

$3/4$ teaspoon freshly ground black pepper

4 pounds salmon fillet, pin bones removed, with skin intact

2 tablespoons mixed minced fresh herbs such as tarragon, basil, flat-leaf parsley, and thyme

2 tablespoons fennel seeds, cracked (page 224)

1 teaspoon salt

$1/2$ teaspoon freshly ground black pepper

Rock or kosher salt for lining pan

2. YAQUINA BAY:
THE OREGON OYSTER COMPANY

Louis Charles Wachsmuth enjoys a fine cigar while inspecting his oyster beds in Olympia, Washington, c. 1935.

My great-great-grandfather, Meinert Wachsmuth, had a seafaring wanderlust that led him to ports around the world before he permanently settled in Oysterville. Records show that during the mid-1800s, his travels took him around Cape Horn seven times.

On one fateful journey in 1865, Meinert was aboard the *Annie Doyle* schooner when it shipwrecked off the central Oregon coast in an area called Yaquina Bay. In a twist to the usual story, it was the shipwreck that led to a new discovery for Meinert: vast quantities of native oysters nestled in the salty waters of the bay. These small aquatic jewels were already well known in the area, and their briny, Yaquina Bay flavor made a lasting impression on Meinert.

Soon after the accident, Meinert returned to Oysterville; his desire for travel had waned, and it was time to settle and raise his family. It would be fifty-seven years before Meinert's son, Louis Charles Wachsmuth, would go in search of the jewels his father had left behind. It was 1922, and the family's Oregon Oyster Company was a fast-growing business in downtown Portland. Louis Charles needed more oysters to meet his customers' demands. He soon realized that, by buying property in Yaquina Bay, he could cultivate a desirable commodity while eliminating the middleman. According to family stories, Louis Charles used various names to purchase the bay's prime oyster beds so as not to alert the local sellers to his massive takeover.

Although his actions were financially motivated, Louis Charles had a deep respect for the waters he claimed. A fanaticism for quality coupled with his insistence on avoiding waste from overproduction led Louis Charles to oversee the seeding and harvesting of his own oyster beds. Numerous family photographs show his involvement in each stage of the harvesting process, from unloading seed bags to posing by a mountain of shells outside the shucking room. The backdrops seem endless, as do the oysters.

As I look at those photographs today, I feel Louis Charles's pride and remember sharing that feeling the first time I was old enough to help in the beds. Harvesting was a summer job that I found to be great fun and a marvelous change of scenery from the city. I vividly remember the early mornings when the bay was shrouded in fog. An occasional seagull would pass overhead and screech to break the silence of the waters. When the midmorning sun began to burn off the cloud cover, the bay became alive with activity, as workers arrived for their daily shift.

The Wachsmuth family passes a leisurely afternoon in the streets of Newport, on Yaquina Bay, c. 1938. The little girl in the back of the group is my mother, LouAnn Wachsmuth Schreiber.

The work was backbreaking. Heavy rainfall during the winter and spring drives mud from the surrounding hills into the bay every year. Add to that the buildup from the tides, and the task of shaking the oyster trays free was an arduous one. The trays weighed close to three hundred pounds each, and it took two people to pull one from the muddy grip of the bay floor.

After working in the beds, I loved to visit the shucking room, a rust-colored, weatherbeaten house perched on pilings buried in the bay. A wooden ramp extended from the building and rose over the mudflats at low tide. Stacks of stained wooden oyster boxes and netted crab pots greeted me at the doorway, as bleached white oyster shells crunched underfoot.

Most shucking rooms are empty except for a concrete floor and a shucking table. Fresh oysters filled with bay water create an intense briny odor, the type of smell that brings back a flood of memories with one familiar whiff. The shuckers, men and women of all ages and backgrounds, shared idle conversation while a radio droned in the background. The rhythmic cracking of the shells and scraping of the oysters added a sharp percussion to their soothing voices: crack, scrape, crack, scrape. This rhythm kept its steady beat more than eight hours of each working day. I would at times try to keep pace with the speed of those committed shuckers, but I was no match for their practiced hands.

Storage methods for oysters and other shellfish play a critical part in ensuring their quality. When oysters are harvested, they are usually kept in tanks that circulate bay water and provide oxygen. This helps keep them in their natural environment. You can replicate a saltwater soak at home by mixing 1 tablespoon of salt with 4 cups of water. The shellfish can soak up to 2 days, but you must change the water twice a day to keep it oxygenated.

Uncle Chet and Louis Arthur Wachsmuth on Yaquina Bay, 1935.

A high point of each summer visit to Yaquina Bay was going fishing with Uncle Chet. He'd always greet me with a hearty "Poke a Hoy," which he claimed was a Native American word for "hello." Uncle Chet loved to collect expressions and work them into his own vocabulary. Some translations still elude me and are probably best left a family mystery.

Uncle Chet owned a prized fishing boat named White Bird. When we set out on our fishing expeditions, we never

Louis John Wachsmuth tending the Yaquina Bay beds, c. 1973.

ventured out too far, a mile at the most, with the coastline in full view. I remember one gray summer day when the salmon were running close to shore, and the splash of the waves was rocking the boat in all directions. I stared intently on my line as it thrashed around in the turmoil. Suddenly, it jerked violently and Uncle Chet jumped to his feet; he knew this was a big one. That fish took me around the boat two times as I fought to bring it in. When the battle was over, I had landed a twenty-four-pound wild king salmon.

The flavor of wild king salmon is exquisite, and the rich orange color and dense yet flaky texture of the flesh are unmistakable. The wild salmon is symbolic of the Pacific Northwest, with varieties including chinook, silver, chum, and sockeye, which vary in their texture, color, and firmness. Firm wild salmon are most desirable for cooking purposes. The firmness of a fish depends on the foods it has consumed during its ocean voyage and the water temperatures it has experienced. Always touch the outer or inner flesh of the salmon to see whether it is firm or soft. In general, softer salmon should be baked or sautéed, while a firm cut will shine either poached or on a grill.

Regardless of the variety you are cooking, salmon is at its best cooked over medium heat, until the meat is just set. Cooked to this point, the salmon will appear opaque on the outside and slightly translucent in the center, and will be firm to the touch. One of the most critical tasks that will dictate the quality of salmon is how the fish is handled when it is brought out of water. The fish should be bled, cleaned, and iced immediately after it is caught in order to preserve the flesh from deteriorating rapidly.

When I visit Yaquina Bay now, it is astonishing to think of the link my family has had with this region for more than 120 years. Although we no longer own the oyster beds, I purchase oysters, Dungeness crab, and rock cod from the current owners. The beds still thrive and produce more oysters than ever. I often think that my great-grandfather's vision for the region has grown far beyond what he might have imagined. Or, might this be exactly what he had in mind from the beginning?

My sister, Meredith, and I show off our prized trout from a day spent on the water, 1974.

Tucker and Louis John Wachsmuth, c. 1974.

Louis Arthur Wachsmuth (left) spreading oyster seed in Yaquina Bay, 1935.

Oysters on the Half Shell
with Black Pepper–Lemon Vinaigrette

**BLACK PEPPER–LEMON
  VINAIGRETTE**

$1/2$ cup extra-virgin olive oil

Grated zest of 1 lemon

Juice of 2 lemons

1 tablespoon white wine vinegar

2 teaspoons coarsely ground
  black pepper

2 shallots, minced, or $1/4$ cup finely
  chopped red onion

1 tablespoon minced fresh
  flat-leaf parsley

$1/2$ teaspoon salt

24 medium-sized Pacific oysters or
  other medium-sized oysters,
  scrubbed

From a very young age, it was obvious to me that the love of eating raw oysters was in my blood. Safe practice dictates that oysters should be served chilled on ice, but there's nothing quite like the sensation of plucking them out of the beds and enjoying them on the spot. It is the epitome of eating from the source.

The Pacific oyster is predominant on the West Coast, and I like to serve it at Wildwood with a black pepper–lemon vinaigrette. The lemon creates a citrus bite, while the cracked black pepper adds a little heat. Throw in some fresh parsley and you'll have a vinaigrette suitable for all raw-oyster occasions.

To make the vinaigrette: In a small bowl, combine all the ingredients and whisk lightly. Let stand for 15 minutes to allow the flavors to blend.

To shuck the oysters: Place one oyster at a time on a dry cloth with the wide rounded end of the shell pointed away. Using an oyster shucking knife, locate the point of insertion (where the top and bottom shell are not as closely sealed) and insert the shucking knife between the groove of the shell. Twist the knife to the right, attempting to pop the shell open. After this is accomplished, run the shucking knife between the two shell halves to separate them completely. The oyster should now be sitting in the deeper of the two shells. Run the knife under the connecting muscle to release the oyster from the bottom shell. Leave the oyster in this bottom shell and place it on crushed or cracked ice until it is to be served. (If you are shucking the oysters for a recipe that doesn't call for them to be served on the half shell, remove the oyster completely and use as directed.)

To serve, distribute the oysters onto plates and spoon the vinaigrette over each oyster.

Golden Potato, Leek, and Oyster Hash Cakes

SERVES 4 AS AN APPETIZER

A hard day's work in the oyster beds requires a hearty breakfast, and the staple of our diet was right at our fingertips. Oysters are not often thought of as a breakfast ingredient, yet this recipe for potato, leek, and oyster hash creates a flavorful start to the day. Add a poached egg on top for a complete meal that will carry any appetite past lunchtime.

1 tablespoon unsalted butter

1/2 bulb fennel, trimmed and thinly sliced

1 leek (white part only), washed and thinly sliced

Pinch of salt

1 tablespoon water

2 unpeeled Yukon Gold potatoes, scrubbed and coarsely shredded

1 teaspoon minced fresh thyme

1 teaspoon salt

1 teaspoon freshly ground black pepper

12 small oysters, shucked and well drained (opposite)

4 tablespoons vegetable oil

In a 10-inch skillet, melt the butter over medium heat. Add the fennel, leek, salt, and water. Cook the vegetables without coloring until softened, 6 to 8 minutes; set aside. This can be done 1 day ahead and refrigerated.

To prepare the hash cakes: In a medium bowl, combine the potatoes, thyme, salt, and pepper. Divide the potato mixture into 4 portions. For each cake, take a little over half of each portion and form into a flat disk about 1/4 inch thick. Top with one-quarter of the cooked vegetables and 3 oysters. Use the remaining potato to form the top of the cake, pressing lightly to form a rounded top. Prepare all 4 cakes and refrigerate for 15 minutes.

In each of 2 small (6-inch) sauté pans or skillets, heat 2 tablespoons of the oil over medium-high heat. Cook the hash cakes until golden brown on one side, about 3 minutes. Then turn and cook the other side for an additional 3 minutes. Transfer to a plate and keep warm in a low oven while cooking the remaining cakes. Serve at once.

Salad of Field Greens with Crispy Fried Oysters, Aioli, and Smoky Bacon on an Herbed Crepe — SERVES 6 AS A SALAD APPETIZER

Hangtown fry is another breakfast dish historically associated with oysters. Created during the gold rush days in California, the traditional fry combines scrambled eggs, fried oysters, and bacon. At Wildwood, I prepare this rich combination in a salad served on an herbed crepe.

To make the vinaigrette: In a medium bowl, combine all the ingredients and whisk lightly. (The vinaigrette can be made up to 5 days ahead and refrigerated.)

To make the crepe batter: In a small sauté pan or skillet, heat the butter over medium heat and cook until lightly browned; let cool. In a medium bowl, whisk together the milk and egg. Blend in the butter and salt. Strain the batter through a fine-meshed sieve and then whisk in the flour and herbs. Cover, refrigerate, and let rest for 1 hour.

To cook the crepes: Spray a 7-inch nonstick or seasoned crepe pan with vegetable-oil cooking spray and heat over medium heat. Stir the batter and pour $^1/4$ cup of the batter into the pan, swirling to coat the bottom of the pan and $^1/2$ inch up the edge. Cook the crepe for 1 to 2 minutes, or until lightly browned, then turn and cook the other side until set, about 30 seconds. Turn out onto a kitchen towel and let cool. Repeat to use all the remaining batter. Stack between sheets of waxed paper. (The crepes can be made 1 day ahead, cooled, and stored in a self-sealing plastic bag in the refrigerator.)

To cook the bacon: Preheat the oven to 350°. Put the bacon or pancetta on a wire rack and bake for about 20 minutes, or until crisp.

To make the aioli: In a small bowl, blend the mayonnaise, milk, lemon juice, and garlic; set aside.

To prepare the oysters: In a medium bowl, combine the flour, cornmeal, cayenne, and salt. Toss several oysters at a time in the coating and place on a wire rack to dry for 5 minutes. In a 12-inch skillet over medium heat, heat the oil to 350° and fry the oysters in small batches for 1 minute on each side. Drain on paper towels and keep warm in a low oven.

To serve: In a salad bowl, toss the greens with the vinaigrette. Put 1 crepe on each of 6 plates and portion the greens onto each crepe. Place 3 hot oysters around the greens and top with 2 strips of bacon. Drizzle with aioli. Serve at once.

RED WINE VINAIGRETTE

$^1/3$ cup extra-virgin olive oil

3 tablespoons red wine vinegar

1 teaspoon Dijon style mustard

$^1/2$ teaspoon salt

$^1/2$ teaspoon freshly ground black pepper

CREPE BATTER

1 cup milk

1 large egg

3 tablespoons unsalted butter

1 teaspoon salt

$^3/4$ cup flour

$^1/4$ cup minced mixed fresh tarragon, chives, and flat-leaf parsley

12 slices applewood-smoked bacon or pancetta

AIOLI

$^1/4$ cup mayonnaise

2 tablespoons milk

1 tablespoon fresh lemon juice

1 clove garlic, minced

CRISPY FRIED OYSTERS

1 cup flour

1 cup stone-ground yellow cornmeal

$^1/4$ teaspoon cayenne pepper

$^1/4$ teaspoon salt

24 medium-sized Pacific oysters or other medium-sized oysters, shucked and well drained (page 20)

1 cup canola oil

10 cups (10 ounces) mixed baby greens

Oysters on the Half Shell
with Fresh Tomato Cocktail Sauce — SERVES 4 TO 6 AS AN APPETIZER

FRESH TOMATO COCKTAIL SAUCE

3 small, very ripe tomatoes

2 ribs celery, chopped

1/2 yellow onion, chopped

1 tablespoon fresh lemon juice

2 teaspoons extra-virgin olive oil

1 teaspoon grated fresh or prepared
   horseradish

1 teaspoon cayenne pepper

1 teaspoon salt

24 extra-small cocktail oysters,
   scrubbed and shucked, left intact
   in bottom shell (page 20)

Commercial cocktail sauces tend to be an overly sweetened mixture of puréed tomatoes, spices, horseradish, and lemon juice. This version reintroduces the fresh tomato flavor, which is a perfect accent to raw or cooked oysters.

Any variety of extra-small cocktail oysters is a fine accompaniment to this recipe. Meaty Pacific varieties, such as skookum, Willapa Bay, or Pearl Bay, are wonderful; firm Atlantic varieties will also pair well.

To make the cocktail sauce: Using a paring knife, make an X in the skin on the blossom end of each tomato. Using a fork, pierce through the stem end. Immerse each tomato in boiling water for about 30 seconds. Plunge immediately into ice water and peel off the skins. Cut the tomatoes in half crosswise and squeeze the juice into a sieve placed over a bowl. Reserve the juice and pulp separately and discard the seeds.

In a blender or food processor, purée the celery, onion, and tomato juice. Pour the mixture into a bowl. Purée the tomato pulp and add to the celery-onion mixture. Mix in the lemon juice, oil, horseradish, cayenne, and salt. Let stand for 30 minutes. Taste and adjust the seasonings.

To serve, distribute the oysters onto plates and spoon approximately 1 teaspoon of the sauce over each oyster. Any remaining cocktail sauce can be refrigerated for up to 3 days.

Panfried Oysters with Lemon Aioli and Wildwood Coleslaw — SERVES 6 AS AN APPETIZER

Most oysters are shucked and sold packed into $^1/_2$- or 1-pint jars. These oysters are generally larger than those sold in the shell and are intended for cooking rather than for eating raw. The following recipe is a basic preparation for preshucked oysters. Tartar sauce and coleslaw are two classic accompaniments to this dish, but here a lemony aioli stands in for tartar sauce. The coleslaw is best made at least 1 hour before serving to allow the flavors to blend.

To make the coleslaw: Halve the cabbage lengthwise and cut out the core. Cut the cabbage into thin crosswise slices. In a large bowl, combine the cabbage, carrots, onion, and parsley. In a small bowl, blend the mayonnaise, vinegar, fennel seeds, salt, and pepper. Add to the cabbage mixture and toss. Cover and refrigerate for at least 1 hour before serving. The coleslaw will keep for up to 3 days in the refrigerator.

To make the aioli: In a small bowl, combine all the ingredients and stir to blend. Use now, or cover and refrigerate for up to 2 days.

To make the oysters: In a medium bowl, combine the flour, cornmeal, cayenne, and salt. Toss several oysters at a time in the coating, making sure that each oyster is completely coated in the breading.

In a 12-inch skillet over medium heat, heat the oil to 350° and fry the oysters in small batches for 1 minute on each side. Drain on paper towels and keep warm.

To serve, portion the coleslaw onto 6 plates. Top each serving with 4 oysters and drizzle with the aioli. Garnish with lemon wedges.

WILDWOOD COLESLAW

1 small head cabbage (preferably Savoy), tough outer leaves removed

2 carrots, peeled and coarsely grated

1 small red onion, cut in half and thinly sliced lengthwise

$^1/_4$ cup chopped fresh flat-leaf parsley

$^1/_4$ cup mayonnaise

$^1/_4$ cup red wine vinegar

1 tablespoon fennel seeds, toasted and coarsely ground (page 224)

$^3/_4$ teaspoon salt

$^1/_2$ teaspoon freshly ground black pepper

LEMON AIOLI

$^1/_2$ cup mayonnaise

$^1/_4$ cup fresh lemon juice

1 clove garlic, minced

1 cup flour

1 cup stone-ground yellow cornmeal

$^1/_2$ teaspoon cayenne pepper

$^1/_2$ teaspoon salt

24 shucked medium-sized Pacific oyster or other medium-sized oysters (about 1 pint), well drained

1 cup canola oil

Lemon wedges for garnish

Oysters with Crème Fraîche, Lemon, and Tarragon

➤ SERVES 4 AS AN APPETIZER

This recipe for baked oysters, which receives accolades each time it appears on the Wildwood menu, accents the shellfish flavor with citrus and cream. Flavor combinations aside, the dish provides the perfect opportunity to use large oysters in the shell. These oysters are sometimes referred to as grilling oysters. When baked, oysters tend to shrink; in the case of smaller oysters, the heat application may not leave much oyster. The larger oysters will hold up fine to the heat with plenty of meat to complement the crème fraîche topping.

Preheat the broiler. In a mixer bowl, using an electric mixer on medium-high speed, beat the crème fraîche or sour cream until soft peaks form. Stir in the tarragon, lemon zest, orange juice concentrate, salt, and cayenne; set aside.

In a jelly-roll pan, layer the kosher or rock salt ¹/₄ inch thick. Gently press the oyster shells into the salt to hold them in place. Broil the oysters 6 inches from the heat source for 4 to 5 minutes, or just until they begin to release their juices and the shells pop open slightly. Remove from the broiler and remove the top oyster shell by inserting a butter knife and popping the shell off. Top each oyster with a spoonful of crème fraîche topping and serve immediately.

¹/₂ **cup crème fraîche or sour cream**

1 **tablespoon minced fresh tarragon**

Grated zest of 1 lemon

1¹/₂ **teaspoons undiluted orange juice concentrate**

¹/₂ **teaspoon salt**

Dash of cayenne pepper

Kosher or rock salt for layering

18 **large oysters, scrubbed and shucked, oysters left intact in bottom shell (page 20)**

Oyster Pan Roast

2 ribs celery, julienned

1 carrot, peeled and julienned

1 small yellow onion, finely chopped

$^3/_4$ cup fish stock (page 221) or
   vegetable stock (page 222)

$^1/_4$ cup dry Sauvignon Blanc

$^3/_4$ cup heavy cream

Grated zest of 1 lemon

24 extra-small oysters, shucked and
   well drained (page 20)

$^1/_2$ teaspoon salt

Freshly ground black pepper to taste

4 slices Potato Bread (opposite)
   or other country bread, toasted
   or grilled

I originally learned to make this dish while working in New England many years ago. The oyster pan roast is strongly associated with Northeast cookery. As I recall, the feast was prepared with heavy cream and plump Wellfleet oysters from Cape Cod, and served on toasted brioche—a rich yet satisfying dish during a particularly cold New England winter. I offer my own Oregonian version here. The ingredient that seems to change most often from recipe to recipe is the type of bread on which it is served. I prefer to use a dense bread, such as the potato bread that follows, but any country-style bread will work nicely.

In a 10-inch stainless-steel skillet, combine the celery, carrot, onion, stock, and wine and simmer over medium heat for about 15 minutes, or until the vegetables are softened and the liquid is slightly reduced. Stir in the cream and lemon zest and bring to a simmer. Add the oysters and poach until the edges curl and the oysters are firm to the touch. Season with salt and pepper.

To serve, place a slice of bread in a shallow soup bowl. Spoon the oysters and sauce over the bread.

Potato Bread — MAKES 2 LOAVES

Because of its density, this bread tends to stay fresh for up to 2 days and is ideal for toasting, grilling, or including in warm preparations like the Oyster Pan Roast on the opposite page. It also makes a fine sandwich bread.

To make the sponge: In a mixer bowl, combine the water and yeast. Let stand for 5 minutes, or until the top surface has a thin layer of foam, indicating that the yeast is active. Using a heavy-duty mixer fitted with a paddle, on low speed, mix in the flour for about 2 minutes. Transfer to a large oiled bowl and cover tightly with plastic wrap. Let stand at room temperature overnight.

To make the dough: In a large saucepan, combine the potatoes with water to cover and add the 1 teaspoon salt. Bring to a boil and cook for about 20 to 25 minutes, or until the potatoes are just tender. Drain, reserving 1 cup water. Force the potatoes through a ricer or mash them. Let cool.

Warm the reserved potato water to 110°, if necessary. In a mixer bowl, combine the potato water and yeast; let stand for 5 minutes. Add the sponge and use a heavy-duty mixer fitted with a paddle to mix on low speed for 4 minutes, or until the sponge is fully incorporated. Add the mashed potatoes, cheese, and sage; mix on low speed for 3 minutes, or until the dough pulls away from the sides of the bowl. Gradually add 7 cups of the flour and mix in, then beat on medium speed for 4 minutes, or until the flour is fully incorporated and a stiff dough is formed. Cover with plastic wrap and let rest for 20 minutes to relax the dough.

Switch to a dough hook. Add the olive oil and the 1 tablespoon salt and mix for 8 minutes, or until the dough pulls together. Add the remaining flour if the dough is still sticking to the sides of the bowl and continue mixing for 10 minutes. Place in a large oiled bowl and turn the dough to coat with oil. Cover with plastic wrap and let rise in a warm place for 1 1/2 hours, or until doubled in size; the dough will be sticky.

Place the dough on a floured board and knead about 25 times, or until smooth and elastic, incorporating more flour, 1 tablespoon at a time, as necessary. Divide the dough in two. Place in two 12-by-4-inch greased loaf pans and cover with plastic wrap. Let rise in a warm place for 1 1/2 hours, or until doubled in size.

Preheat the oven to 400°. Bake for 35 to 45 minutes, or until golden brown. Let cool in the pans for 5 minutes. Turn out onto a wire rack and let cool for 1 hour before slicing.

SPONGE

2 1/4 cups warm (110°) water

3/4 teaspoon active dry yeast

3 1/2 cups plus 2 tablespoons bread flour

DOUGH

1 1/2 pounds russet potatoes, peeled, and cut into 2-inch pieces

1 teaspoon plus 1 tablespoon salt

3/4 teaspoon active dry yeast

3/4 cup grated Asiago cheese

1 1/2 tablespoons minced fresh sage

9 1/2 cups bread flour

1/4 cup olive oil

Cedar-Planked Salmon — SERVES 4 AS AN ENTRÉE

Vegetable oil, for coating

4 salmon fillets (about 6 ounces each), pin bones removed, with skin intact

Salt and freshly ground black pepper

Rosemary, thyme, or tarragon sprigs

For hundreds of years, Native Americans living in the Northwest have prepared salmon using cedar planking. The traditional preparation is laborious. Huge quantities of hardwood are burned in pits built into the ground. When the embers and coals are hot, cedar planks or branches are driven into the ground around the perimeter of the pit. The cedar planks are split, and whole sides of salmon are skewered, affixed to the wood, and roasted slowly next to the fire. The finished salmon has a wonderful odor of smoked cedar that permeates the fish.

Fortunately, there is a simpler way to replicate this flavor at home, using your oven and untreated cedar boards. Often lumberyards or hardware stores can cut pieces for you from their scrap or odd-size cedar pieces. Many gourmet cooking stores also carry cedar planks cut specifically for baking salmon. You will need four 1-inch-thick cedar planks, each 12 inches long, soaked in water overnight. Any size piece of salmon works for this recipe, including individual fillets or a whole side. This preparation also works for other types of fish such as whole trout, cod, or halibut, and I have even seen it used for cooking chicken breasts. Serve with rice or a pasta salad.

~~~~~~

Soak the cedar pieces in water overnight; drain. Preheat the oven to 400°. Lightly oil the salmon and season with salt and pepper. Put the salmon on the cedar boards, placing some herb sprigs under meat to accent the flavor. Bake for 15 to 20 minutes, or until the salmon is firm to the touch and cooked through. The board may start to darken in color as it loses water. For an attractive presentation, serve the salmon on the board.

Poached Salmon with
Warm Clam and Bacon Vinaigrette — SERVES 4 AS AN ENTRÉE

The following recipe juxtaposes the delicate texture of salmon with a robust vinaigrette made with bacon and clams. If king salmon is not available at your local market, any type of wild or farm-raised salmon will work for this recipe.

To prepare the poaching liquid: In a large skillet, combine the parsley stems, water, salt, celery, carrot, onion, leek, pepper, coriander, and bay leaf. Bring to a boil, reduce heat to a simmer, and cook for 30 minutes. Let cool slightly and strain the liquid, reserving both the liquid and the vegetables. In a colander placed over a skillet, press the vegetables with the back of a large spoon to extract the flavors, then discard. Return the poaching liquid to the skillet and add the wine; set aside.

To prepare the clams: In a large saucepan, combine the clams with the water. Bring the water to a boil over medium heat. Cover and steam the clams until they open, 3 to 4 minutes. Discard any clams that do not open after 10 minutes of cooking. Strain the liquid and remove the clams from their shells. Put the clams into the clam juice to keep them moist; set aside.

To poach the salmon: Bring the poaching liquid barely to a simmer. Add the salmon, skin-side down (the liquid should cover the salmon), and cook for 9 to 10 minutes per inch of thickness. Do not overcook, as the salmon will continue to cook after it is removed from the liquid. Check for doneness by flaking the meat with a fork; the interior color should be even and cooked through completely. Remove the salmon from the liquid and place on paper towels to dry. Remove and discard the skin.

To prepare the vinaigrette: In a heavy sauté pan or skillet, cook the bacon over medium heat until crisp. Remove the bacon from the pan and drain on paper towels. Pour off the bacon drippings, reserving 2 tablespoons, and wipe out the pan. Return the reserved bacon drippings to the pan, add the shallots, and sauté for 3 minutes, or until translucent. Remove from heat and stir in the olive oil, vinegar, mustard, thyme, and bacon. Drain the clams and add them as well.

To serve, place each salmon fillet on a plate and spoon the warm vinaigrette evenly over the fillets.

POACHING LIQUID

10 parsley sprigs, chopped

4 cups water

2 teaspoons salt

2 ribs celery, chopped

1 carrot, peeled and chopped

1 unpeeled white onion, trimmed and chopped

1 leek (white part only), washed and chopped

1 teaspoon coarsely ground black pepper

1 teaspoon coriander seeds, or $^1/_2$ teaspoon ground coriander

1 bay leaf

1 cup Chardonnay

1 pound Manila or other small clams in their shells, scrubbed

$^1/_2$ cup water

4 salmon fillets (about 6 ounces each), pin bones removed, with skin intact

4 slices smoky bacon, cut into $^1/_2$-inch strips

4 shallots, thinly sliced

$^1/_4$ cup olive oil

$^1/_4$ tablespoons red wine vinegar

2 teaspoons Dijon mustard

$1^1/_2$ teaspoons minced fresh thyme

Whole Roasted Rockfish
with Celery, Fennel, and Thin Potatoes — SERVES 4 AS AN ENTRÉE

8 tablespoons olive oil

4 whole rock cod or salmon fillets (about 1 pound each), cleaned and patted dry, heads removed

5 teaspoons salt

5 teaspoons freshly ground black pepper

2 tablespoons unsalted butter

3 ribs celery, julienned

2 leeks (white part only), washed, halved lengthwise, and julienned

2 bulbs fennel, trimmed and thinly sliced

1 red onion, cut vertically into thin crescents

3 cups fish stock (page 221)

$^1/_2$ cup Chardonnay

2 Yukon Gold potatoes, sliced very thin (use a mandoline, if possible)

6 sprigs thyme

3 tablespoons minced fresh flat-leaf parsley

Juice of 1 lemon

When I wasn't out with Uncle Chet or working in the oyster beds, I fished for rockfish from the docks on Yaquina Bay. Rockfish is a generic term applied to many species, including ocean perch. My uncles and aunts never seemed as interested in helping to clean rockfish as the larger, more prized wild salmon. I was often left to fillet these fish myself, and this is probably why I still prefer to roast them whole!

Ethnic markets (especially Asian) are generally the best places to acquire good-quality whole fish. Make sure the fish are packed on ice and that the exposed flesh is somewhat translucent. The fish should smell like fresh seawater and be firm to the touch. The variety I enjoy most is the canary rockfish, which has a beautiful orange and yellow color and a firmer texture than other rockfish.

I like to purchase whole fish in the 1- to 1 $^1/_2$-pound range. At this weight, 1 fish per person is plenty. If a fish weighs closer to 2 pounds, it can generally feed up to 3 people. Use one pan per fish, or if you have a 14-inch or larger pan, you can prepare 2 whole fish per pan. This next preparation works nicely for any type of whole fish including black bass, perch, and flounder.

To prepare the fish: Preheat the oven to 350°. In a large, heavy ovenproof braising pan or skillet, heat 2 tablespoons of the olive oil over high heat, almost to the point of smoking. Season each fillet with $^1/_2$ teaspoon of salt and $^1/_2$ teaspoon of pepper on each side and place in the pan. Brown the fish on one side. When you can release it from the pan with relative ease, turn and brown on the other side. Remove the fish from the pan and wipe out the pan. Repeat the process to cook the remaining fish.

In the same pan, melt 1 tablespoon of the butter over medium heat and sauté the celery, leeks, fennel, and onion for 3 minutes, or until the onion is translucent. Season with the remaining 1 teaspoon salt and 1 teaspoon pepper. Stir in the fish stock, wine, potatoes, and thyme. Bring to a simmer and transfer the mixture to a roasting pan large enough to hold the fish. Place the fish over the vegetables. Bake, uncovered, for 20 to 30 minutes, or until the fish flakes easily with a fork and is opaque throughout.

Transfer the fish to a platter and cover loosely with aluminum foil to keep warm. Place the roasting pan over medium heat. Add the remaining 1 tablespoon butter, the parsley, and lemon juice, and cook for 2 to 3 minutes, or until the butter has melted and the sauce is fragrant. Remove from heat and adjust the seasoning.

To serve, portion the vegetable stew into 4 deep serving plates and place the fish on top of each.

Pan-Roasted Halibut with Red Wine Butter and Red Potatoes — SERVES 4 AS AN ENTRÉE

RED WINE BUTTER

1 cup Pinot Noir

1/4 cup red wine vinegar

4 tablespoons unsalted butter,
    at room temperature

Purée from 2 heads roasted garlic
    (page 223)

2 teaspoons minced thyme leaves

1 teaspoon salt

1 teaspoon coarsely ground
    black pepper

2 pounds small red potatoes

2 1/2 teaspoons salt

1 tablespoon minced fresh
    flat-leaf parsley

4 halibut fillets or steaks (about
    6 ounces each), seasoned with salt
    and freshly ground black pepper
    to taste

2 tablespoons olive oil

1 bunch sautéing greens such as
    kale, mustard greens, or white
    chard, stemmed and cut crosswise
    into 1-inch-wide shreds

Freshly ground black pepper
    to taste

Halibut is another popular fish found on both the East and West coasts. It has a firm ivory or white flesh and holds up well in cooking. The halibut season in Oregon is extremely short, sometimes running only one to two days in midsummer. The quality of these fish is impeccable, and the flesh appears almost translucent and is very firm. Alaskan Halibut is a staple fish at Wildwood and is used in recipes in many ways, from grilled to wood-roasted to sautéed. It's extremely versatile and contributes to many great flavor combinations.

You can purchase halibut in either steak form or fillets. The bone in the steaks adds flavor and helps keep the fish moist after it is cooked. Steaks also tend to flake less and are good for grilling. When preparing fillets, I like to pan-roast them with red wine butter and red-skinned potatoes. This recipe uses Pinot Noir in the butter, but any good-quality red table wine will work nicely.

To make the red wine butter: In a small saucepan, combine the wine and vinegar. Bring to a boil, reduce heat, and simmer until reduced to a syrup, about 20 minutes. Remove from heat and let cool.

In a mixer bowl, using an electic mixer on medium speed, blend the butter, garlic, thyme, salt, pepper, and reduced wine mixture. This can be refrigerated for several days or frozen for several weeks.

To prepare the potatoes: In a large pot, cover the potatoes with water. Add 2 teaspoons of the salt. Bring the water to a boil, reduce heat, and simmer for 15 to 20 minutes, or until fork-tender. Drain well. Add 2 tablespoons red wine butter and the parsley; set aside and keep warm.

Meanwhile, preheat the oven to 350°. In a large ovenproof skillet, heat 1 tablespoon of the olive oil over high heat. Put the halibut in the pan and brown until it releases from the pan, 4 to 5 minutes. In a small saucepan, melt 1 1/2 tablespoons of the wine butter. Turn the fillets over and baste with the red wine butter. Place in the oven and cook for 7 to 10 minutes, or until opaque throughout. Remove from the oven and cover loosely with aluminum foil to keep warm.

To prepare the greens: In a 10-inch skillet, heat the remaining tablespoon of olive oil over medium-high heat. Add the greens, stir, and cook until wilted. Season with the remaining 1/2 teaspoon of salt and pepper to taste.

To serve, portion the potatoes, wilted greens, and halibut onto each plate. Melt the remaining wine butter and drizzle over the halibut.

Ocean Perch with Red Onion–Lemon Vinaigrette and Smashed Yukon Gold Potatoes — SERVES 4 AS AN ENTRÉE

At Wildwood, the day on which the ocean perch, freshly pulled from the Pacific, is delivered is always an exciting one. We know whatever we purchase will be gone by the end of the evening, as the fish is highly appreciated for its firm texture and sweet flesh. This recipe is unique in that it incorporates a crispy potato base, seared firm white fish, and a chunky vinaigrette. The lemon and red onion flavors refresh the fish and infuse the potatoes. Although the recipe calls for ocean perch, sea bass, snapper, or rockfish fillets will also work well.

To prepare the potatoes: In a large pot, combine the potatoes, garlic, rosemary, bay leaf, salt, pepper, and water to cover. Bring to a boil, reduce heat, and simmer for 25 to 30 minutes, or until the potatoes are firm but tender when pierced with a paring knife. Drain, discard the herbs, and cool the potatoes in the refrigerator. When cool, crumble by hand into pieces the size of quarters; set aside.

To make the vinaigrette: In a small bowl, combine the olive oil, lemon zest, lemon segments, onion, thyme, salt, and pepper. Set aside.

To cook the fish and potatoes: Preheat the oven to 350°. In a large ovenproof sauté pan or skillet large enough to hold the fillets, heat 1 tablespoon of the oil over medium-high heat. Add the fish and brown on one side. Look for the edges of the fish to curl up when browned. Turn the fillets over and place the pan in the oven for 7 to 10 minutes, or until opaque throughout; you will need to cook thicker fillets such as sea bass longer. Meanwhile, in a large sauté pan or skillet, heat the remaining 1 tablespoon olive oil over medium-high heat. Add the potatoes and garlic and cook, turning, until golden brown. Stir in the rosemary and remove from heat.

Portion the potatoes onto 4 plates and top with the fish. Spoon on the vinaigrette and serve.

4 unpeeled Yukon Gold potatoes, scrubbed

2 unpeeled heads garlic, halved crosswise

1 sprig rosemary

1 bay leaf

1 teaspoon salt

1 teaspoon freshly ground black pepper

RED ONION-LEMON VINAIGRETTE

2 tablespoons extra-virgin olive oil

Grated zest of 2 lemons

4 lemons, peeled and segmented (page 224)

1 small red onion, finely chopped

1 teaspoon minced fresh thyme

3/4 teaspoon salt

3/4 teaspoon freshly ground black pepper

2 tablespoons olive oil

4 ocean perch fillets

2 cloves garlic, minced

1 teaspoon minced fresh rosemary

DAN & LOUIS OYSTER BAR

3. DAN & LOUIS OYSTER BAR: SPANNING THE CENTURY

Overleaf: (bottom right) *Louis Arthur and Dan Wachsmuth, sons of Louis Charles, stuck in the mudflats of Willapa (Shoalwater) Bay, c. 1922; (top right) the shucking room of the original Oyster Bar, with Louis Arthur and Dan Wachsmuth, second from the right and far right; (left) the interior of the Oyster Bar, 1999.*

*W*hen the Yaquina Bay oyster business was firmly established, Louis Charles focused his energies on distribution. His tactic was reminiscent of his oyster-bed takeovers: He hired individuals to dine at Portland-area restaurants that did not offer Yaquina Bay oysters. Their directive was to order the oysters by name and to become outraged when told they were not available. The final act of the diners' performance included an ultimatum: Either the oysters would be added to the menu, or the restaurant would no longer enjoy their patronage. It proved to be a successful means of promoting

Louis Charles Wachsmuth, far left, and employees of the Oregon Oyster Company standing in front of the storefront on Ankeny Street, c. 1910.

business in those days, and eventually Louis Charles was shipping oysters as far east as the Waldorf Astoria Hotel in New York City.

Louis Charles founded the City Oyster Company in 1907, and by 1910, he bought out his silent partner and changed the name to the Oregon Oyster Company. He ran his growing "empire" from the Bickle Building in downtown Portland, adding a small food bar in 1919 and calling it Louis' Oyster Bar. In 1938, it was rechristened Dan & Louis Oyster Bar as a tribute to Louis Charles's son Dan, who had died that same year. Today, Dan & Louis Oyster Bar is still in the family and remains a Portland dining institution.

The original Oyster Bar was a tiny L-shaped storefront facing onto Ankeny Street, with just enough space for a cooler, a shucking room, a few tables, a counter, and two pots of piping-hot milk for oyster stew. But by the 1930s, Portlanders had developed a huge appetite for local seafood, and Louis Charles responded to the call by expanding his storefront operation and hiring a retired ship builder to oversee the design. The result was an interior brimming with seafaring artifacts. But perhaps the most impressive sight of all was the open kitchen resembling the outer hull of a ship, complete with a gold-leafed mermaid on the bow.

This was a grand time for the restaurant. The kitchen was state of the art, and the menu offered new and diverse items including panfried Yaquina Bay oysters (of course!), milk-based stews, oyster cocktails, and crab and shrimp Louis. I've often been asked if my great-grandfather was the originator of the now-classic seafood salad. It makes for a nice story, but the truth is I don't know to whom the credit belongs.

As at Yaquina Bay, the shucking room was one of my favorite places at the restaurant. By the time I was working at the Oyster Bar, shucking was a one-person show in the capable hands of Ed Sorge, a man who spent the better part

The Oyster Bar, c. 1938.

of twenty-five years working in the restaurant. You could find Ed in the front window on most days and evenings, with a shucking knife in one hand and a rubber glove on the other, popping shells to keep pace with the restaurant demand. During the evenings, long lines formed outside the front door as people waited for their tables. Ed would entertain them with anecdotes, commentary, and personal advice. When asked if he had ever found a pearl, his answer was "Yes, of course," leaving expectant patrons to wonder whether, if they waited long enough, Ed might find a pearl as they watched. Imagine a restaurant where people wanted to wait in line!

According to James Beard, Portland was a culinary capital in the first decades of the twentieth century. In *Delights & Prejudices*, he recalls his early gastronomic experiences in the 1920s when Louis Charles and other Portland restaurateurs were at work. He compliments Don Daniel, the chef at Meier & Frank department store, for having a "true sense of the seasonal aspect of menu building." He mentions classic dishes of the time, such as veal birds with cream sauce flavored with dill or tarragon, local squab with rice stuffing, salmon soufflé with hollandaise sauce, and local clams cooked in parsley butter and served with tartar sauce.

Beard particularly enjoyed dining in the grandeur of Portland's great hotels. One such landmark was the Benson Hotel, owned by the lumber baron Simon Benson. Beard befriended Mr. Benson's son Chester and enjoyed many an evening dining in the hotel restaurant on Chester's expense account. The chef at the time was Henri Thiele, who would later become a prominent name in Portland with the establishment of his own restaurant in the 1930s. In his book, Beard fondly recollects evenings spent sampling paupiettes of sole garnished with native Olympia oysters, crabmeat Newburg on toasted brioche, fillets of king salmon stuffed with salmon mousse, and delicate pastries ranging from Princess Charlotte pudding to puff pastry tarts with hazelnuts, pastry cream, melted sugar, and nut topping.

Long after the days when Henri Thiele created those feasts for Benson and Beard, I became an apprentice chef at the hotel under the watchful eye of chef Xavier Bauser, who, like Thiele, was Swiss born and trained. As I worked in the basement kitchens, I envisioned Beard feasting in the hotel restaurant on such Northwest delicacies as wild salmon and sturgeon from the Columbia River, shellfish from the Oregon coast, and wild mushrooms from the outlying forests. These were the flavors I had grown up with and have come to appreciate even more as I write my own menus.

My formal apprenticeship at the Benson Hotel proved to be the cornerstone of my technical and professional training, but my passion for cooking arose out of my early experiences working at the Oyster Bar. My baby shower even took place in the restaurant in the summer of 1960, so I guess you could say I was born into the business.

The author during his days as a bus boy at the Oyster Bar, c. 1976.

Harry Wachsmuth, brother of Louis Charles, c. 1910.

Dan & Louis Crispy Jumbo Dungeness Crab Legs

(ADAPTED BY CORY SCHREIBER) — SERVES 4 AS AN ENTRÉE

1 cup milk

2 large eggs

3 tablespoons flour

1/2 teaspoon salt

2 cloves garlic, minced

2 cups cracker crumbs

2 tablespoons minced fresh
flat-leaf parsley

16 cooked jumbo Dungeness or
Alaskan king crab legs

Vegetable or canola oil for
deep-frying

Lemon wedges for serving

Tartar sauce (page 7)

This recipe is an Oyster Bar classic. It is easy to prepare and works well with any type of crab.

In a medium bowl, beat the milk, eggs, flour, salt, and garlic together. In another medium bowl, combine the crumbs and parsley. Dip the crab legs in the batter and drain off the excess. Gently roll the crab legs in the crumbs until dry.

In a large skillet, heat 2 to 3 inches of oil to 375°. Fry a few crab legs at a time (do not crowd them) until golden brown. Using a slotted spoon, transfer to a baking sheet lined with paper towels. Keep warm in a low oven while frying the remaining crab legs.

Serve piping hot with lemon wedges and tartar sauce.

Dan & Louis Oyster Stew

(ADAPTED BY CORY SCHREIBER) — SERVES 6

8 cups milk

2 cups heavy cream

4 tablespoons unsalted butter

3/4 teaspoon seasoned salt

1/2 teaspoon ground white pepper

1 pint shucked oysters and
their juice

Louis Charles, dishing out his famous oyster stew, 1940.

Over the years, many Oyster Bar patrons have quizzed my family about the secret seasoning in our oyster stew. When Uncle Chet was commanding the ladle, he threw in a little something extra that I've since deduced was Schilling's seasoned salt. The quality of the oysters is the key to this stew, however, so make sure they are packed in lots of juice. If you are feeling adventurous, add a secret seasoning of your own. After more than ninety years, this stew is still available at the Oyster Bar.

In a double boiler, combine the milk and cream, and heat until small bubbles form around the edge of the pan. Stir in the butter, salt, and pepper. Gently add the oysters and their juice and simmer for 5 minutes, or until the oysters are firm yet tender. Stir and serve in soup bowls.

Olympia Oyster, Fennel, and Bacon Chowder — SERVES 4

Here is a dish that James Beard would have enjoyed, as he was known to delight in Olympia oyster stew during the Christmas season. These tiny oysters are native to an ocean inlet near the town of Olympia, Washington. Since the waters from which they come have a lower salt content than the Pacific Ocean proper, Olympia oysters taste less briny. Their slightly sweet flavor makes them wonderful either cooked or raw on the half shell.

In a 6-quart soup pot, cook the bacon over medium heat until crisp. Using a slotted spoon, transfer the bacon to paper towels to drain. Pour off the bacon drippings, reserving 1 tablespoon. Wipe out the pan.

In the same pan, heat the reserved bacon drippings over medium-low heat and add the onion, leek, fennel, and water. Cover and cook for about 10 minutes, or until the vegetables are soft; stir often so they do not brown. Mix in the stock, milk or cream, potatoes, 1 teaspoon of the salt, the thyme, fennel seeds, and bay leaves. Simmer, stirring occasionally, for 15 to 20 minutes, or until the potatoes are tender. Add the oysters, lemon zest, remaining 1 teaspoon salt, and the white pepper; simmer for an additional 5 minutes. Remove the bay leaf.

Ladle into soup bowls and sprinkle with the cooked bacon. Serve.

4 slices bacon, halved lengthwise and cut into 1-inch pieces

1 white onion, chopped

1 leek (white part only), washed and thinly sliced

1 bulb fennel, trimmed and chopped

$^{1}/_{4}$ cup water

4 cups fish stock or chicken stock (page 221)

2 cups milk or heavy cream

2 cups peeled, chopped Yukon Gold potatoes (about 4 small potatoes)

2 teaspoons salt

2 teaspoons minced fresh thyme

2 teaspoons fennel seeds, cracked (page 224)

1 bay leaf

$^{1}/_{2}$ pint Olympia or other shucked oysters and their juice (page 20)

1$^{1}/_{2}$ tablespoons grated lemon zest

1 teaspoon ground white pepper

Baked Oysters with Bread Crumbs, Herbs, and Lemon — SERVES 4 AS AN APPETIZER

$^1/_2$ cup homemade dried bread crumbs (page 223)

1 tablespoon minced fresh chives

1 tablespoon minced fresh tarragon

1 tablespoon grated lemon zest

$^1/_2$ teaspoon fennel seeds, toasted and ground (see page 224)

$^1/_2$ teaspoon salt

$^1/_8$ teaspoon cayenne pepper

5 tablespoons unsalted butter, melted

Kosher or rock salt for lining pan

16 oysters, scrubbed and shucked, left intact in bottom shell (page 20)

The success of the following recipe relies on the use of freshly dried coarse bread crumbs, which will remain crisp when combined with melted butter, oyster liquor, herbs, and lemon juice. The result should be a textural surprise, with the briny oysters broiled until they are just set and the bread crumbs are crunchy.

Preheat the broiler. In a small bowl, combine the bread crumbs, chives, tarragon, lemon zest, fennel seeds, salt, and cayenne. Mix in the butter and set aside.

On a jelly-roll pan, layer kosher or rock salt $^1/_4$ inch thick. Nest the oyster shells in the salt to hold them in place. Top each oyster with $^1/_2$ tablespoon of the crumb mixture. Broil the oysters 6 inches from the heat source until the topping is brown and the juice of the oysters is bubbling, about 4 minutes. Serve immediately.

Louis Charles, right, discusses the complex flavor differences between oyster varieties with an associate.

Scallops in Their Shells Steamed with Tomatoes, White Wine, and Leeks — SERVES 4 AS AN ENTRÉE

Singing, or spiny, scallops are farm-raised in the Puget Sound area in Washington state. These scallops are sold in their shells and are generally smaller than the varieties usually found at the local fish market. They are a rare treat, so if you find them, buy them and cook them the same day, as they are extremely perishable. In this recipe, the scallops are steamed open in white wine with some chopped tomatoes, leeks, and butter. The thin membrane around each opened scallop should be removed before eating by taking one side of the membrane and pulling it around to separate it from the scallop.

If scallops in their shells are not available, substitute 2 1/2 pounds of small clams.

In a 12-inch skillet, melt 1 teaspoon of the butter over low heat. Add the leeks, garlic, and $1/2$ teaspoon of the salt. Cook for 5 minutes, or until soft and translucent, being careful not to brown. Stir in the tomatoes and juice, wine, water, 2 teaspoons of the tarragon, 2 teaspoons of the chives, the remaining 1 teaspoon salt, and the red pepper sauce. Bring to a boil, reduce heat, and simmer for 5 minutes. Add the scallops, cover, and cook for an additional 4 to 6 minutes, or until the shells open. Discard any scallops that do not open after 10 minutes of cooking. When the shells are open, remove the scallops from the pan. Set aside and keep warm.

Cook the sauce over medium heat for 3 minutes to reduce it slightly. Swirl in the remaining 1 teaspoon butter, 1 teaspoon tarragon, 1 teaspoon chives, and the lemon juice. Put the scallops in bowls, spoon on the sauce, and serve.

2 teaspoons unsalted butter

2 leeks (white part only), washed, halved lengthwise, and thinly sliced

3 cloves garlic, minced

$1^1/2$ teaspoons salt

2 large vine-ripened tomatoes, cored, seeded (reserve juice), and chopped

$1^1/2$ cups Chardonnay

$1/2$ cup water

3 teaspoons minced fresh tarragon

3 teaspoons minced fresh chives

8 drops red pepper sauce

16 scallops in the shell, scrubbed

$1/4$ cup fresh lemon juice

Seared Scallops with Cider Brown Butter — SERVES 4 AS AN ENTRÉE

1 cup apple cider

6 tablespoons unsalted butter

1 pound sea scallops, patted dry with paper towels

1 Granny Smith apple, cored and julienned

3/4 teaspoon salt

1/2 teaspoon ground white pepper

16 small fresh sage leaves

2 tablespoons fresh lemon juice

Until recently, most store-bought scallops came from the East Coast, including Atlantic varieties of sea scallops, bay scallops, and calico scallops. Fortunately, sea scallops are returning to the Oregon Coast in small quantities after not being available for many years.

Scallops found in stores are often treated with tripolyphosphate, a preservative that affects their sweet flavor. This treatment also causes the scallops to retain water and to weigh a little more on the store scales. For this reason, you may hear them referred to as "wet scallops," because they release a lot of excess water into the pan during cooking. The water is problematic when sautéing because it prevents the scallops from achieving a nice caramelized color and texture. I prefer to use nontreated, dry-packed scallops. They are more difficult to find but well worth the hunt.

I generally don't pair fish and fruit, yet I find that the apple flavor in this recipe, and the orange in the next, blend well with the meaty quality of the scallops. Among Wildwood seafood lovers, these dishes are favorites.

In a large skillet, bring the cider to a boil over medium-high heat. Boil for 6 to 8 minutes, or until reduced to about 3 tablespoons. Pour into a bowl and set aside.

In another large skillet, melt 2 tablespoons of the butter over medium heat. Season the scallops with the salt and pepper. Cook the scallops until lightly browned on the outside and opaque throughout, about 2 minutes on each side (do not overcook). Remove from the pan and keep warm.

Add the remaining 4 tablespoons butter to the skillet. Brown the butter over medium heat, being careful not to burn. Stir in the reduced cider, half of the julienned apple, the sage, and lemon juice. Simmer until the apple is tender and the sauce is slightly thickened, about 1 minute. Taste and adjust the seasoning.

To serve, put the scallops in a serving dish and spoon on the sauce. Garnish with the remaining julienned apple.

Warm Scallop and Endive Salad
with Oranges, Walnuts, and Pomegranate — SERVES 4

VINAIGRETTE

1/4 cup olive oil

3 tablespoons undiluted orange juice concentrate

2 tablespoons red wine vinegar

1 teaspoon coriander seeds, toasted and cracked (page 224)

3/4 teaspoon salt

1/2 teaspoon freshly ground black pepper

SALAD

3 oranges, peeled and segmented (page 224)

2 endives (red or green leaf), cut lengthwise into 1/4-inch-thick slices

1 red onion, halved crosswise and cut vertically into thin crescents

1/2 cup coarsely chopped walnuts, toasted (page 224)

1 pomegranate, seeded, or 1/4 cup dried cranberries or cherries, for garnish

16 sea scallops, patted dry with paper towels

1 teaspoon salt

3/4 teaspoon freshly ground black pepper

2 tablespoons olive oil

This recipe is a good dish to prepare when citrus season and pomegranate season overlap in November. The lively colors and innovative combination of flavors make this dish a winter treat. If pomegranates are not available, dried cranberries or cherries are good substitutes.

To make the vinaigrette: In a small bowl, whisk together the vinaigrette ingredients; set aside.

To make the salad: In a salad bowl, combine the oranges, endives, and red onion. Gently toss with three-fourths of the dressing. Let stand while cooking the scallops.

To make the scallops: Season the scallops with the salt and pepper. Using 2 large skillets, heat 1 tablespoon of the oil in each skillet over medium-high heat. Cook several scallops at a time, being careful not to crowd, until lightly browned on the outside and opaque throughout, about 2 minutes on each side (do not overcook). Remove the scallops from the pan and cover to keep warm. Continue the cooking process until all of the scallops are prepared.

To serve, add the walnuts to the salad. Portion the salad mixture onto 4 plates and arrange 4 scallops around the edge of each salad. Sprinkle with the pomegranate seeds or cranberries or cherries and spoon on the remaining dressing.

Baked Spot Prawns with
Potato-Saffron Aioli — SERVES 4 AS AN APPETIZER

The meaty flesh of spot prawns is similar to lobster meat. Their sizes vary and are referred to by how many are in a pound. For example, a 16–20 count would mean 16 to 20 per pound. I have seen spot prawns that would fit a 2 count, as they can be jumbo in size, yet most spot prawns are in the former category.

I have found that spot prawns are best when baked in the shell and eaten while still warm. Adding potato purée to this garlic mayonnaise sauce gives it a unique texture that helps it to stay on the shrimp instead of landing on you! Any type of medium-sized shrimp with shell still intact may be substituted.

To make the aioli: In a small saucepan, combine the vinegar and saffron. Bring to a boil, reduce heat, and simmer until the liquid is reduced to about 1 tablespoon; remove from heat. In a bowl, blend the potato purée, saffron mixture, garlic, capers, salt, and pepper. Spoon the aioli into a serving bowl; set aside.

Meanwhile, preheat the oven to 400°. In a large bowl, combine the olive oil, lemon juice, garlic, salt, and pepper. Add the prawns or shrimp and toss to coat. Spread out on a jelly-roll pan and bake until pink and opaque throughout, 5 to 8 minutes, depending on the size of the prawns or shrimp.

Place the prawns or shrimp on a platter and serve with the aioli.

POTATO–SAFFRON AIOLI

1 russet potato, baked, cooled, skinned, and puréed in a food mill, sieve, or ricer

1 cup mayonnaise

1/4 cup white wine vinegar

1/8 teaspoon powdered saffron

1 teaspoon minced garlic

3 tablespoons capers, drained

1 teaspoon salt

1 teaspoons freshly ground black pepper

2 tablespoons olive oil

2 teaspoons fresh lemon juice

1 teaspoon minced garlic

1 teaspoon salt

1 teaspoon freshly ground black pepper

16 (16–20 count) spot prawns or Gulf shrimp

Shrimp Soup with Carrots, Fennel, and Oranges — SERVES 8

2 pounds large shrimp in the shell

SHRIMP BROTH

3 tablespoons unsalted butter

Reserved shells and tails from
    shrimp, above

3 carrots, peeled and chopped

3 ribs celery, chopped

2 yellow onions, chopped

2 unpeeled heads garlic, chopped

1 bulb fennel, trimmed and chopped

1 leek (white part only), washed
    and chopped

2 teaspoons salt

1/4 cup tomato paste

1 tablespoon paprika

1/2 to 1 teaspoon cayenne pepper

8 cups water

2 cups Chardonnay

2 unpeeled oranges, cut into wedges

1 tablespoon fennel seeds

1 tablespoon cumin seeds

8 flat-leaf parsley sprigs

1 carrot, peeled and cut into
    1/2-inch dice

1 bulb fennel, trimmed and cut
    into 1/2-inch dice

1 to 2 teaspoons salt

3 tablespoons coarsely chopped
    fresh flat-leaf parsley

Shrimp shells can be removed either before or after the shrimp are cooked. If you shell the shrimp while raw, the shell still has a fair amount of flavor that can be put to good use. In the following recipe, tomato, orange, fennel seeds, bay leaf, carrot, and onion are combined to make a wonderful broth that becomes the base for a flavorful shrimp soup.

Remove the shells and tails from the shrimp.

To make the broth: In a 6-quart soup pot, melt the butter over medium heat. Add the reserved shrimp shells and tails, the carrots, celery, onions, garlic, fennel, leek, and salt. Cover, reduce heat to low, and cook, stirring frequently, for 30 minutes, or until the vegetables are soft. Whisk in the tomato paste, paprika, and cayenne, and cook for another 5 minutes. Stir in the water, wine, oranges, fennel seeds, cumin seeds, and parsley stems. Bring to a boil, reduce heat, and simmer for 35 minutes. Let cool slightly. Strain the soup through a sieve, pressing down on the shrimp shells and the vegetables with the back of a large spoon to extract all the flavors.

In a soup pot, combine the shrimp broth, diced carrot and fennel, and salt. Cook for 7 minutes, or until the vegetables soften slightly. Bring to a boil, add the shrimp, remove from heat, and let stand for 5 minutes, or until the shrimp are translucent and completely firm.

To serve, ladle the soup into bowls and sprinkle with the parsley.

Boiled Dungeness Crab — SERVES 4 AS AN ENTRÉE

Dungeness crab is the prized shellfish in the Pacific Northwest. The sweet, succulent meat, especially from the legs, is unmatched in the crab kingdom and holds up well in any dish. The commercial Dungeness crab season lasts from November to March, and many stores offer crab both live and cooked. Cooking live crab takes a little extra effort, but the results are well worth it. The flavor is more robust than that of precooked crab because you only cook it once; precooked crab needs to be reheated and tends to lose some of its sweetness and tenderness in the process. So if the chance arises, cook your crabs live and enjoy the ceremonious act of shelling them at the dining table.

2 live Dungeness crabs

1 gallon court bouillon (page 222)

Melted butter and lemon wedges or
   Potato-Saffron Aioli (page 49)
   for serving

In a large stockpot, bring the court bouillon to a boil. Drop the crabs into the court bouillon and boil until the shells turn bright red; a 3- to 5-pound crab takes 8 to 10 minutes to cook. Remove from the pot and let cool to the touch. If you prefer, boil the crabs for 5 minutes, remove from heat, and let cool in the bouillon to allow the meat to absorb the flavors.

To clean the crabs, first cut off the legs with kitchen shears. Cut lengthwise through the top shell of each leg to remove the meat. Although the leg meat is prized for its size, the body also houses lots of meat, if you are willing to work for it. Pull the shell off by placing two fingers under the front, near the eyes, and pull up on the shell as you would open the lid of a box. There are gills on either side of the inner shell. They are dark green in color and look similar to the gills of fish. Remove and discard the gills and any other debris. Cut the body into quarters.

Serve with melted butter and lemon wedges or aioli.

Wildwood Dungeness Crab Cakes with Orange, Fennel, and Watercress Salad

— SERVES 6 AS A LUNCH ENTRÉE OR DINNER APPETIZER

Each region of the country offers a different method for assembling and cooking crab cakes. At Wildwood, we serve our crab cakes wrapped in potatoes, as the blanched strings offer a wonderful, crunchy texture when panfried. The contrast between the crispy outside of the cake and the creamy inside is irresistible, and the dish remains a best-seller on our menu.

These crab cakes also make a great passed hors d'oeuvre without the salad. They can be paired with other salads, too, such as Roasted Corn and Basil Salad, page 92. Bread crumbs can be substituted as a coating for the cakes with good results.

To form the crab cakes: In a small sauté pan or skillet, melt the butter over low heat. Add the shallots and cook for 2 minutes, or until translucent. In a large bowl, combine the shallots, bread crumbs, cheese, lemon juice, mayonnaise, egg, mustard, bell pepper, parsley, salt, and cayenne. Gently mix the crabmeat into the mixture. Divide the mixture into 12 equal portions and form into balls. Cover and refrigerate for at least 30 minutes or up to 24 hours.

Bring a large pot of water to a boil. Salt the water and blanch the potato strings for 2 minutes. Transfer to an ice-water bath; set aside.

To prepare the salad: Whisk together the lemon juice, oil, salt, and pepper; set aside. In a salad bowl, combine the orange segments and juice, fennel, watercress or greens, and onion. Set aside to toss just before serving with the cakes.

To cook the crab cakes: In a shallow bowl, beat the remaining 2 eggs until blended. Put the flour and potato strings in 2 separate shallow bowls. Remove the crab balls from the refrigerator. Flatten each ball to make a $^3/_4$-inch-thick cake. Dip each crab cake in the flour, then the eggs. Pack a layer of potato strings around each cake.

In a large skillet, heat 2 tablespoons of the oil over medium heat. Cook the crab cakes, turning once, until golden brown on each side, about 6 minutes total, adding more oil as needed to prevent sticking.

To serve, toss the salad with the dressing and distribute evenly among 6 plates. Top each salad with two cakes and serve immediately.

CHEF'S NOTE: If using a box grater to prepare the potatoes, don't blanch the potatoes, as they are likely to fall apart.

CRAB CAKES

1 tablespoon unsalted butter

2 shallots, minced

$^1/_2$ cup homemade dried bread crumbs (page 223)

$^1/_2$ cup grated Asiago or pecorino cheese

$^1/_4$ cup fresh lemon juice

$^1/_4$ cup mayonnaise

1 egg, beaten

2 tablespoons Dijon mustard

2 tablespoons minced green bell pepper

2 tablespoons chopped fresh flat-leaf parsley

1 teaspoon salt

$^1/_8$ to $^1/_4$ teaspoon cayenne pepper

1 pound fresh lump Dungeness or other crabmeat

4 Russet potatoes, peeled, cut into strings on a Japanese turning slicer or box grater, and soaked in water until ready to use

ORANGE, FENNEL, AND WATERCRESS SALAD

3 tablespoons fresh lemon juice

2 tablespoons extra-virgin olive oil

$^3/_4$ teaspoon salt

$^1/_2$ teaspoon freshly ground black pepper

4 oranges, peeled and segmented, juice reserved (page 224)

1 bulb fennel, trimmed and thinly sliced by hand or on a mandoline

4 cups (4 ounces) watercress or mixed baby greens

1 yellow onion, thinly sliced

$^1/_2$ cup flour

2 eggs

4 to 5 tablespoons canola oil

Crab and Braised-Artichoke Salad
with White Beans — SERVES 6

WHITE BEANS

4 to 5 cups chicken stock (page 221)

6 cloves garlic, chopped

1 small yellow onion, chopped

1 carrot, peeled and chopped

1 teaspoon salt

1 teaspoon freshly ground
black pepper

1¼ cups dried navy beans, soaked
in water overnight and drained

BRAISED ARTICHOKES

12 baby artichokes (about 1 pound)

1 lemon, halved

3 cups olive oil

½ cup white wine vinegar

8 cloves garlic, crushed

1 small yellow onion, sliced

1 teaspoon salt

1 teaspoon freshly ground
black pepper

1 teaspoon fennel seeds, cracked
(page 224)

1 tablespoon grated lemon zest

⅓ cup fresh lemon juice

2 teaspoons Dijon mustard

1 teaspoon salt

1 teaspoon freshly ground
black pepper

8 ounces fresh lump Dungeness or
other crabmeat

8 cups (8 ounces) mixed baby greens

Although artichokes are most at home in Mediterranean climates, they grow quite well in the buffered zones of the Northwest Coast Range. However, I've noticed that Northwest artichokes do not seem to have the interior meatiness of their southern counterparts.

Here, the artichokes are braised in oil and white wine vinegar, creating a flavored vinaigrette for the salad. The sweetness of the crab and bitterness of the artichoke make for an exhilarating flavor combination.

To make the beans: In a medium pan, combine the stock, garlic, onion, carrot, salt, and pepper; bring to a boil. Add the drained beans, reduce heat, and simmer for 35 to 40 minutes, or until the beans are tender, adding more stock or water as needed. Remove the pan from heat and let the beans cool in the seasoned liquid. Cover and refrigerate. (The beans can be made 1 day ahead.)

To make the artichokes: Clean the artichokes by peeling back and removing 2 to 3 layers of the outer leaves until the lighter yellow-green leaves appear. Trim off the thorns on the tips of the artichoke leaves. Trim off the outer skin and bottom of the stem. Rub each artichoke with lemon to prevent discoloring, and place in cold water.

In a 12-inch skillet, combine the oil, vinegar, garlic, onion, salt, pepper, and fennel seeds. Bring to a boil, reduce heat, and simmer for 10 minutes. Drain the artichokes well and pat dry with paper towels. Cut into quarters. Carefully add the artichokes to the simmering oil mixture. Bring back to a simmer and cook for 10 to 15 minutes, or until the artichokes are tender. Remove the artichokes from the oil, cover, and refrigerate. Reserve ½ cup of the oil for the salad dressing and save the remainder for other cooking uses. This can be done 1 day ahead.

In a small bowl, whisk together the ½ cup reserved oil, lemon zest and juice, mustard, salt, and pepper; set aside.

Drain the beans. In a large salad bowl, combine the optional cooked beans, quartered artichokes, crabmeat, and greens. Toss with the dressing and serve.

Creamed Crab on Wildwood Brioche
with Wild Mushrooms and Thyme — SERVES 4 AS AN APPETIZER

I still get a craving for the creamed crab I used to savor on the days I worked at the Oyster Bar. This dish is traditionally prepared by heating the crabmeat in a béchamel sauce and spooning it on top of a piece of toast. I use heavy cream instead of béchamel sauce. The cream requires time to reduce, but it has just the right consistency to bind the crabmeat. Wild mushrooms, another great accompaniment to crab, give this dish a rich flavor that will warm your soul on a cold winter's day.

Preheat the broiler. Wipe the mushrooms clean. If using wild mushrooms, leave whole; if using portobello, dice. In a large sauté pan or skillet, melt the butter over medium heat. Add the shallots and cook, stirring, for 1 minute. Add the mushrooms and cook until they wilt and reduce in size, 3 to 4 minutes. Stir in the wine and simmer until reduced by half. Add the cream and cook over medium-high heat until the cream is reduced by half. Stir in the crabmeat, cheese, and lemon zest and juice; cook for 1 minute. Blend in the parsley, thyme, salt, and pepper; remove from heat. The mixture should be thick and creamy. If the mixture is too thin, return to heat and cook until thickened.

Preheat the broiler. Brush both sides of the bread slices with the olive oil. Broil on each side until lightly browned.

To serve, place a slice of bread on each plate and top with one-quarter of the crab mixture. Toss the salad greens with the vinaigrette dressing and place one-quarter on each serving of crab.

CHEF'S NOTE: To use the crab mixture as an appetizer, serve it with toasted baguette slices. Dried mushrooms may be substituted for fresh mushrooms. Use 2 ounces (dried mushrooms are more concentrated), and skip the wilting step—the dried mushrooms should be added along with the wine.

4 ounces wild mushrooms, such as morels, black trumpet, or chanterelle or 1 portobello mushroom, about 4 ounces

1 teaspoon unsalted butter

3 shallots, minced

1/4 cup dry white wine

2 cups heavy cream

8 ounces fresh lump crabmeat

1/3 cup grated Asiago or pecorino cheese

1 tablespoon grated lemon zest

1 tablespoon fresh lemon juice

2 teaspoons minced fresh flat-leaf parsley

2 teaspoons minced fresh thyme

2 teaspoons salt

1 teaspoon freshly ground white pepper

Four 1/2-inch-thick slices Wildwood Brioche (page 56) or thick-crusted country bread

2 tablespoons olive oil

10 cups (10 ounces) mixed baby greens

1/4 cup red wine vinaigrette (page 23)

Wildwood Brioche — MAKES TWO 8-BY-4-INCH LOAVES

SPONGE

1/4 cup warm (110°) water

1 package active dry yeast
(2 1/4 teaspoons)

1 teaspoon sugar

1/2 cup bread flour

DOUGH

2 large egg yolks

1/4 cup sugar

5 large eggs

3 1/4 cups bread flour

1 tablespoon salt

1 cup (2 sticks) unsalted butter,
at room temperature, cut into
tablespoon-sized slices

Brioche is a versatile bread that can be used in French toast, sandwiches, or more delicate preparations, such as the creamed crab on toast on the previous page. It's rich with butter and eggs, so if you're feeling indulgent, this is the recipe for you!

To make the sponge: In a mixer bowl, combine the water, yeast, and sugar. Let stand for 5 minutes, or until the top surface has a thin layer of foam, indicating that the yeast is active. Using a heavy-duty mixer fitted with a paddle, on low speed, add the flour and beat for about 2 minutes. Transfer to a large oiled bowl, cover tightly with plastic wrap, and let rise in a warm place until doubled in size, about 1 1/2 hours.

To make the dough: In a mixer bowl, using a heavy-duty mixer fitted with a paddle, combine the sponge, egg yolks, and sugar and beat on low speed until well mixed. Add the eggs, one at a time, beating until combined.

Change to a dough hook. Start kneading on medium-low speed, adding the flour, 1/2 cup at a time, and the salt. Increase speed to medium and knead the dough until smooth. Add the butter gradually and knead until the butter is almost incorporated. The dough will be somewhat streaky. Remove from the bowl and form the dough into a ball. Place in an oiled bowl and turn the dough to coat with oil. Cover tightly with plastic wrap and let rise in a warm place for 1 1/2 hours, or until doubled in size. Punch down and put in a large self-sealing plastic bag; refrigerate overnight.

Punch the dough down and divide it into 2 portions. Form each into an 8-inch-long loaf. Spray two 8-by-4-inch loaf pans with vegetable-oil cooking spray. Place a loaf, seam-side down, in each pan and let rise in a warm place until doubled, about 1 1/2 hours.

Preheat the oven to 350°. Bake the loaves for 35 to 45 minutes, or until a tester inserted in a loaf comes out clean. Let cool in the pans for 5 minutes, then turn out onto wire racks. Let cool for 1 hour before slicing.

CHEF'S NOTE: For a shiny crust, brush the loaf with an egg glaze before baking. To make the glaze, whisk together 1 egg and 2 teaspoons water.

THE WILLAMETTE VALLEY

4. THE WILLAMETTE VALLEY: SPRING VEGETABLES

*I*t's impossible to count the many shades of green in the Willamette Valley in early spring. As rain clouds gently shower the fertile landscape, the earth's hues blend like a cool and hazy watercolor. Suddenly, a ray of sunshine breaks through with a brilliance that brings everything into sharp focus—greens mixed with splashes of red, pink, and white from the flowering fruit trees. The immediacy of the transformation seems to be a sign of the earth's pent-up energy after a long and dormant winter. The days are becoming warmer in the valley, and rows of turned soil are now fully planted with the promise of a bountiful and flavorful summer harvest. The nights are still cool, but the days are getting longer, allowing the farmers to tend their wealth of produce. The valley is beginning to awaken, bringing the anticipation of tender spring vegetables.

I think of spring as a time of culinary reinvention. My visits to the valley renew my cooking senses and restore the excitement of planning menus based on new produce. Daily conversations with local farmers resume, and plans are made

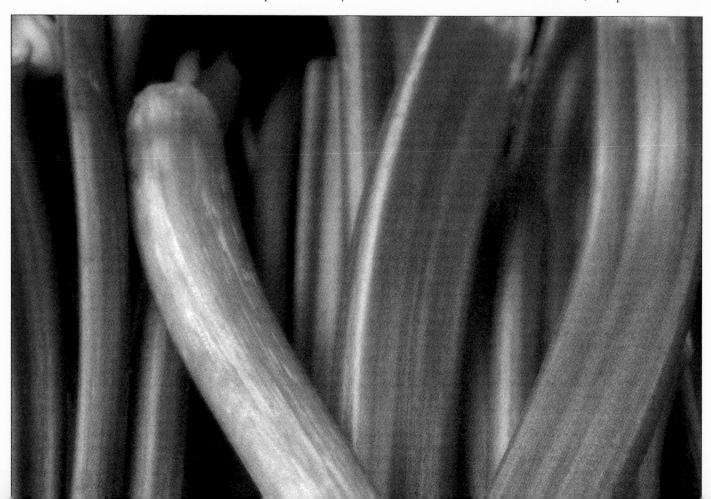

for the season. Soon, deliveries of fresh-picked leeks, onions, garlic, lettuce, and fennel will be arriving daily at Wildwood, and we will begin experimenting with new ways to bring out their subtle spring flavors.

❦ ❦ ❦

Sheldon Marcuvitz and Carole Laity own Your Kitchen Garden Farm in the northern Willamette Valley near Canby and the banks of the Willamette River. The farm is their home, and they lovingly tend to five acres of rich alluvial soil watered by local springs. They till the land with age-old equipment handed down with the farm, but the bulk of their painstaking work is done by hand, which shows in the impeccable quality of their produce.

Sheldon and Carole are part of a breed of growers that I refer to as "direct organic farmers." They made a commitment when they purchased the farm not only to grow high-quality produce, but to establish ongoing relationships with their customers. They do not have a sales staff, packager, or distributor, but deal with consumers directly. I have visited the farm on a few occasions and have admired their passion for the product and their genuine desire to connect with the people who live and work around them in the valley.

The leek is one of the first spring crops to arrive at the restaurant from Your Kitchen Garden Farm. It seems that this black sheep of the onion family is rarely allowed to stand on its own for fear that its flavor will prove too strong for most palates. Actually, leeks are mild when compared to the onion, and the tender spring leeks have an almost sweet quality. Sheldon and Carole plant theirs deep into the soil so the white of the leek is much larger than the green, producing a vegetable that has a high yield and is very tender.

When shopping for leeks, select those that are medium-sized and about an inch in diameter at the center, and look for long white stalks. You may find that the stalks have accumulated a fair amount of soil, so I recommend splitting each leek lengthwise with a knife and washing it thoroughly in running water. Whenever I come across extremely tender leeks, I like to grill them over a wood fire for a simple, yet flavorful treat. Leeks this tender are rare, however, so I generally recommend cooking them slowly in butter or olive oil until they are soft, and then adding a little

lemon juice and some sorrel or fines herbes at the end. Baby leeks, available in specialty and organic food stores, are exquisitely tender, and I give them a place of honor on the Wildwood menu whenever they turn up on produce lists from local farms. Unlike their larger counterpart, baby leeks can and should be eaten in their entirety, green and white parts alike.

Wild sorrel, also known as sheep's sorrel, is quite abundant in the Pacific Northwest, and offers a hint of lemon that enhances the flavor of leeks. Considered both an herb and a salad green, depending on how it is used, sorrel is somewhat of an undiscovered flavor, for it is not often available in many markets in the United States.

On my visits to the valley in early spring, I always marvel at the tiny young fennel bulbs pushing their way through the soil. Fennel is at its best in the spring and again in the fall, when the bulbs are small (about the size of a lemon) and their layers are tender. You can usually identify a young bulb by the rich green color of its outer ribs. As the season progresses, the bulbs tend to grow larger and lose some of their coloring. If a bulb has reached this stage, simply strip away the tough outer ribs to reach the tender insides.

Lettuce is one of the first leafy greens to appear in spring and grows throughout the summer and fall. A walk through a farmer's market may introduce you to many members of the lettuce family, including arugula, miner's lettuce, watercress, spinach, young romaine, and curly endive. Each offers a subtle differ-ence in flavor, ranging from the sharp bite of arugula to the peppery flavor of cress to the slight bitterness of curly endive. Each can be enjoyed on its own, or blended with others for a fresh layering of flavors. It may take some experimentation on your part to find the best blend for you. Many stores now offer mesclun, or mixed baby greens, which is a nice way to sample the different lettuce varieties.

Saffron-Braised Leeks with Celery, Capers, and Chopped Egg

1/2 cup Chardonnay

1/2 cup white wine vinegar

1/4 teaspoon saffron threads

1/2 cup olive oil

4 sprigs thyme

12 baby leeks, washed and left whole, or 4 regular leeks, white part only, washed and each cut into long, thin strips

4 ribs celery, julienned

1 small red onion, thinly sliced

2 tablespoons capers, drained

8 cups (8 ounces) mixed baby greens

1 teaspoon salt

1/2 teaspoon freshly ground black pepper

2 hard-cooked large eggs, chopped

I recommend using baby leeks in this dish since they stand up to braising quite well. Use any leftover braising liquid as a vinaigrette for salads, or brush it on baguette slices and toast in the oven to serve with salads or appetizers.

Preheat the oven to 350°. In a large ovenproof skillet, combine the wine, vinegar, and saffron. Heat over medium-low heat for 5 to 6 minutes, or until the saffron blooms and the liquid is a bright yellow. Mix in the oil, thyme, and leeks. Bring to a boil. Remove from heat and transfer to the oven to braise for 8 to 10 minutes. Mix in the celery, onion, and capers; braise an additional 10 minutes. Let the vegetables cool in the braising liquid. Cover and refrigerate for 2 hours or overnight.

One hour before serving, remove from the refrigerator. Using a slotted spoon, remove the vegetables from the braising liquid, setting the leeks aside. To assemble, place 3 baby leeks or leek strips on each plate. In a large salad bowl combine the greens and the remaining braised vegetables with 3 to 4 tablespoons of the braising liquid. Season with the salt and pepper. Toss the salad and place on top of the leeks. Garnish with the chopped egg. Serve.

Leek and English Pea Soup
with Asparagus and Curly Pasta — SERVES 4

2 tablespoons unsalted butter

4 leeks (white part only), washed and cut into long, thin strips

2 cloves garlic, thinly sliced

1 teaspoon salt

1/2 teaspoon ground white pepper

4 cups vegetable stock (page 222)

1 1/2 cups cooked fusilli or corkscrew pasta

12 ounces English peas, shelled, or 10 ounces frozen peas

4 ounces asparagus, trimmed and cut into 1/2-inch-long pieces

4 to 5 leaves fresh sorrel or basil, finely shredded

Leeks are perhaps best known as a soup ingredient, and they usually end up puréed with potatoes or other white vegetables such as parsnips, celery root, or turnips. In this modest role, the leek's flavor is often hard to detect and acts more as a backdrop for the other elements in the soup. This soup is designed to bring out the flavor of the leek and to give it a little of the attention it deserves. The vegetables are cooked in the broth to ensure that the flavors and nutrients do not escape.

In a 3-quart saucepan, melt 1 tablespoon of the butter over medium heat. Add the leeks, garlic, salt, and pepper. Sauté for 4 to 5 minutes, stirring to prevent the vegetables from browning. Stir in the vegetable stock. Bring to a boil and cook for 8 minutes. Mix in the pasta, peas, and asparagus, reduce heat, and simmer for 3 to 4 minutes, or until bright green and just tender. Swirl in the remaining 1 tablespoon of butter.

To serve, ladle into soup bowls and garnish with the sorrel or basil.

Marinated Raw Fennel Salad
with Radishes, Carrot, and Spring Greens — SERVES 4

A first encounter with a fennel bulb usually involves a look of consternation and the question "What do I do with that?" If you smell this mysterious little vegetable, you'll quickly notice the familiar scent of licorice. The fennel bulb, though small, can be packed with flavor. Many cooks like to mellow the taste by slowly braising the fennel in milk. I prefer a more pronounced flavor and often serve it raw or lightly cooked.

This next recipe is perfect for anyone who delights in the anise flavor of fennel. I thinly slice the bulb with a sharp knife or a mandoline, then toss the slices with lettuce, radish, raw carrot, and red onion. The mixture is then marinated in a vinaigrette accented with toasted fennel seeds before serving.

In a small bowl, whisk together the oil, vinegar, fennel greens, and fennel seeds; set aside.

In a medium bowl, combine the sliced radishes, sliced fennel, onion, and carrot. Toss with the vinaigrette and marinate for 1 hour. Just before serving, stir in the lemon juice, salt, and pepper.

To serve, toss together the greens and marinated vegetables in a large bowl and distribute onto 4 plates.

1/4 cup extra-virgin olive oil

2 tablespoons white wine vinegar

2 tablespoons chopped fennel greens

1 teaspoon fennel seeds, toasted and ground or cracked (page 224)

4 or 5 radishes, thinly sliced

1 fennel bulb, trimmed and thinly sliced

1 small red onion, thinly sliced

1 carrot, peeled and thinly sliced

2 teaspoons fresh lemon juice

1 teaspoon salt

1/2 teaspoon freshly ground black pepper

8 cups (8 ounces) mixed baby greens

Pan-Braised Spring Fennel
with Olive Oil, Honey, and Orange — SERVES 4 AS AN APPETIZER OR SIDE DISH

1 cup fresh orange juice

$^1/_4$ cup Riesling

1 tablespoon honey

$^1/_4$ cup olive oil

1 teaspoon fennel seeds, toasted and
  ground or cracked (page 224)

1 teaspoon minced fresh thyme

1 teaspoon salt

$^1/_2$ teaspoon freshly ground
  black pepper

2 large bulbs fennel, trimmed and
  cut into quarters, or 4 small bulbs
  (6 to 8 ounces each), trimmed
  and halved

2 tablespoons coarsely chopped
  fennel greens for garnish

When "Your Kitchen Garden" produce begins to arrive to Wildwood in March and April, their rich, green young fennel is quickly ushered into numerous preparations, including this braised fennel recipe. This dish is wonderful served on its own or as an accompaniment to chicken, game, or pork.

Preheat the oven to 350°. In a small saucepan, cook the orange juice, wine, and honey over medium heat until the honey melts. Stir in the oil, fennel seeds, thyme, salt, and pepper.

In a 7-by-11–inch baking dish, arrange the fennel pieces. Pour the hot mixture over the fennel pieces. Cover tightly with aluminum foil and bake for 35 to 40 minutes, or until the fennel is tender.

To serve, use a slotted spoon to transfer the fennel to a platter. Pour some of the sauce over the fennel and garnish with the chopped fennel greens.

CHEF'S NOTE: Use the remaining fennel sauce as a basting sauce for grilled poultry or seafood.

Opposite: *The Swan Restaurant, owned by Moss Freeland, stood across from the post office.*

Red Lentil and Fennel Ragout
with Bacon, Carrots, and Thyme — SERVES 4 AN AS ENTRÉE OR SIDE DISH

Here is a quick stew that combines fennel with red lentils, bacon, and carrots. Dried red lentils are available in most stores. The dish is hearty enough to stand alone, or pair it with a poultry or pork preparation.

In a large skillet, cook the bacon over medium heat until crisp. Using a slotted spoon, transfer the bacon to paper towels to drain. To the bacon drippings, add the carrots, fennel, onion, and salt. Sauté for 6 to 8 minutes, stirring occasionally. Stir in the stock, thyme, pepper, and lentils. Bring to a boil, reduce heat, and simmer for 10 minutes, stirring frequently. Look for the lentils to double in size and to absorb most of the stock.

Mix in the lemon zest, lemon juice, and bacon and serve.

4 ounces sliced bacon, cut into
 ¹/₂-inch strips

2 carrots, peeled and thinly sliced

1 bulb fennel, trimmed, halved,
 and thinly sliced

1 small yellow onion, thinly sliced

1 teaspoon salt

2 cups chicken stock (page 221) or
 vegetable stock (page 222)

1 teaspoon minced fresh thyme

¹/₂ teaspoon freshly ground
 black pepper

1 cup dried red lentils, soaked in
 warm water for 1 hour and
 drained

1 teaspoon grated lemon zest

3 tablespoons fresh lemon juice

Wilted Young Spinach Salad with Hazelnuts, Smoked Trout, and Oregon Blue Cheese — SERVES 4

Young spinach is a treat well worth tracking down at your local store or farmer's market. I am particularly fond of the wrinkly-leafed Savoy spinach, which has a firmness and sweetness that adds texture and flavor to a dish. Because spinach can be a bit too firm for a cold salad, however, I like to wilt it slightly with a warm vinaigrette. This recipe includes smoked trout and hazelnuts—two staples of Pacific Northwest cuisine. If you cannot find smoked trout in your local store, substitute smoked salmon.

In a large salad bowl, combine the greens, onion rings, and trout or salmon; cover and refrigerate.

In a small saucepan, whisk together the oil, vinegars, salt, and pepper. Add the nuts and warm over medium heat. Pour over the greens and trout or salmon.

To serve, toss the salad. Divide evenly among 4 plates. Top each serving with a portion of cheese.

1 pound baby spinach or arugula (or a combination), stemmed, washed, and dried

1 small red onion, thinly sliced and separated into rings

8 ounces smoked trout or smoked salmon fillet, skinned and cut into 1-inch pieces

1/4 cup hazelnut or olive oil (or a combination)

2 tablespoons sherry vinegar

1 tablespoon balsamic vinegar

3/4 teaspoon salt

1/4 teaspoon freshly ground black pepper

1/4 cup hazelnuts, toasted, skinned, and chopped (page 224)

4 ounces chilled Oregon Blue cheese or other mild blue cheese, cut into 4 portions

Sweet-Onion Sandwich — MAKES 4 SANDWICHES

Like spring garlic and leeks, sweet onions are mild in flavor and soft in texture. In my neck of the woods, the sweet Walla Walla onion is well known. The flavoring of the earliest varieties is often so subtle that they can be enjoyed raw, as is the case in this recipe.

Split the rolls and spread the cut sides with the mayonnaise. Arrange the onions and lettuce in layers on the bottom half of each roll. Season with salt and pepper. Add the top half of each roll and slice.

4 Soft Rye Torpedo Rolls (page 81)

1/4 cup mayonnaise, preferably homemade

1 sweet white onion (Walla Walla, Maui, Vidalia, or Texas Sweet), thinly sliced

4 ounces lettuce, such as arugula, mizuna, or shredded romaine

Salt and freshly ground black pepper to taste

Blanched New Asparagus with Olive Oil, Lemon, and Cracked Black Pepper — SERVES 4 AS AN APPETIZER

3 tablespoons olive oil

2 teaspoons grated lemon zest

3 tablespoons fresh lemon juice

1^1/2 teaspoons salt

^{1}/4 teaspoon freshly ground black pepper, plus more to taste

1 pound pencil-thin asparagus, trimmed

^{1}/4 cup shaved Parmesan or pecorino cheese

With wet springs in the Willamette Valley, I look east of the Cascades to the high desert regions to see what vegetables might be appearing in the drier terrain of eastern Oregon and Washington. One of the first signs of late spring is the arrival of asparagus from eastern Washington. When the first thin spears show up at your local market, treat yourself to this simple preparation.

In a small bowl, whisk together the oil, lemon zest, lemon juice, ^{1}/2 teaspoon of the salt, and ^{1}/4 teaspoon pepper; set aside.

To blanch the asparagus, fill a large skillet with about 1 inch of water and add the remaining 1 teaspoon salt. Bring the water to a boil. Carefully place the asparagus in the boiling water and cook for 1 minute. Immediately remove the asparagus and drain well.

To serve, arrange the asparagus on 4 warm plates. Spoon the vinaigrette over the asparagus. Garnish with shaved cheese. Top with freshly ground pepper to taste.

Asparagus with Spring Onion–Lemon Vinaigrette, Sorrel, and Goat Cheese — SERVES 4 AS AN APPETIZER

Yet another great debate on the vegetable front is which size asparagus, thick, thin, or medium, is the most desirable. The answer is a matter of personal taste, of course, but I have found that some preparations work better than others depending on the size of the stalk. Pencil-thin asparagus is the most tender and usually does not need to be peeled. Medium stalks are easy to handle and are also sometimes tender enough that they do require peeling. Jumbo asparagus should be peeled and is excellent in a vegetable sauté, on the grill, or oven roasted with olive oil, salt, and pepper.

In this dish, thin asparagus is blanched and chilled with a vinaigrette to make a nice first course or luncheon plate. Spring onions are mild and flavorful and can be used raw, as they are here, without being overwhelmingly strong or bitter.

1/4 cup olive oil

2 teaspoons grated lemon zest

3 tablespoons fresh lemon juice

1 3/4 teaspoons salt

1/4 teaspoon freshly ground black pepper, plus more to taste

2 to 3 spring onions or baby leeks (white part only), thinly sliced

1 pound pencil-thin asparagus, trimmed

4 ounces fresh white goat cheese, crumbled (about 1 cup)

4 or 5 sorrel leaves, ribs removed, thinly sliced

To prepare the vinaigrette: In a small bowl, whisk together the oil, lemon zest, lemon juice, 3/4 teaspoon of the salt, and 1/4 teaspoon pepper. Stir in the onions or leeks and let stand for 30 minutes.

To blanch the asparagus: Fill a large skillet with about 2 inches of water and add the remaining 1 teaspoon salt. Fill a large bowl with water and ice cubes; set aside. Carefully place the asparagus in boiling water and cook for 1 minute. Immediately remove from the skillet and plunge into ice water to cool. When fully cooled, drain well.

To serve, arrange the asparagus on chilled plates. Spoon the vinaigrette over the asparagus. Top with the cheese, sorrel, and freshly ground pepper to taste.

Warm Asparagus and Bacon Toast
with Red Pepper–Shallot Vinaigrette — SERVES 4 AS AN APPETIZER

RED PEPPER–SHALLOT VINAIGRETTE

$1/3$ **cup olive oil**

3 tablespoons sherry vinegar

$3/4$ **teaspoon salt**

$1/4$ **teaspoon freshly ground black pepper**

$1/4$ **cup minced fresh chives**

$1/4$ **cup pitted kalamata or black olives, chopped**

3 shallots, thinly sliced

1 red bell pepper, roasted, peeled, and cut into thin strips (page 224)

12 ounces thin or medium asparagus, trimmed

4 slices bacon, halved crosswise

Four $3/4$-inch-thick slices thick-crusted Salted Rosemary Bread (opposite), Potato Bread (page 29), or other country bread

2 tablespoons olive oil

1 clove garlic, minced

4 slices mozzarella or Monterey Jack cheese

This recipe was a bit of a fluke—the kind of dish created at the spur of the moment, before a busy restaurant service, that ends up selling very well. So well, in fact, customers have asked for it again and again. The recipe works best with small- to medium-sized asparagus and should be served warm.

To make the vinaigrette: In a medium bowl, whisk together the oil, vinegar, salt, and pepper. Stir in the chives, olives, shallots, and bell pepper; set aside.

Preheat the oven to 350°. Place the asparagus on a baking sheet in 4 bunches of 4 or 5. Place 2 pieces of bacon over each bunch, forming an X. Bake for about 15 minutes, or until the asparagus is partially cooked. Remove from the oven, leaving the oven on.

Lightly toast the bread in the oven. In a small bowl, combine the oil and garlic and brush on the bread. Transfer each bundle of asparagus and bacon to a slice of bread and top with a slice of cheese. Place on the baking sheet and bake for an additional 3 to 5 minutes, or until the cheese is melted.

To serve, spoon one-quarter of the vinaigrette on each of 4 plates. Place a warm toast on each pool of vinaigrette.

Salted Rosemary Bread — MAKES 2 ROUND LOAVES

This rosemary bread makes a nice accompaniment to the preceding asparagus toast or to many of the salads included in this chapter. You can either toast a slice or cube it and grill it with a little olive oil and garlic to make tasty salad croutons. The sponge needs to be prepared the day before the bread is made.

To make the sponge: In a mixer bowl, combine the water and yeast. Let stand for 5 minutes, or until the top surface has a thin layer of foam, indicating that the yeast is active. Using a heavy-duty mixer fitted with a paddle, at low speed, gradually add the flour and mix for about 2 minutes. Transfer to a large oiled bowl and cover tightly with plastic wrap. Let stand at room temperature overnight.

To make the dough: In a mixer bowl, combine the water and yeast. Let stand for 5 minutes, or until the top surface has a thin layer of foam, indicating that the yeast is active. Using a heavy-duty mixer fitted with a paddle, mix in the sponge, flour (in $1/2$-cup increments), and cornmeal on low speed for 5 minutes. Cover and let rest for 20 minutes.

Change to a dough hook and mix in the rosemary and salt on medium speed for 8 to 9 minutes, or until the dough leaves the sides of the bowl. Form the dough into a ball and place in a large oiled bowl, turning the dough so that all surfaces of the dough are coated with oil. Cover tightly with plastic wrap and let rise in a warm place for $1 1/2$ to 2 hours, or until doubled in size.

Punch the dough down, cut it in half, and form into 2 rounds. Place each round smooth-side down in a floured proofing basket or bowl lined with a tea towel and covered lightly with another tea towel, and let rise in a warm place for $1 1/2$ to 2 hours, or until doubled in size.

Preheat the oven to 500° for 1 hour. Gently turn out the loaves onto a greased baking sheet. Sprinkle the tops of the loaves with kosher salt. Just before putting the loaves into the oven, spritz the oven heavily with water, being careful not to spritz the oven-light area. Put the loaves on the highest rack and reduce the oven temperature to 450°. Spritz the oven 2 more times during the first 5 minutes of baking. Check the bread after 20 minutes of baking and rotate the loaves if necessary for even browning. Bake an additional 15 to 20 minutes, or until the crust is fully browned and dense to the touch. Transfer the loaves to a wire rack and let cool for 1 hour before slicing.

SPONGE

$1 1/2$ cups warm (110°) water

$3/4$ teaspoon active dry yeast

$2 1/4$ cups unbleached organic flour

DOUGH

$1 1/3$ cups warm (110°) water

$1/2$ teaspoon active dry yeast

$5 1/3$ cups bread flour

$3/4$ cup cornmeal

2 tablespoons minced fresh
  rosemary

1 tablespoon plus $3/4$ teaspoon salt

Kosher salt for sprinkling

Olive Oil–Basted Asparagus with Grated Hard Cheese and Sherry Vinegar — SERVES 4 AS AN APPETIZER OR SIDE DISH

1 pound thick asparagus, peeled halfway up stalk and trimmed

2 tablespoons olive oil

1 tablespoon sherry vinegar

1/4 cup shaved hard cheese such as Parmesan or pecorino

Salt and freshly ground black pepper to taste

Jumbo asparagus has a rich, mature flavor, and the firmness of the stalk adds an enjoyable texture to a dish. The thick stalk is great for slicing and sautéing, or for roasting with olive oil, as in the following recipe.

Preheat the oven to 400° Place the asparagus on a baking sheet. Brush with the olive oil. Bake for 8 to 10 minutes, or until crisp-tender.

To serve, place the asparagus on a serving platter. Sprinkle with the vinegar, shaved cheese, and salt and pepper.

Spring Lettuce Salad with Marinated Beets and Ricotta Crouton — SERVES 4

VINAIGRETTE

1/3 cup hazelnut oil or extra-virgin olive oil

3 tablespoons red wine vinegar

2 teaspoons grated orange zest

3 tablespoons fresh orange juice

3/4 teaspoon salt

1/2 teaspoon freshly ground black pepper

8 ounces small beets (red or yellow), trimmed to 1 inch of greens and scrubbed

2 teaspoons salt

Four 1/2-inch-thick slices walnut or country bread

1/4 cup fresh whole-milk ricotta

8 cups (8 ounces) mixed baby greens

3 tablespoons hazelnuts, toasted, skinned, and chopped (page 224)

This salad pairs the subtle flavors of early spring lettuces and vegetables with whole-milk ricotta, which tends to taste sweeter due to the lush green grass that reappears as a staple food for Willamette Valley milk cows. Arugula, watercress, and miner's lettuce tend to be fairly mild in the early spring, and their subtle flavors offer a wonderful complement to the tang of the marinated beets.

To prepare the vinaigrette: In a small bowl, whisk together the oil, vinegar, orange zest, orange juice, salt, and pepper; set aside.

In a medium saucepan, cover the beets with water and add the salt. Bring to a boil, reduce heat, and simmer for 20 to 35 minutes, or until tender. Let cool slightly and peel. Cut into 1/2-inch-thick wedges and place in a medium bowl. While the beets are still warm, gently toss with 1/3 cup of the vinaigrette and allow to marinate for 30 minutes.

To serve, toast the bread and spread with the ricotta. Toss the greens with the remaining dressing. Divide the greens among 4 plates. Portion the beets and dressing onto each plate and top with a crouton. Sprinkle with hazelnuts.

Spring Onion, Radish, and Arugula Salad with Walnuts and Corn Bread Croutons — SERVES 4

Spring onions are often referred to as salad onions because they are mild and sweet enough to eat raw. Slice them thin and toss with radishes, arugula, walnuts, and a mustard vinaigrette for a lovely salad. If you can locate spring Walla Walla onions, you will be in for a real treat!

Corn bread croutons are a good way to use day-old corn bread, and to add color and texture to the greens.

To prepare the vinaigrette: In a small bowl, whisk together the oil, vinegar, mustard, salt, and pepper; set aside.

To make the croutons: Preheat the oven to 350°. In a medium bowl, combine the oil, salt, and pepper. Add the corn bread and toss lightly to coat. Place on a baking sheet and toast in the oven for about 10 minutes, or until crispy; set aside.

In a large salad bowl, combine the greens, walnuts, radishes, onions, and corn bread croutons. Toss lightly with the vinaigrette. Serve.

VINAIGRETTE

1/4 cup olive oil

3 tablespoons sherry vinegar

1 teaspoon Dijon mustard

1/2 teaspoon salt

1/4 teaspoon freshly ground black pepper

CORN BREAD CROUTONS

2 tablespoons olive oil

1/2 teaspoon salt

1/4 teaspoon freshly ground black pepper

1 1/4 cups 1-inch cubed Wildwood Corn Bread (page 80)

8 cups (8 ounces) baby greens or arugula

1/4 cup toasted walnuts, coarsely chopped (page 224)

5 radishes, thinly sliced

2 red or white spring onions or 2 mature yellow or red onions, thinly sliced crosswise

Baked Stuffed Chard Leaves with Spring Garlic, Potatoes, Goat Cheese, and Black Olive Vinaigrette

SERVES 4 AS AN APPETIZER OR LUNCH ENTRÉE

After enduring the fall and winter, early garlic sends up its fragile shoots to announce where the tender bulbs are hiding. Because the bulbs are still fairly young, their flavor is much milder than the more mature summer garlic.

This recipe is adapted from a dish prepared by Robert Reynolds, a chef instructor who resides in Portland. It takes full advantage of the subtle taste of baby garlic, which is added to a potato filling that is mixed with onion and goat cheese and stuffed into blanched red chard leaves. The stuffed leaves are baked, then topped with a black olive and garlic vinaigrette.

You can find chard year-round, but it is particularly good in early spring. This leafy vegetable works well in this dish because it is sturdy when blanched and can be used as a wrapping for most fillings.

To make the vinaigrette: In a small bowl, whisk together the oil, vinegar, salt, and pepper. Mix in the olives and shallots; set aside.

To prepare the filling: Preheat the oven to 400°. Bake the potatoes for 45 to 60 minutes, or until tender. Let cool slightly. Cut the potatoes in half and scoop out the potato flesh into a medium bowl. Mash with a fork; set aside.

In a small saucepan, melt the butter over medium heat. Add the garlic, onion, salt, and pepper; sauté for 6 to 8 minutes, or until the onion is tender. Blend the onion mixture, nutmeg, goat cheese, basil, and chives into the mashed potatoes; adjust seasoning and set aside.

To blanch the chard, fill a 3-quart pot three-fourths full with water. Stir in the salt and bring to a rolling boil. Fill a large bowl with ice cubes and water. Carefully dip the chard leaves in the boiling water, 3 or 4 at a time, for about 30 seconds. Immediately plunge them into ice water to cool. Drain well on paper towels.

Divide the potato mixture into 8 portions. Place 8 leaves on a flat surface (piece some of the leaves together if necessary, or cut the leaves in half to make 8 portions). Place a portion of potato filling in the center of each leaf. Fold the sides in and roll up. Repeat the process to make 8 portions. (This can be done 1 day ahead, covered, and refrigerated.) Place the stuffed chard on a buttered baking sheet. Bake for 20 to 30 minutes, or until heated through.

To serve, place 2 stuffed chard leaves on each plate and spoon on the vinaigrette.

BLACK OLIVE VINAIGRETTE

1/4 cup olive oil

3 tablespoons white wine vinegar

1/2 teaspoon salt

1/4 teaspoon freshly ground black pepper

1/4 cup pitted kalamata or other black olives, chopped

3 shallots, thinly sliced

FILLING

2 russet potatoes, scrubbed and pierced

1 tablespoon unsalted butter

3 stalks spring garlic (both green and white parts), minced, or 4 cloves mature garlic, minced

1/2 cup minced yellow onion

1 teaspoon salt

1/2 teaspoon ground white pepper

1/4 teaspoon grated nutmeg

4 ounces fresh white goat cheese

2 tablespoons minced fresh basil

2 tablespoons minced fresh chives

1 teaspoon salt

1 bunch red chard leaves, stemmed

Wildwood Corn Bread — SERVES 8

1 cup flour

1 cup yellow cornmeal

1/4 cup brown sugar

1 tablespoon baking powder

1/2 teaspoon baking soda

1/2 to 1 teaspoon cayenne pepper

1 teaspoon salt

1/2 cup milk

1/2 cup buttermilk

3/4 cup sour cream

2 large eggs

1/4 cup corn oil or vegetable oil

Place a pan of corn bread in front of me and it'll be gone by the end of a meal. I can't seem to resist a warm slice slathered with honey and butter, and the first is usually followed by another and another. Here is a recipe from Wildwood for this classic bread. It can also be used to make colorful croutons, as in the recipe on page 77.

Preheat the oven to 375°. In a large bowl, combine the flour, cornmeal, brown sugar, baking powder, baking soda, cayenne, and salt; set aside.

In a medium bowl, beat together the milk, buttermilk, sour cream, eggs, and oil. Add the wet ingredients to the dry ingredients, mixing just until the dry ingredients are moistened; the batter will be slightly lumpy. Grease a 9-inch square baking pan. Pour in the batter. Bake for 20 to 25 minutes, or until a toothpick inserted in the center comes out clean.

Let cool. Cut into 8 portions and serve.

Oven-Roasted Spring Sweet Onions — SERVES 4 AS A SIDE DISH

4 bulbs red or white spring sweet onions (Walla Walla, Maui, Vidalia, or Texas Sweet)

2 tablespoons olive oil

1 tablespoon white wine vinegar

3/4 teaspoon salt

1/4 teaspoon freshly ground black pepper

12 sprigs thyme

12 cloves garlic, peeled

Spring sweet onions are wonderful roasted in the oven with a little olive oil and herbs. This recipe also works for mature red or yellow onions at any time of year; adjust the cooking time by allowing the firmer onions to roast a few minutes longer.

Preheat the oven to 400°. Trim the dark green tops off of the onions and save them for stock or vegetable soup. Remove the outer layer of skin from the bulb, but leave the root intact (this will keep the onion from falling apart). Cut each bulb into quarters. In a baking dish, arrange the onions in a single layer. Sprinkle with the oil, vinegar, salt, and pepper, and place the thyme sprigs and garlic cloves around the onions. Bake for about 25 minutes, turning occasionally, or until tender. Serve immediately.

Soft Rye Torpedo Rolls — MAKES ABOUT 12 ROLLS

It goes without saying that the key ingredient of a good sandwich is the bread on which it is made. Here's a soft rye roll recipe from our Wildwood repertoire that is served with many sandwich combinations. Try the rolls with the Sweet Onion Sandwich on page 71.

2 cups warm (110°) water

1 tablespoon olive oil

1 1/2 teaspoons active dry yeast

2 tablespoons honey

4 cups bread flour

2 cups dark or medium rye flour

1 1/2 tablespoon salt

To make the sponge: In a large mixing bowl, combine the water, olive oil, yeast, and honey. Let stand for 8 minutes, or until the top surface has a thin layer of foam, indicating that the yeast is active.

Using a heavy-duty mixer fitted with a paddle, at low speed, mix in 2 cups each of the bread and rye flour. Mix for 3 minutes. (This mixture will be wet and sticky.) Cover tightly with plastic wrap and let sit in a warm place for 45 to 60 minutes, or until doubled in size.

Turn the dough out onto a lightly floured surface. Mix in by hand the remaining 2 cups bread flour, 1/2 cup at a time. Knead the dough until all of the flour has been incorporated. Cover the dough with a floured towel and let rise in a warm place for 1 hour, or until doubled in size.

Portion into 12 equal pieces. Roll each portion into a ball, cover with a tea towel, and let rest for 4 minutes. Press each ball into a disk about 3/4 inch thick. Roll each disk to form a torpedo shape. Place each roll, seam-side down, on a greased baking sheet. Cover with a tea towel and let rise in a warm place for about 45 minutes, until doubled in size.

Preheat the oven to 425°. Just before putting the rolls in the oven, spritz the oven heavily with water, being careful not to spritz the oven-light area. Bake for 15 to 20 minutes, or until golden brown. Transfer the rolls to wire racks and let cool. Serve.

SAUVIE ISLAND

5. SAUVIE ISLAND: AN AGRICULTURAL ISLAND WITH OUTLETS TO THE CITY

Aunt Boots had a home with acreage on the eastern tip of Sauvie Island, on the Willamette River side. The island is a 15-mile-long, 4 1/2-mile-wide piece of solitude just outside the Portland city limits. On the larger scale of things, it sits about halfway between the equator and the North Pole, which, perhaps, explains why the summer sun seems to linger just a little longer here on the evening horizon.

I remember standing in Aunt Boots's garden one summer, surrounded by beanpoles, flowering squash blossoms, and that never-ending twilight overhead. Aunt Boots wasn't really my aunt; she was related to Joan Uhl, a dear friend of my mother's who is a marvelous cook and a food enthusiast. I always enjoyed going out to the farm, experiencing the quiet, and marveling at the wonderful fruits and vegetables the rich soil brought to life.

I remember one particular evening when Boots plucked a red cherry tomato off its vine and handed it to me. I could still feel its warmth from the afternoon sun. "Have you ever tasted anything like that?" she asked, as I bit into its juicy richness. Her smile told me she already knew the answer.

Indulge yourself some late August afternoon, when tomatoes are at their peak, and head out of the kitchen and into the garden with a knife, salt, pepper grinder, and a dose of extra-virgin olive oil. Slice open a ripe tomato and sprinkle it with a little of this and a little of that, then bite into it and experience the full flavor nurtured by the summer sun, the soil, and the vine. This, to me, is one of nature's perfect snacks.

Many small farms still exist on Sauvie Island today. When I buy vegetables for the restaurant, I often go to Sauvie Island Organics. Shari Satir and Beth Gibans have three acres planted on a plot of land that used to be a dairy farm. The farm sits on the midwest section of the island, and is a sight to behold in the summer with greens of all kinds growing in neat little rows. Red mustard greens, curly kale, black kale, stir-fry greens, arugula, mizuna, and garden cress each flourish on their little piece of the landscape. Some of my favorites are the Red Ace beets that seem to grow sweeter here than anywhere else. These fat little beets are a rich burgundy red and sweet enough to eat raw.

During the growing season, Shari and Beth head out early each Saturday morning to sell their produce at the farmer's market in the Portland Park Blocks, a stretch of Park Avenue that runs north to south along the park, creating a natural green belt in the heart of downtown Portland. This is one of my favorite summer marketplaces, due in part to its uniquely picturesque setting surrounded by one-hundred-year-old elm trees that are lovingly protected and maintained by the city.

After a successful day, Shari and Beth have a few deliveries to make before heading back to Sauvie Island. They stop by the restaurant with boxes of lettuce, beets, tomatoes, and peppers, all of which will be part of the evening's menu, ensuring an empty truck on the return trip to the island. Once home, they will begin the cycle again, harvesting another week's crops, which will undoubtedly be as extraordinary as the last.

During the summer months, the landscape of Sauvie Island consists of wavy, windblown trees and lush green dotted with color from the local flower farms. Much of the island is farmland heavily planted with corn, squashes, beans, peaches, flowers, pickling cucumbers, berries, and other fruits and vegetables. Sauvie Island's proximity to the city creates a high demand for these foods from city dwellers craving that "homegrown" flavor.

Strawberries are the first crop to arrive in early summer, followed by raspberries and blackberries. Cauliflower, broccoli, potatoes, beans, and hard and soft squashes eventually join the ranks as summer rolls into autumn, but perhaps the most prized item of all is the corn. Tall fields of sweet varieties span the island and grow seven to eight feet high. Everyone in Portland talks about the corn before its arrival, and when it does arrive, the season is short, too short most would say.

Public markets are popular on the island in summer and early fall. Old barns and storage houses display hand-painted signs extending a friendly offer: "We

Pick or You Pick." Prices are scrawled in bold colors on the sides of the worn wooden buildings. Inside, bins brimming with fruits and vegetables yield an occasional runaway potato or avalanche of apples.

Autumn brings the pumpkin harvest to Sauvie Island. By September, many of the summer crops have thinned, allowing the pumpkin fields to emerge. Glowing balls of deep orange are scattered across the island. I used to spend hours wandering out into the fields looking for the largest ones. Sometimes, if the first frost hadn't arrived yet, I could find a few cherry tomatoes still lingering on their vines. Having lasted this long into the season, their sugar content was high, resulting in what I call tomato candy.

As winter churns its chilly air off the Columbia and Willamette rivers, one crop remains: the trusty potato. Sauvie Island was once known as Wapato Island because of the roots the natives dug from the banks of the two rivers and the wetlands. These wapatos, or "wild potatoes," are not currently part of our culinary repertoire in Oregon, but many other kinds of potatoes are.

In the winter, Sauvie Island is returned to its year-round inhabitants. The Columbia River beaches become empty tracts of sand where you can wander for hours hearing no sound other than that of waves breaking from the occasional cargo ship finding its way through the narrow channel to the city. The farmland folds back into itself to rest for another spring and a new planting season.

Tomatoes with Olive Oil

4 large vine-ripened tomatoes

1/4 cup extra-virgin olive oil

3 tablespoons red wine vinegar

Kosher salt and freshly ground
  black pepper to taste

Like Aunt Boots's tomatoes eaten directly from the vine, warm from the summer sun, the essential ingredient in this very simple recipe is ripe tomatoes at the peak of their flavor.

Slice each tomato into 4 or 5 thick slices and arrange on a plate. Combine the oil and vinegar. Spoon over the tomatoes. Season with salt and pepper. Serve.

Summer Tomato Sauce

MAKES ABOUT 3 CUPS

1 tablespoon extra-virgin olive oil

4 cloves garlic, minced

1 yellow onion, thinly sliced

1/4 cup water

1 teaspoon salt

8 ripe tomatoes, chopped

1/4 cup dry white wine

2 tablespoons red wine vinegar

1/8 teaspoon cayenne pepper

3 herb sprigs (flat-leaf parsley,
  thyme, or basil, or a mixture),
  tied together

Tomato sauce preparations range from uncooked, to briefly cooked, to slowly simmered. This sauce cooks for about 30 minutes but retains much of the fresh flavor of an uncooked sauce. Over the years, I've used it for many dishes, including pastas and pizzas.

In a large skillet, heat the oil over medium-low heat. Add the garlic, onion, water, and 1/4 teaspoon of the salt. Simmer for about 10 minutes, or until the onion is tender, stirring occasionally so that the onion does not brown. Blend in the tomatoes, wine, vinegar, cayenne, and remaining 3/4 teaspoon salt. Cover and simmer for an additional 15 minutes. Remove from heat, add the herb bundle to infuse flavor into the sauce, and let cool. Remove the herb bundle and use the sauce for pasta, soup, or other dishes. To store, cover and refrigerate for up to 3 days.

Tomato and Fennel Seed Vinaigrette

MAKES ABOUT 2 CUPS

The preceding tomato sauce can be cooled and made into a dense vinaigrette by adding olive oil, white wine vinegar, toasted fennel seeds, and basil. The intense flavor, color, and texture of tomatoes and the aroma of fennel seed create a perfect accent for a tossed salad, or grilled meat, fish, or vegetables.

In a food processor, combine all the ingredients. Process for 1 minute. Cover and refrigerate for up to 3 days.

1 cup Summer Tomato Sauce (opposite)

3/4 cup extra-virgin olive oil

1/4 cup red wine vinegar

1/4 cup fresh basil leaves

1 teaspoon fennel seeds, toasted and cracked (page 224)

1 teaspoon salt

1/8 teaspoon cayenne pepper

Grated-Tomato Sauce

MAKES ABOUT 1 1/2 CUPS

I recommend using this uncooked tomato sauce as a vinaigrette or as a sauce for grilled fish, poultry, or vegetables. Because the water is not completely cooked out of the tomatoes, the sauce is too wet for pizza, but it can be added to pasta or made into a cold tomato soup. This recipe is perfect for tomatoes that are a little too ripe for salads.

Place a box grater over a bowl and grate the tomatoes on the large holes, catching the juice and tomato pieces in the bowl. If the seed and skin content are heavy, strain the tomatoes through a sieve. Stir in the onion, parsley, basil, fennel seeds, olive oil, vinegar, salt, and pepper. Let stand for a few minutes to let the flavors blend.

3 large ripe tomatoes (about 1 pound), cut into quarters

1/4 cup minced red onion

2 tablespoons chopped fresh flat-leaf parsley

1 tablespoon chopped fresh basil

1 teaspoon fennel seeds, toasted and cracked (page 224)

1 tablespoon extra-virgin olive oil

2 tablespoons white wine vinegar

Salt and freshly ground black pepper to taste

Fresh-Herb Pizza

1³/4 cups plus 1 tablespoon warm (110°) water

1 package active dry yeast

2¹/2 cups bread flour

³/4 cup semolina flour

1 tablespoon salt

¹/4 cup mixed minced fresh herbs, such as rosemary, thyme, and flat-leaf parsley

2 tablespoons olive oil

¹/4 cup yellow cornmeal for baking the pizza

We prepare many types of pizza at Wildwood, and although the toppings change from day to day, our dough recipe remains the same. This dough yields a crispy, thin crust when baked on a pizza stone in a very hot oven. It is important to select your pizza toppings carefully, as far too many pizzas suffer from an overdose of wet cheeses or oppressively heavy ingredients. Using fewer toppings and just a shaving of a good aged cheese, such as a romano, Parmesan, or goat cheese, creates a subtle, satisfying pizza with a crust that retains its crispness.

I have become so fond of this dough that when I make it at home, I often simply bake it sprinkled with a little salt, freshly ground black pepper, and olive oil, and then I shave fresh Parmesan on top while it's hot from the oven.

In a small bowl, combine the water and yeast and let stand for 5 minutes, or until the top surface has a thin layer of foam, indicating that the yeast is active.

In a mixer bowl, combine the yeast mixture, bread flour, semolina flour, salt, herbs, and olive oil. Using a heavy-duty mixer fitted with a dough hook, mix on low speed for 7 minutes, or until the dough is smooth and elastic. Form the dough into a ball and place in a large oiled bowl, turning the dough so that all the surfaces are coated with oil. Cover tightly with plastic wrap and let rise in a warm place for 1¹/2 to 2 hours, or until doubled in size.

Place a pizza stone, if you have one, in the middle rack of the oven. Preheat the oven to 500°. If you do not have a pizza stone, oil a baking sheet, sprinkle with cornmeal, and set aside.

Punch the dough down and cut into 6 portions. Form into 6 balls and cover with a tea towel while rolling out each pizza. On a floured surface, roll out each ball into a 6-inch round. Top as desired.

If using a pizza stone, transfer the rounds to the oven with a peel or baking sheet sprinkled with cornmeal. If using a baking sheet, transfer the rounds to the oiled sheet with a peel or another baking sheet sprinkled with cornmeal. (Depending on the size of your stone, you will probably have to bake the rounds in 2 batches.) Bake for 10 to 15 minutes, or until golden brown. Cut into wedges and serve immediately.

Zucchini with Thyme, Butter, and Sweet Onions

— SERVES 6 AS A SIDE DISH

How many times has a neighbor, friend, or relative come to you with an armload of zucchini saying, "I have more of these than I know what to do with," as they hand over giant specimens with more seeds than flesh? It may be these generous offerings that have earned the zucchini such a mixed reputation in the vegetable world! This recipe shines the spotlight on zucchini. I'm usually inspired to prepare it around the middle of the summer when the zucchini are 6 to 8 inches long and about 1 1/2 inches wide, and have a sweet flavor that doesn't ask for much more than a little butter and some fresh herbs.

2 tablespoons unsalted butter

1 white sweet onion, thinly sliced (Walla Walla, Vidalia, Maui, or Texas Sweet)

1 teaspoon salt

4 zucchini, halved lengthwise and cut into 1/4-inch-thick slices

1 tablespoon minced fresh thyme

1/2 teaspoon freshly ground black pepper

In a large skillet, melt the butter over medium heat. Add the onion and 1/2 teaspoon of the salt. Sauté for about 5 minutes, stirring occasionally; do not allow it to brown. Stir in the zucchini, thyme, the remaining 1/2 teaspoon salt, and the pepper. Cook for an additional 5 to 6 minutes, or until the vegetables are tender. Serve.

Roasted Corn and Basil Salad

8 ears corn, husks and silk removed

4 tablespoons olive oil

1 large red bell pepper, roasted, peeled, seeded, and cut into thin strips (page 224)

1 red onion, thinly sliced

1/4 cup fresh basil leaves, torn into small pieces

Grated zest and juice of 2 oranges

3 tablespoons fresh lemon juice

2 tablespoons white wine vinegar

1 teaspoon cumin seeds, toasted and cracked (page 224)

1 teaspoon fennel seeds, toasted and cracked (page 224)

1 teaspoon salt

1/2 teaspoon freshly ground black pepper

Corn is one of my favorite vegetables because of its versatility and sweet taste. The variations in corn are vast. This is why, at farmer's markets, I often see vendors encouraging shoppers to pull back a husk and bite into the raw kernels. Starch and sugar play a role in finding the perfect ear. Look for fresh-picked corn with a crisp bite and a good flavor balance.

This recipe for grilled corn salad is accented with orange and basil. It can stand alone as an appetizer or can be served with a roasted chicken or other poultry dish.

Preheat the broiler. Place the corn on a broiler pan and brush with 1 tablespoon of the oil. Broil 4 inches from the heat source, turning as the corn browns to roast all sides. Let cool. Using a sharp knife, cut the kernels from the cobs and put in a large bowl. Add the roasted bell pepper, red onion, and basil; set aside.

In a small bowl, whisk together the orange zest and juice, lemon juice, vinegar, cumin and fennel seeds, salt, and pepper. Pour over the salad ingredients, tossing to coat. Let stand for 30 minutes before serving.

Corn Soup with Red Mustard Greens and Red Potatoes — SERVES 8

Endless rows of cornfields are a common sight on Sauvie Island in the late summer. At Wildwood, we always specify "Sauvie Island Corn" on the menu, since it's a true local specialty.

The lowly corn cob, though sheared of its kernels, retains a surprising amount of flavor that most of us never utilize. In this recipe, the cob is used to create a stock infused with the sweet taste of corn. Any available bitter greens, such as escarole, curly endive, or yellow mustard greens, can be substituted for the red mustard greens in this recipe. The bitterness of the greens offsets the sweetness of the corn. If desired, you can make the stock for this corn soup 1 day ahead.

Using a sharp knife, cut the kernels off the cobs. Divide the kernels into 2 equal portions and set aside. Chop half of the corn cobs into 1-inch-round pieces and set aside. Discard the remainder.

In a 4-quart saucepan, melt the butter over medium heat. Add the chopped corn cobs, onions, leeks, celery, fennel, garlic, and 2 teaspoons of the salt; sauté for 10 minutes, stirring occasionally. Blend in 1 cup of the water and the wine. Bring to a boil, reduce heat to low, and cover the pan. Cook for about 30 minutes, stirring occasionally. Add the stock, the remaining 2 cups water, and the herbs, and simmer, covered, for an additional 30 minutes. Let cool slightly and strain the stock into a large bowl. Discard the cooked vegetables and herbs.

Return the stock to the pot. Add the potatoes, the remaining 2 teaspoons salt, the pepper, and the whole corn kernels. Bring to a boil, reduce heat to medium, and cook for 15 minutes. Add the mustard greens and simmer until the potatoes and greens are tender, about 5 minutes. Taste and adjust the seasoning. Serve.

8 ears corn, husks and silk removed

2 tablespoons unsalted butter

3 yellow onions, chopped

3 leeks (white part only), washed and chopped

3 ribs celery, chopped

1 bulb fennel, trimmed and chopped

8 cloves garlic, chopped

4 teaspoons salt

3 cups water

1 cup dry white wine

4 cups chicken stock (page 221) or vegetable stock (page 222)

4 sprigs each thyme, flat-leaf parsley, and oregano, tied together

4 red potatoes, cut into 1/2-inch slices

2 teaspoons freshly ground black pepper

1 bunch red mustard greens, stemmed and chopped

Creamed Corn with Smoky Bacon, Chanterelles, and Thyme — SERVES 6 AS A SIDE DISH OR LUNCH ENTRÉE

2 thick slices smoky bacon, cut into 1/4-inch strips

Kernels cut from 4 ears yellow or white corn (about 4 cups)

4 ounces chanterelle or portobello mushrooms, wiped clean and chopped into 1/2-inch pieces

1/2 yellow onion, chopped

1 cup heavy cream

1 tablespoon fresh lemon juice

1 teaspoon minced fresh thyme

1 teaspoon salt

1/2 teaspoon freshly ground black pepper

1 tablespoon minced fresh flat-leaf parsley

Creamed corn seems to have become a dish of the past, perhaps because we think of it as a canned food. This version of creamed corn, which combines fresh corn with herbs, heavy cream, chanterelle mushrooms, and a bit of smoky bacon, bears little resemblance to its canned namesake. Serve this as a lunch entrée or as an accompaniment to roasted chicken or pork chops. Any mushroom will work in this recipe, although the flavors of the chanterelles and corn blend especially well together.

In a large skillet, cook the bacon over medium heat until crisp. Remove the bacon from the pan and drain on paper towels. Pour off the bacon drippings and reserve 1 teaspoon.

Add the reserved bacon drippings back to the skillet. Over medium heat, sauté the corn, mushrooms, and onion for 6 minutes, or until the mushrooms appear soft, stirring occasionally. Blend in the cream, lemon juice, thyme, salt, pepper, and bacon. Bring to a simmer and cook the cream to reduce until thick, 3 to 4 minutes. The starch in the corn will help thicken the cream. Add the chopped parsley. Ladle into bowls and serve.

Left: *Creamed Corn with Smoky Bacon, Chanterelles, and Thyme*
Right: *Roasted Beets with Fennel Seed, Oranges, and Goat Cheese* (recipe appears on page 96)

Roasted Beets with Fennel Seed, Oranges, and Goat Cheese

— SERVES 6 AS AN APPETIZER OR SIDE DISH   (PICTURED ON PREVIOUS PAGE)

2 pounds beets (about 6 medium-sized beets or 18 small or baby beets), scrubbed and trimmed

$3/4$ cup fresh orange juice

$1/4$ cup extra-virgin olive oil

2 teaspoons salt

1 teaspoon freshly ground black pepper, plus more for garnish

1 tablespoon grated orange zest, plus orange zest strands for garnish

2 tablespoons red wine vinegar

1 teaspoon fennel seeds, toasted and cracked (page 224)

2 ounces fresh or aged white goat cheese, crumbled (about $1/2$ cup)

With its barn-sized doors, dirt floor, and sunny, open-air feel, Sauvie Island Market is one of my favorite roadside produce stands. Just-picked red and yellow beets, with their greens still intact, teem forth from the large bins starting in midsummer, though they seem to be at their sweetest in October.

For this recipe, I prefer using a medium-sized red variety, as it will hold up well during the hour-long braising.

~~~~~~

Preheat the oven to 350°. In a 7-by-11-by-2-inch baking dish, arrange the beets. Combine $1/2$ cup of the orange juice, the olive oil, 1 teaspoon of the salt, and $1/2$ teaspoon of the pepper and pour over the beets. Cover the pan with aluminum foil. Roast in the oven for 50 to 60 minutes, or until the beets are tender. Remove the beets from the pan, let cool slightly, and peel while still warm. Reserve the liquid from the pan. Cut each medium-sized beet into 4 wedges or leave the baby beets whole; set aside.

To make the vinaigrette: Combine the reserved beet liquid, the remaining $1/4$ cup of orange juice, the grated orange zest, the vinegar, and the remaining 1 teaspoon salt and $1/2$ teaspoon pepper; pour over the beets. Marinate in the vinaigrette for 30 minutes or cover and refrigerate overnight.

To assemble, use a slotted spoon to transfer the beets to a platter. Sprinkle with the fennel seeds and the orange zest strands. Garnish with the crumbled goat cheese and freshly ground pepper. Serve.

Fennel Seed Crackers

MAKES 1 DOZEN CRACKERS

If you're looking for a fun and flavorful alternative to croutons, try these crackers to lend a little extra crunch to your salad. Sprinkle the top of the crackers with your favorite seed or spice mixture to create your own variations of this versatile recipe.

In a mixer bowl, combine the flour, cracked fennel seeds, sugar, and salt. Using a heavy-duty mixer fitted with a paddle, mix on low speed for 1 minute. Add the butter and mix on low speed until the butter is blended, 4 to 6 minutes. Add the fennel greens, if using, and the water; mix until the dough comes together.

Turn the dough onto a floured board and knead until smooth and elastic, about 5 minutes, adding more flour as needed. Cover with a damp tea towel and let rest for 20 minutes. Divide into 12 portions and keep covered with the towel.

Preheat the oven to 400° with a pizza stone inside, if you have one. If you do not have one, lightly oil a baking sheet and set aside. Flour 1 of the dough portions. Using a pasta machine, put the portion through the machine at its widest setting. Put it through at the medium setting, and then again at the thinnest setting, flouring the dough as needed. The dough should now be in irregular rectangular shapes. Repeat until all the dough is used. Put the dough on the pizza stone or the lightly oiled baking sheet. Bake for 5 to 8 minutes, or until the crackers are brittle (they will be pale). Let cool. Serve or store in an airtight container.

2 cups unbleached organic flour

1 tablespoon fennel seeds, cracked (page 224)

1 $3/4$ teaspoons sugar

1 $1/2$ teaspoons salt

2 $1/4$ teaspoons unsalted butter, cut into pieces

2 tablespoons coarsely chopped fennel greens (no stems), optional

$1/2$ cup water

Olive Oil–Braised Bell Peppers

SERVES 6 AS AN APPETIZER OR SIDE DISH

3 cups olive oil

3/4 cup white wine vinegar

1 yellow onion, thinly sliced

Peeled whole cloves from
   1 bulb garlic

1 teaspoon fennel seeds, cracked
   (page 224)

1 teaspoon coriander seeds, cracked
   (page 224)

2 teaspoons salt

1 teaspoon freshly ground black
   pepper

2 red bell peppers, seeded, deribbed,
   and cut into 1/2-inch-wide strips

2 yellow bell peppers, seeded,
   deribbed, and cut into
   1/2-inch-wide strips

2 green bell peppers, seeded,
   deribbed, and cut into
   1/2-inch-wide strips

8 herb sprigs (thyme, basil, oregano,
   rosemary, flat-leaf parsley,
   tarragon, and/or bay leaves),
   tied together

You can serve these peppers on a platter by themselves, or use them as a garnish or to top pastas or pizzas. To serve with a salad, toss the peppers with baby lettuce and shave Parmesan or Asiago cheese on top. Use some of the braising liquid as a dressing. Any leftover liquid can become the braising liquid for other vegetables, such as artichokes, tomatoes, or red onions.

In a 12-inch skillet, combine the oil, vinegar, onion, garlic, fennel seeds, coriander seeds, salt, and pepper; bring to a simmer. Add the bell pepper strips and herb bundle. Simmer for 15 minutes, or until the peppers are tender when pierced with the tip of a paring knife. Let cool in the liquid and discard the herb bundle. Cover and refrigerate overnight to allow the flavors to blend.

To serve, use a slotted spoon.

Potato Dumplings with Pumpkin, Hazelnuts, Bacon, and Brown Butter — SERVES 4 AS AN APPETIZER OR SIDE DISH

Field pumpkins are meant for carving, but sugar pumpkins make a nice accompaniment to a game dish. This recipe uses one of my favorite flavor combinations: pumpkin, bacon, sage, and brown butter. The dumplings can be made 1 day ahead.

To make the dumplings: Preheat the oven to 325°. In a large pot, cover the potatoes with water. Bring to a boil, reduce heat, and simmer for about 15 minutes, or until tender when pierced with a knife. Drain well and let stand at room temperature to dry for 5 minutes. When the potatoes are cool enough to handle, pass them through a food mill or grate them on the large holes of a box grater. Cover a large baking sheet with waxed paper or parchment paper. Spread out the grated potatoes on it, and place in the oven to dry out for 5 minutes. Place in the refrigerator to cool, about 15 minutes.

Put the potatoes in a large bowl. Form a well in the center and add the sage, salt, cayenne, allspice, nutmeg, and pepper. Add half of each of the flours and stir the mixture for 1 minute. Stir in the egg and the remaining flours. Transfer the dough to a lightly floured board and knead, working to incorporate all of the ingredients. Wrap in plastic wrap and refrigerate for 1 1/2 hours or overnight.

Meanwhile, preheat the oven to 350°. Put the pumpkin in a baking pan. Baste lightly with the olive oil and season with 3/4 teaspoon of the salt and 1/4 teaspoon of the pepper. Bake for 25 to 35 minutes, or until slightly soft. Leave the oven on. Let cool and cut off the skin. Cut the pumpkin or squash into 1/2-inch dice and set aside.

To form the dumplings, remove the dough from the refrigerator and cut into 4 pieces. Dust a board with semolina flour and roll each piece of dough into a rope 1/2 inch in diameter. Cut into 1-inch pieces and place on an oiled jelly-roll pan. (At this point, the dumplings can be refrigerated overnight.) Bake the dumplings for 20 to 25 minutes, or until lightly browned and cooked through.

Just before the dumplings are ready, in a 12-inch skillet, cook the bacon until crisp. Transfer the bacon to paper towels to drain, then crumble. Discard the drippings and wipe out the pan. Add the butter and cook over medium heat until it begins to brown. Add the bacon, lemon juice, hazelnuts, parsley, diced pumpkin or squash, and the remaining 1 teaspoon salt and 1/2 teaspoon pepper. Cook to heat through.

To assemble, spoon the dumplings into pasta bowls and top with the pumpkin brown butter sauce. Garnish with the cheese and serve.

POTATO DUMPLINGS

1 1/2 pounds Yukon Gold potatoes, peeled and quartered

2 teaspoons chopped fresh sage

1 teaspoon salt

1/4 teaspoon cayenne pepper

1/4 teaspoon ground allspice

1/4 teaspoon ground nutmeg

1/4 teaspoon freshly ground black pepper

1/2 cup all-purpose flour

1/4 cup semolina flour

1 large egg, beaten

1 sugar pumpkin (3 to 4 pounds), seeded and cut into 6 pieces

1 tablespoon olive oil

1 3/4 teaspoons salt

3/4 teaspoon freshly ground black pepper

4 slices bacon

1/2 cup (1 stick) unsalted butter

2 tablespoons fresh lemon juice

1/2 cup hazelnuts, toasted, skinned, and chopped (page 224)

2 tablespoons chopped fresh flat-leaf parsley

1/4 cup shaved Asiago or pecorino cheese

Acorn Squash and Cider Soup

4 pounds acorn squash (4 or 5 squash), halved and seeded

3 teaspoons salt

1 teaspoon freshly ground black pepper

2 tablespoons unsalted butter

6 cloves garlic, chopped

4 carrots, peeled and chopped

3 leeks (white part only), washed and chopped

2 yellow onions, chopped

1 bulb fennel, trimmed and chopped into 1/2-inch pieces

4 cups chicken stock (page 221) or vegetable stock (page 222)

4 cups apple cider

1/4 cup undiluted orange juice concentrate

2 teaspoons fennel seeds

1/4 teaspoon ground cloves

1 tablespoon sherry vinegar

1 tablespoon fresh lemon juice

1/2 teaspoon cayenne pepper

1 unpeeled red apple, cored and chopped into 1/4-inch pieces for garnish

I prefer winter squashes to pumpkin for soup, as they provide more meat for flavor and thickening, and can offer different textures, depending on the kind you use. Butternut squash creates a smooth texture. Delicata, Sugar Loaf, and dumpling seem to work better for baking and serving on their own. The kabocha, a large, dark green, pumpkin-shaped squash found in Asian markets, offers a dry flesh that is well suited to baking.

This recipe breaks with traditional soup-making techniques by calling for the squash to be roasted in the oven before it is added to the soup base. The flesh of the roasted squash is then puréed into the base, infusing it with a robust, smoky squash flavor. I use one of my favorite squashes, the acorn (also known as the Danish squash), and combine it with apple cider to create an autumn soup with slightly sweet overtones and a velvety texture.

Preheat the oven to 375°. Season the squash with 1 teaspoon of the salt and the black pepper. Lightly oil a jelly-roll pan and place the squash, cut-side down, on the pan. Bake for about 45 minutes, or until tender. Let cool completely, scrape out the squash flesh, and set aside.

In a heavy 3-quart pan, melt the butter over medium heat. Add the garlic, carrots, leeks, onions, chopped fennel, and 1 teaspoon of the salt. Cover, reduce heat to low, and simmer, stirring occasionally, for 25 to 30 minutes, or until the vegetables are soft. Mix in the cooked squash, stock, cider, orange juice concentrate, fennel seeds, and cloves. Simmer, covered, for 20 minutes. Add the vinegar, lemon juice, cayenne, and remaining 1 teaspoon salt. Let cool completely. In a food processor or blender, purée the soup, in batches if necessary, until smooth. Press through a fine-meshed sieve. Heat the soup and add more stock if the soup is too thick. To serve, ladle into soup bowls and garnish with the chopped apple.

Roasted Yellow Finn Potatoes
with Garlic, Rosemary, and Olive Oil — SERVES 8 AS A SIDE DISH

When I first moved back to Oregon to open Wildwood, local potato offerings were for the most part limited to Yukon Golds, russets, sweet potatoes, and red potatoes. Since that time, many potato varieties have come onto the market, including fingerlings, bananas, and Yellow Finn.

This recipe is uncomplicated and tasty. Yellow Finns are good for a quick roast because of their small size and buttery texture. Rosemary and garlic are a natural pairing that goes well with hearty meat dishes such as roasted loin of pork or leg of lamb.

3 pounds unpeeled Yellow Finn, Yukon Gold, fingerling, or red potatoes, scrubbed and halved

12 cloves garlic, smashed (see page 224)

2 tablespoons minced fresh rosemary

1/4 cup olive oil

1 1/2 teaspoons salt

1 teaspoon freshly ground black pepper

Preheat the oven to 400°. In a large bowl, combine the potatoes, garlic, rosemary leaves, olive oil, salt, and pepper. Toss well to coat. Place in a large roasting pan or in the bottom of a broiler pan and roast in the oven for 40 minutes, or until golden brown, stirring twice.

Spoon onto a platter and serve.

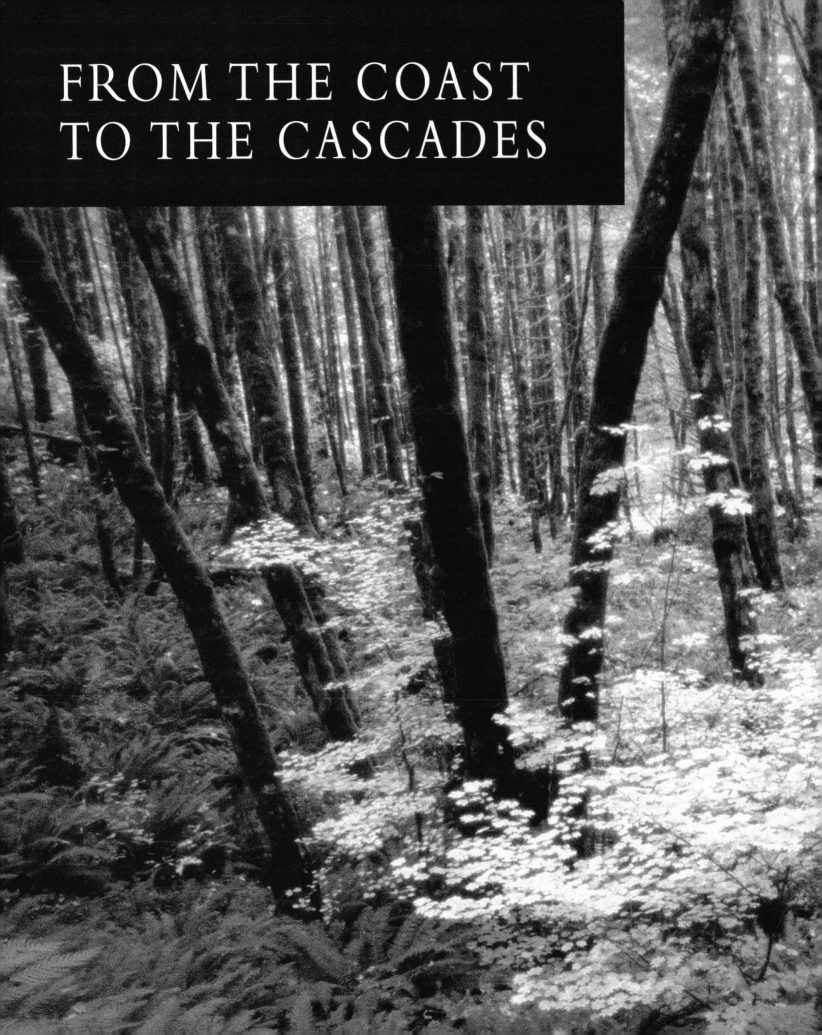

FROM THE COAST
TO THE CASCADES

6. FROM THE COAST TO THE CASCADES: IN SEARCH OF THE WILD MUSHROOM

Oregon's Coast Range begins at the northwest tip of the state where the Pacific Ocean meets the mouth of the Columbia River. As it moves south, it buffers the lush Willamette Valley from ocean storms, and its diverse terrain is home to a wide variety of wild mushrooms. Hedgehogs, black trumpets, lobsters, white oysters, yellowfoots, and chanterelles are only a few of the inhabitants of its many microclimates.

If you move east, away from the coast mountains and across the valley floor, you come to the foothills of the Cascades, home to the alpine branch of Oregon's mycological family. Among these timberline dwellers is a variety whose name befits this lofty setting: the king boletus, also known as the porcini mushroom.

A much sought after, yet often elusive ingredient, wild mushrooms are a culinary cornerstone of the Pacific Northwest. Though the mushroom season can last year-round, with different varieties peaking at different points along the way, their growth depends on many factors that can vary greatly from year to year. A forest fire can mean a prosperous morel season, while excess rain in the Coast Range can literally turn a chanterelle season to mush.

Although yields may vary, the reward is always consistent. The varietal cavalcade of mushrooms that thrive in the cool, damp climes of the Pacific Northwest offers adventurous cooks the opportunity to experiment with each mushroom and to conjure up their own preparations. The rich flavors and unique textures of wild mushrooms hold foragers and chefs in thrall to the tasty possibilities lurking on the forest floor. Wild mushrooms are easily paired with almost any other indigenous ingredient of the region, including wild fish, game, and vegetables. Whether earthy, nutty, buttery, or pinelike, wild mushrooms contribute a complexity and depth to any dish of which they are a part.

I am particularly fond of the summer chanterelles that come into season in late July. This mushroom variety tends to be a little drier than most, and I have found that, when served with a vinaigrette, it soaks up the liquid like a sponge without becoming overly wet and soft. The intense apricot-orange color of nutty-flavored chanterelles livens up salads and any other dishes in which they are included.

The king boletus, referred to as the *porcino* in Italy, and as the *cèpe* in France, is the granddaddy of the edible mushroom varieties that thrive in the Pacific Northwest. Porcini are found at high altitudes in the coastal and Cascade

Mountains from midsummer into fall. They tend to grow beneath fir and pine trees just below the timberline. I often refer to the porcini as the steak of mushrooms because of their firm texture and earthy, robust flavor. When purchasing porcini, select those that are four to six inches long, with a firm texture and a mahogany to nut-brown coloring on their outside cap. Good-quality porcini have pure white stems, often with light brown streaks.

Black trumpet mushrooms, thin, delicate, and mysterious, remind one of the freshness of a forest after a heavy rain. If you are lucky enough to find fresh matsutake mushrooms, you'll be treated to the almost hypnotic allure of their pine-like perfume.

The hunt for wild mushrooms requires patience and education. These little fungi are as deceptive as they are elusive, and professional foragers are careful not to be taken in by poisonous impostors. Fortunately, many local retailers are removing the guesswork by offering an increasing number of mushroom varieties to their customers.

When shopping for wild mushrooms, look for ones that are firm, fairly dry, and unblemished. Smell one or two of them to make sure they have a pleasant and full-bodied odor. A chanterelle should have a nutty and buttery aroma; morels tend to have a piney, almost soillike smell and seem to thrive in the Pacific Northwest climate. As a result, the region is making a name for itself as one of the

leading suppliers of morels in the nation. The season peaks in late spring, and you can identify these tasty morsels by their honeycomb texture and hollow insides.

Mushrooms should be stored in your refrigerator or a cool dry place that allows for plenty of air circulation. If you are keeping them in a container, make sure that it is open or perforated to allow for adequate aeration. Most mushrooms will last for about a week before they begin to turn or dry out. The less-meaty varieties, such as the black trumpet and the yellowfoot, can begin to dry out sooner; place a slightly damp paper towel over them when storing. If the mushrooms are coated with debris and impossible to brush clean, soak them for 3 to 5 minutes in cold water, then gently dry them in a lettuce spinner.

Dried mushrooms are an excellent substitute if fresh varieties are not available or are out of season. The drying process does not include preservatives, and the mushroom flavor tends to intensify as the moisture evaporates. As a result, dried mushrooms can be even more flavorful than fresh varieties.

When buying dried mushrooms, inspect them for color, making sure that it is true to what you would expect from fresh mushrooms of the same variety. The smell will be more intense, but it should not be stale. The price may seem exorbitant, but remember that a little goes a long way when you rehydrate them. As a rule of thumb, there is a 4 to 1 ratio between fresh and dried mushrooms, so 4 cups fresh mushrooms equals about 1 cup dried.

The best way to rehydrate dried mushrooms is to soak them in warm water for 20 to 30 minutes. You can also reconstitute them by adding them directly to a stock, or by grinding them in a coffee grinder or food processor and adding them as a flavoring in pastas, breads and vinaigrettes. It is important to remember that dried mushrooms excrete flavor into their soaking liquid, so try to include the liquid in your preparation.

When preparing dishes using wild mushrooms, you may notice that the mushrooms (both fresh and dried) release varying amounts of water as they begin to cook. This liquid has a great deal of flavor and is a valuable part of the cooking process, so don't throw it out! I recommend two options for recapturing the flavors in the liquid; the one you choose will depend on how firm you want the mushrooms to be when served. For softer mushrooms, continue to cook the mushrooms until the liquid evaporates and the flavor is reabsorbed. For firmer mushrooms, remove them from heat, strain the mushroom water, and continue to cook the liquid separately until almost dry, then add the liquid back to the mushrooms as a glaze.

Sautéed Chanterelles with Shallots and Fines Herbes

— SERVES 4 AS AN APPETIZER OR SIDE DISH

1 teaspoon olive oil

1 pound chanterelle or porcini mushrooms, wiped clean and cut into 1/2-inch pieces

1 teaspoon salt

2 shallots, minced

2 teaspoons unsalted butter

1/4 cup minced mixed fresh tarragon, chives, chervil, and flat-leaf parsley

1/2 teaspoon freshly ground black pepper

Whenever I can get my hands on mushrooms pulled fresh from the earth, I lean toward a simple preparation that preserves their true flavors. The following recipe for chanterelles sautéed with shallots, butter, and herbs is a prime example. I like to serve this dish with rice pilaf.

In a 12-inch skillet, heat the oil over medium-high heat. Add the mushrooms and season with salt to dry out the moisture. Cook and stir for 2 to 3 minutes. Add the shallots, butter, and herbs. Cook for 1 additional minute. Season with the pepper and serve.

Chanterelle Soup with Dried Apples, Hazelnuts, and Apple Brandy ⟶ SERVES 8

Although it may seem luxurious to use the pricey chanterelle in a soup, I think you'll find it well worth the splurge. This potato-based soup accents the mushroom's unique flavor with dried apples, hazelnuts, and apple brandy. This soup can be made several days ahead and refrigerated.

In a heavy 4-quart pot, melt 2 tablespoons of the butter over low heat. Add the celery, parsnips, onions, fennel, leek, and 1 teaspoon of the salt and sauté for 5 minutes. Stir in the water and $1/2$ pound of the mushrooms, cover, and cook, stirring occasionally, for 20 minutes, or until the vegetables begin to soften. Add the stock and cider and bring to a boil. Reduce heat and simmer for 10 minutes. Add the potatoes and fennel seeds and simmer for 20 to 25 minutes, or until the potatoes are soft. Let cool. In a food processor or blender, purée the soup, in batches if necessary. Press through a fine-meshed sieve; set aside.

In a heavy 4-quart pot, melt the remaining 1 tablespoon butter over medium heat. Add the remaining mushrooms and sauté until soft, about 8 minutes. Add the brandy or cider, vinegar, pepper, and the remaining 2 teaspoons salt and simmer for about 5 minutes. Pour in the puréed soup; heat until warm.

To serve, ladle into soup bowls. Garnish with the apples, hazelnuts, and sage.

3 tablespoons unsalted butter

3 ribs celery, chopped

2 parsnips, peeled and chopped

2 yellow onions, chopped

1 bulb fennel, trimmed and chopped

1 leek (white part only), washed and chopped

3 teaspoons salt

2 tablespoons water

2 pounds fresh chanterelle or cremini mushrooms, or a mixture, wiped clean and thinly sliced

8 cups chicken stock (page 221)

1 cup apple cider

3 medium-sized Yukon Gold or russet potatoes, peeled and chopped

1 tablespoon fennel seeds, toasted and ground (page 224)

$1/4$ cup apple brandy or hard apple cider

1 tablespoon apple cider vinegar

2 teaspoons freshly ground black pepper

$1/4$ cup chopped dried apples

$1/2$ cup hazelnuts, toasted, skinned, and finely chopped (page 224)

6 fresh sage leaves, thinly sliced crosswise

Warm Chanterelle Salad with Onions, Summer Berries, and White Cheddar Toast — SERVES 4

1 white onion, sliced $1/4$ inch thick and separated into rings

3 tablespoons grapeseed or canola oil

$1^1/4$ teaspoons salt

$1^1/2$ teaspoons freshly ground black pepper

1 tablespoon grated orange zest

$1/3$ cup fresh orange juice

$1/4$ cup olive oil

2 tablespoons red wine vinegar

2 teaspoons Dijon mustard

1 pound chanterelle or cremini mushrooms, or a mixture, wiped clean and sliced

4 cups (4 ounces) mixed baby greens

2 cups fresh raspberries or blackberries

Two $1/4$-inch-thick slices thick-crusted country bread, halved and toasted

$1/4$ cup shredded sharp white Cheddar cheese, grated Parmesan cheese, or crumbled fresh white goat cheese

This salad is ideal when the firm, nutty summer chanterelles become available in July and August. These early-season chanterelles are firm due to lack of rain; combine them with plump, juicy berries, warm Cheddar toast, and wilted onions for a dish with delightful texture and temperature contrasts.

Preheat the broiler. Line a broiler pan with aluminum foil. In a medium bowl, toss the onion slices with 1 tablespoon of the grapeseed or canola oil, $1/4$ teaspoon of the salt and $1/4$ teaspoon of the pepper. Put the onion rings on the prepared pan and broil 4 inches from the heat source for 5 to 6 minutes, or until slightly charred and softened. Let cool; set aside. Leave the broiler on.

To prepare the vinaigrette: In a small bowl, whisk together the orange zest, orange juice, olive oil, vinegar, mustard, $1/2$ teaspoon of the salt, and $3/4$ teaspoon of the pepper; set aside.

In a 12-inch skillet, heat the remaining 2 tablespoons grapeseed or canola oil over medium-high heat. Add the mushrooms and season with the remaining $1/2$ teaspoon salt and $1/2$ teaspoon pepper. Cook for 3 to 4 minutes, or until lightly browned. Remove from heat and drain.

In a salad bowl, toss the greens, berries, warm mushrooms, and onions with the vinaigrette.

Quickly top the toast with the cheese and melt under the broiler.

To serve, portion the salad onto 4 plates. Top each serving with a toast.

Lentil Flat Breads

$1/2$ cup dried green lentils, soaked in very hot water for 30 minutes, drained, and dried on paper towels

2 tablespoons semolina flour

1 cup plus 2 tablespoons warm (110°) water

$1/2$ teaspoon sugar

$1 1/2$ teaspoons active dry yeast

$2 3/4$ cups bread flour

1 tablespoon coarsely chopped fresh rosemary

$1 1/2$ teaspoons grated lemon zest

1 teaspoon freshly ground black pepper

$1/2$ teaspoon salt

2 tablespoons olive oil

Caramelized onions (page 120), fresh herb leaves such as rosemary, basil, or oregano, or sliced roasted red bell peppers (page 224) for toppings

Lentils offer an earthy flavor component that pairs well with any of the warm mushroom salads in this chapter. Here, they are ground and mixed with flour to make a crisp flat bread.

In a food processor, finely grind together the lentils and semolina flour; set aside.

In a small bowl, combine the water and sugar; stir to dissolve. Add the yeast and let stand for 5 minutes, or until the top surface has a thin layer of foam, indicating that the yeast is active.

In a mixer bowl, combine the bread flour, rosemary, lemon zest, pepper, and salt. Using a heavy-duty mixer fitted with a paddle, blend in the yeast mixture on low speed for 3 minutes. Change to a dough hook and add the lentil mixture and olive oil; mix on medium speed for 6 minutes, or until the dough is smooth and slightly sticky. Place the dough in a large oiled bowl. Cover tightly with plastic wrap and let rise in a warm place for $1 1/2$ to 2 hours, or until doubled in size.

Preheat the oven to 500° with a pizza stone inside, if you have one, for 45 minutes. If you do not have a pizza stone, oil a baking sheet and set aside. Punch the dough down and cut into 12 portions. Cover with a tea towel and let the dough rest for 15 minutes.

On a lightly floured surface, roll out each dough portion into a $1/4$-inch-thick oblong. Top with one of the suggested toppings. Just before putting the bread into the oven, spritz the oven heavily with water, being careful not to spritz the oven-light area.

Sprinkle the pizza stone or oiled baking sheet with cornmeal and place the oblongs on the stone or sheet, set on the middle rack of the oven. Bake for 7 to 10 minutes, or until lightly browned. Let cool on a wire rack. Serve.

Wild Rice and Chanterelle Salad with Dried Fruit, Goat Cheese, and Walnuts — SERVES 4 AS AN APPETIZER OR SIDE DISH

As autumn approaches and the availability of fresh summer produce wanes, I begin to incorporate grains and dried fruits into salads. This next recipe pairs chanterelles with wild rice, dried fruits, nuts, and goat cheese. Because the salad does not include lettuce, you can use the wetter fall mushrooms without making the salad soggy. Serve as an accompaniment to grilled pork chops or roasted chicken.

~~~~~~

To prepare the rice: Wash the rice under cold water for 2 minutes. Bring 4 cups of water to boil and add the salt, bay leaf, and thyme. Add the washed rice to the boiling water and simmer for 40 minutes, or until tender. Drain the rice and remove the bay leaf and thyme; let cool. (This can be done 1 day ahead of time and refrigerated.) You should have 3 1/2 cups cooked rice.

In a 12-inch skillet, heat the grapeseed or canola oil over medium-high heat. Add the mushrooms and cook, stirring occasionally, for 5 to 6 minutes, or until lightly browned. Remove from heat, drain well, and set aside.

To make the vinaigrette: In a small bowl whisk together the olive oil, vinegar, shallots, fennel, cumin, thyme, the remaining 1 teaspoon salt, and the pepper. Add the dried fruits.

In a salad bowl, combine the cooled wild rice, cooked mushrooms, and walnuts. Toss with the vinaigrette and fruits.

To serve, portion the salad onto 4 plates. Top with the greens and sprinkle with the goat cheese.

WILD RICE

1 cup wild rice

1 teaspoon salt

1 bay leaf

6 sprigs thyme

2 teaspoons grapeseed or canola oil

1 pound chanterelle or portobello mushrooms, wiped clean and chopped

1/4 cup olive oil

3 tablespoons balsamic vinegar

2 large shallots, thinly sliced

1 teaspoon fennel seeds, toasted and cracked (page 224)

1 teaspoon cumin seeds, toasted and cracked (page 224)

1 teaspoon coarsely chopped fresh thyme

1 teaspoon freshly ground black pepper

1/2 cup mixed dried fruits, such as cherries, cranberries, raisins, chopped figs, or chopped apricots

1/2 cup chopped walnuts, toasted (page 224)

8 cups (8 ounces) stemmed arugula or watercress

4 ounces fresh white goat cheese, crumbled (about 1 cup)

Wild Mushroom and Apple Potato Cake

3 tablespoons olive oil

1 pound portobello or cremini
mushrooms, or a mixture, wiped
clean and chopped

1 cup minced or grated yellow
onions, squeezed dry

1 Granny Smith or pippin apple,
peeled, cored, and shredded

1 teaspoon minced fresh thyme

2 teaspoons salt

1¼ teaspoons freshly ground
black pepper

1 teaspoon unsalted butter

1 pound Yukon Gold or Yellow Finn
potatoes, peeled and thinly sliced
by hand or on a mandoline or
grated and squeezed dry

The following recipe works well with any mushroom variety. The key is to cook the mushrooms until they are dry before placing them between the potato layers. This cake can be served with a salad as a lunch entrée or as an accompaniment to game dishes such as roasted venison or quail.

In a 10-inch skillet, heat 1 tablespoon of the oil over medium-high heat. Add the mushrooms and $^1/_2$ cup of the onions; reduce heat to medium. Sauté, stirring occasionally, for 15 to 20 minutes. At first, the mushrooms will release moisture; as they continue to cook, the moisture will evaporate. When the mixture is almost dry, stir in the apple, minced thyme, $^1/_2$ teaspoon of the salt, and $^1/_4$ teaspoon of the pepper; set aside.

In a medium bowl, combine the potatoes and the remaining $^1/_2$ cup onions, $1^1/_2$ teaspoons salt, and 1 teaspoon of pepper; set aside.

Preheat the oven to 400°. In a 10-inch nonstick ovenproof skillet, heat the remaining 2 tablespoons oil and the butter over medium-high heat. Reduce heat to low and add one-third of the potatoes in an even layer. Spoon on half of the mushroom mixture. Top with even layers of one-third of the potatoes and the remaining mushroom mixture. Top with the remaining potatoes.

Place the skillet in the oven and bake for 20 minutes, or until the bottom layer of potato is lightly browned and comes loose from the pan. Remove from the oven and carefully place a pizza pan over the top of the skillet. Invert both to unmold the potato cake onto the pizza pan. Gently slip the potato cake back into the pan with the golden side up. Bake for an additional 10 minutes, or until the cake is crispy on the outside and well set inside. Remove from the oven and let cool in the pan for 5 minutes.

To serve, turn the potato cake out onto a plate and cut into wedges.

Mushroom Bread Pudding

SERVES 8 AS A SIDE DISH

One of my favorite uses for morels is in mushroom bread pudding. This dish is popular on the restaurant's spring menu and can be adapted to chanterelles in the summer and fall. Cultivated mushroom varieties also work well in this preparation, including portobellos and basic field mushrooms. Regardless of the variety you use, the mushrooms must be cooked until they are almost dry before adding them to the custard. This condenses their flavor and ensures that the custard does not become too loose or watery.

At the restaurant, we serve this dish with roasted chicken from our wood-fired ovens, but I find that it also holds up well on its own or as an accompaniment to any other meat, game, or poultry preparation. The apple cider bread is a nice accompaniment to the earthy tones of the mushrooms. To create your own variation of this pudding, try adding dried fruit such as raisins, currants, or dried apples.

1 tablespoon olive oil

6 ounces fresh morel or white mushrooms, wiped clean and chopped, or 2 ounces dried mushrooms, rehydrated (page 107)

$1^1/_2$ teaspoons salt

$1^1/_2$ teaspoons freshly ground black pepper

2 cups half-and-half

4 large eggs

2 tablespoons roasted garlic purée (page 223)

1 tablespoon grated lemon zest

$^1/_2$ teaspoon fresh thyme leaves

$^1/_4$ teaspoon ground nutmeg

2 cups 1-inch-cubed stale Apple Cider–Raisin Bread (page 116), nut and/or dried-fruit bread, or brioche or egg bread

1 cup shredded white or yellow Cheddar cheese

$^1/_4$ cup chopped green onions

In a 10-inch skillet, heat the oil over medium-high heat. Add the mushrooms, $^1/_2$ teaspoon of the salt, and $^1/_2$ teaspoon of the pepper. Cook for 8 to 10 minutes, stirring occasionally, until the mushrooms are soft and the juices are reduced by half. Remove from the pan and let cool.

In a blender or food processor, combine the half-and-half, eggs, garlic purée, lemon zest, thyme, nutmeg, and the remaining 1 teaspoon salt and 1 teaspoon pepper; blend until smooth and set aside.

Preheat the oven to 350°. Butter a $8^1/_2$-by-$4^1/_2$-inch loaf pan.

In a large bowl, toss together the bread cubes, cheese, mushrooms, and green onions. Pour the mixture into the pan. Pour the cream mixture over the bread and press lightly on the bread to submerge. Cover with parchment paper or waxed paper, then aluminum foil. Place the loaf pan in a baking pan and add hot water to the baking pan to reach halfway up the sides of the loaf pan. Bake for 30 minutes. Uncover and bake for an additional 20 minutes, or until the pudding is golden brown, the custard is set, and a knife inserted into the center comes out clean. Let stand for 10 minutes. Using a large spoon, distribute the pudding onto 8 plates and serve.

Apple Cider–Raisin Bread

SPONGE

2 1/2 cups warm (110°) water

1/2 teaspoon active dry yeast

3 cups bread flour

1 cup whole wheat flour

DOUGH

1 cup apple cider

4 cups bread flour

2 tablespoons salt

1 teaspoon active dry yeast

1 cup golden raisins

Although this bread is excellent when used in the Mushroom Bread Pudding, page 115, it's also a fine table bread. In fact, when we serve it at the restaurant in the fall, we often have to take certain precautions—our customers fill up on the bread so quickly that we have to wait to put it on the table until after they have ordered their food! If you have any bread left over, use it the next morning for french toast.

To make the sponge: In a mixer bowl, combine the water and yeast. Let stand for 5 minutes, or until the top surface has a thin layer of foam indicating that the yeast is active.

Using a heavy-duty mixer fitted with a paddle, on low speed, mix in the flours in 1/2-cup batches for about 2 minutes. Place in a large oiled bowl, cover tightly with plastic wrap, and let stand at room temperature overnight. The next day the sponge will be slightly thick and bubbly.

To make the dough: In a mixer bowl, combine the sponge, apple cider, and bread flour. Using a heavy-duty mixer fitted with a dough hook, mix on low speed for 1 minute. Add the salt and continue mixing for 6 minutes. Add the raisins and mix on medium speed for 2 to 3 minutes, or until the dough starts to pull away from the sides of the bowl. Place in a large oiled bowl. Cover tightly with plastic wrap and let rise in a warm place for 1 1/2 to 2 hours, or until doubled in size.

Punch the dough down and let rise for 1 more hour. Cut the dough in half and place on a lightly floured surface. Form the dough into 2 round loaves, folding the dough under to form a smooth top. Place the rounds on a baking sheet 6 inches apart. Cover with damp tea towels and let rise in a warm place for 1 hour, or until doubled in size.

Preheat the oven to 450°. Bake for 35 to 40 minutes, or until golden brown. Transfer the loaves to wire racks and let cool 1 hour before slicing.

Creamed Morels with Apple Brandy, Thyme, and Roasted Garlic — SERVES 4 AS AN APPETIZER OR SIDE DISH

I was introduced to morels when I was an apprentice chef at the Benson Hotel. There, I learned to prepare these mushrooms using the classic technique of cooking them in white wine and cream. Twenty years later, the pairing still sticks in my mind because of its shear decadence. In this recipe, a little roasted garlic purée is added for a mild flavoring, along with diced apples and apple brandy. The garlic purée does not overwhelm morels as raw garlic can, and it helps to thicken the sauce.

In a 12-inch skillet, melt the butter over medium heat. Add the mushrooms, salt, and pepper and sauté for 4 to 5 minutes, or until the mushrooms release their liquid and become soft. Stir in the shallots and apple brandy or cider. Cook for 2 minutes. Blend in the cream or crème fraîche and garlic purée. Simmer until the sauce thickens and coats the mushrooms, about 2 minutes. Stir in the herb mixture and lemon juice. Serve immediately.

CHEF'S NOTE: If fresh morel mushrooms are not available, use 4 ounces dried mushrooms. Cover with warm water and soak for 1 hour. Strain, reserving the mushroom liquid for use in soups or sauces. Drain the mushrooms on paper towels. Proceed as directed in the recipe.

2 tablespoons unsalted butter

1 pound morel or cremini mushrooms, wiped clean and halved

$1/2$ teaspoon salt

$1/4$ teaspoon freshly ground black pepper

2 shallots, minced

1 apple, peeled, cored, and finely chopped

2 tablespoons apple brandy or hard apple cider

$1/2$ cup heavy cream or crème fraîche

2 tablespoons roasted garlic purée (page 223)

$1/4$ cup minced mixed fresh thyme, tarragon, chives, and flat-leaf parsley

1 teaspoon fresh lemon juice

Roasted Chicken Thighs with Morel Mushrooms, Asparagus, and Garlic — SERVES 4 AS AN ENTRÉE

As if to suggest her own perfect pairing, Mother Nature brings morels and asparagus into season together. The grassy undertones of the tender asparagus complement the earthiness of the morels, resulting in a flavorful rite of spring.

~~~~~~

In a large self-sealing plastic bag, combine the oil, vinegar, rosemary, and pepper. Add the chicken, seal the bag, and rotate to coat the chicken. Refrigerate for 2 to 24 hours, turning the bag occasionally.

One and a half hours before serving, preheat the oven to 375°. Place the chicken in a roasting pan. Roast in the oven for 25 to 30 minutes, or until the juices run clear when the chicken is pierced with a knife.

Meanwhile, to make the vinaigrette: In a small bowl, whisk together the oil, vinegar, basil, mustard, salt, and pepper; set aside.

In a large pan, cover the potatoes with water. Add the salt. Bring to a boil, reduce heat, and simmer for 10 to 15 minutes, or until just fork-tender (do not overcook). Drain well. Place the potatoes in a large bowl and gently toss with 1/3 cup of the vinaigrette; set aside.

In a large skillet, heat 1 tablespoon of the olive oil over medium heat. Sauté the garlic, red onion, and asparagus for 4 minutes, or until just tender. Add to the cooked potatoes.

Using the same skillet, add the remaining 1 tablespoon oil and sauté the mushrooms over medium heat for 6 to 8 minutes, or until soft. Add to the potatoes and gently toss together with the greens and the remaining vinaigrette.

To serve, portion the warm salad onto 4 large plates. Top each serving with 1 or 2 pieces of chicken. Distribute the crumbled goat cheese over the greens and serve.

2 tablespoons olive oil

2 tablespoons balsamic vinegar

1 tablespoon minced fresh rosemary

1/2 teaspoon freshly ground black pepper

8 chicken thighs, or 4 boneless chicken breast halves

VINAIGRETTE

1/3 cup olive oil

3 tablespoons red wine vinegar

2 tablespoon chopped fresh basil leaves

2 teaspoons Dijon mustard

1/2 teaspoon salt

1/2 teaspoon freshly ground black pepper

6 Yukon Gold or new potatoes, peeled and quartered

1 teaspoon salt

2 tablespoons olive oil

2 cloves garlic, minced

1 red onion, thinly sliced

8 ounces asparagus, trimmed and cut on the diagonal into 2-inch lengths

1 pound morel mushrooms, wiped clean and halved, or 1 pound portobello mushrooms, sliced

5 cups (5 ounces) mixed baby greens

4 ounces fresh white goat cheese, crumbled (about 1 cup)

Wild Mushroom Toast with Roasted Garlic, Caramelized Onions, and Goat Cheese — SERVES 6 AS AN APPETIZER OR LUNCH ENTRÉE

CARAMELIZED ONIONS

2 tablespoons unsalted butter

2 yellow onions, thinly sliced

$^1/_2$ teaspoon salt

$^1/_2$ teaspoon freshly ground
   black pepper

2 tablespoons balsamic vinegar

1 tablespoon Dijon mustard

1 teaspoon chopped fresh thyme

1 pound morel, chanterelle, cremini,
   or portobello mushrooms, wiped
   clean and coarsely chopped

$^1/_2$ teaspoon salt

1 teaspoon freshly ground black
   pepper

Six $^3/_4$-inch-thick slices round
   thick-crusted country bread

1 tablespoon olive oil

2 tablespoons roasted garlic purée
   (page 223)

4 ounces fresh white goat cheese,
   cut into 6 rounds

VINAIGRETTE AND SALAD

$^1/_4$ cup olive oil

3 tablespoons red wine vinegar

2 teaspoons Dijon mustard

$^1/_2$ teaspoon salt

$^1/_4$ teaspoon freshly ground
   black pepper

10 cups (10 ounces) mixed
   baby greens

This recipe offers a layering of perfectly matched flavors and makes a great luncheon dish or first course for dinner. You can prepare much of it ahead of time and assemble just before serving. Pour an Oregon Pinot Noir at the table.

To make the caramelized onions: In a large skillet, melt the butter over medium heat. Add the onions and season with the salt and pepper. Cook for 5 minutes, or until the onions begin to sweat. Reduce heat to low and cook the onions, stirring frequently, until they caramelize to a coffee color, 25 to 30 minutes. Stir in the vinegar, mustard, and thyme. Cook about 5 additional minutes, or until the onion mixture is thick and glazed; set aside.

To roast the mushrooms: Preheat the oven to 350°. Place the mushrooms on a baking sheet; season with the salt and pepper. Roast in the oven for 10 to 15 minutes, or until lightly browned and dry; set aside.

To make the toast: Brush the bread slices with the oil and toast on both sides under a broiler or on a grill until lightly browned. Increase the oven temperature to 375°. Spread each slice with a portion of roasted garlic purée, caramelized onions, cooked mushrooms, and a slice of goat cheese. Place on a baking sheet and bake for 5 to 8 minutes, or until the cheese begins to brown.

To make the vinaigrette and salad: In a small bowl, whisk together the olive oil, vinegar, mustard, salt, and pepper. In a large bowl, toss the greens with the vinaigrette until evenly coated.

To assemble, place a portion of the tossed salad greens onto 6 large plates. Top each with a wild mushroom toast and serve.

Roasted Porcini on Garlic Mashed Potatoes

Because of their large size and meaty texture, I like to cut porcini in half and roast or grill them. The marinade that follows includes garlic, rosemary, thyme, balsamic vinegar, and olive oil to enhance the full-bodied flavor of the mushrooms. These garlic mashed potatoes are a Wildwood favorite that is included on our steak plate and requested often.

To make the potatoes: In a large pan, cover the potatoes with water. Add the garlic and salt. Bring to a boil, reduce heat, and simmer for about 25 minutes, or until the potatoes are tender. Drain well and let stand for 5 minutes. Place the potatoes and garlic in a food mill and purée to a fine consistency or mash with a pastry cutter. Heat the half-and-half or milk and butter until steaming. Gradually add the milk mixture and cayenne to the mashed potatoes, continuing to stir until light and fluffy. Taste and adjust the seasoning. Set aside and keep warm.

To make the mushrooms: Preheat the oven to 400°. In a large bowl, combine the oil, vinegar, garlic, rosemary, thyme, salt, and pepper. Add the mushrooms and toss to coat; let stand for 20 minutes. Place the mushrooms, oil, and herbs in a large roasting pan. Roast in the oven for 15 to 20 minutes, or until the mushrooms begin to shrivel around the edges and brown lightly.

To serve, spoon the mashed potatoes onto a platter, creating a shallow bowl for the mushrooms. Pour the mushrooms and liquid onto the mashed potatoes.

GARLIC MASHED POTATOES

2 pounds Yukon Gold potatoes, peeled and quartered

8 to 10 cloves garlic, halved

1 teaspoon salt

$3/4$ to 1 cup half-and-half or milk

2 tablespoons unsalted butter

$1/8$ to $1/4$ teaspoon cayenne pepper

ROASTED PORCINI

3 tablespoons olive oil

2 tablespoons balsamic vinegar

2 cloves garlic, minced

1 teaspoon fresh rosemary leaves

1 teaspoon fresh thyme leaves

1 teaspoon salt

$3/4$ teaspoon freshly ground black pepper

1 pound porcini or portobello mushrooms, wiped clean and halved

Whole Roasted Portobello Mushrooms with Soft Polenta and Wilted Spinach

SOFT POLENTA

2 cups water

2 cups milk

1 cup polenta

$^1/_4$ cup grated Asiago or pecorino cheese

$^1/_4$ cup fresh lemon juice

1 teaspoon salt

1 teaspoon freshly ground white pepper

WHOLE ROASTED PORTOBELLO MUSHROOMS

2 teaspoons olive oil

2 teaspoons balsamic vinegar

4 portobello mushrooms (3-inch caps), stemmed and wiped clean

1 teaspoon salt

1 teaspoon freshly ground black pepper

WILTED SPINACH

1 teaspoon unsalted butter

1 bunch spinach, washed, dried, and stemmed

$^1/_2$ teaspoon salt

$^1/_2$ teaspoon freshly ground black pepper

1 cup mushroom stock, heated (page 222)

Shavings of aged Monterey Jack or other grating cheese for garnish

One of my favorite recipes for roasted portobellos includes a bed of soft polenta topped with sautéed spinach and mushroom stock. I like to shave aged Monterey Jack or other grating cheese on top and let the tasty combination of flavors emerge.

To make the polenta: In a heavy 3-quart pan, combine the water and milk. Whisk in the polenta. The polenta will be thin at this point. Cook over low heat, stirring frequently, until the polenta is thick, 25 to 30 minutes. Stir in the cheese, lemon juice, salt, and white pepper. Set aside and keep warm.

Meanwhile, to make the mushrooms: Preheat the oven to 350°. Whisk the oil and vinegar together. Brush on the mushrooms. Place the mushrooms on a baking sheet. Sprinkle with the salt and pepper. Roast in the oven for 12 to 15 minutes, or until the mushrooms are lightly browned.

To make the spinach: In a 12-inch skillet, melt the butter over medium-high heat. Add the spinach, stir, and cook until wilted. Season with the salt and pepper.

To assemble, spoon the polenta into 4 warm bowls. Top each with a portion of spinach and a mushroom cap. Ladle $^1/_4$ cup of hot mushroom stock over each mushroom cap. Sprinkle with the cheese shavings. Serve.

Mushroom and Barley Soup
with Red Wine and Parsnips — SERVES 6

Though this recipe calls for cremini or shiitake mushrooms, any mixture of wild mushrooms, fresh or dried, will yield a delicious soup. Prepare the mushroom stock in advance, and you'll have only two simple steps between you and a hearty, satisfying soup.

In a heavy 4-quart pan, melt the butter over medium heat. Add the onions, parsnips, and carrots and sauté for 6 to 8 minutes, or until tender. Add the mushrooms and sauté for 5 additional minutes, or until tender. Remove from the pan and set aside.

Add the stock, wine, vinegar, barley, salt, pepper, thyme, and bay leaf to the pan. Bring to a boil, reduce heat, and simmer for 40 to 45 minutes, or until the barley is tender. Remove the bay leaf and stir in the vegetables. Simmer the soup for 5 minutes, then serve.

1 tablespoon unsalted butter

2 cups chopped yellow onions

$1^{1}/2$ cups finely chopped peeled parsnips (about 3 parsnips)

$1^{1}/4$ cups finely chopped peeled carrots (about 2 carrots)

1 pound cremini or shiitake mushrooms, wiped clean and sliced

6 cups mushroom stock (page 222)

$^{3}/4$ cup Pinot Noir

3 tablespoons sherry vinegar

$^{1}/4$ cup pearl barley

1 teaspoon salt

1 teaspoon freshly ground black pepper

1 teaspoon chopped fresh thyme

1 bay leaf

OREGON WINE COUNTRY

7. OREGON WINE COUNTRY: TRUE FLAVOR FROM THE SOIL

I remember driving home from Yaquina Bay in the early 1970s after spending a week working in my family's oyster beds. As I dropped out of the Coast Range into the rolling landscape of Eola Hills and Yamhill County, I was struck by how quickly the terrain and climate were changing around me. Forests of Douglas fir gave way to grassy hillsides, and the hot valley air seemed to melt away the chill of the cool coastal waters.

Little did I know that as I wound my way through those rural roads, other, more subtle, changes were beginning to take shape. In the late 1960s, a group of Oregon winemakers recognized the great potential of this arid valley. Cool nights and hot afternoons, coupled with the natural barrier of the coastal mountains, create a long ripening season ideal for grape growing. Through patience and hard work, these early visionaries put the region on the winemaking map. Today, Yamhill County is world renowned for its Pinot Noir grapes, and other grape varieties are quickly gaining recognition, including Pinot Gris, Sauvignon Blanc, and Chardonnay.

I've long thought that the wine of a region is a good indicator of that area's indigenous cuisine. The rich soils of Oregon's wine country produce grape flavors that seem to pair naturally with our local foods. The crisp fruitiness of the Pinot Gris nicely complements our flavorful hazelnuts, apricots, and goat cheese. The more robust and earthy tones of the Pinot Noir blends well with the wild mushrooms, berries, and game of the area.

Pairing foods and wines is an exciting aspect of cooking, because each can so easily influence the flavor of the other. The trick lies in finding a blend of flavors that does not overpower the unique characteristics of the individual components. The recipes included in this chapter use a variety of techniques for cooking with wine. Most good-quality wines work nicely in these preparations, but for the true flavor of the Northwest, treat yourself to one of the fine wines from our great Oregon vineyards.

When cooking with wine, it is important to remember that wine begins as a fruit. Although it is somewhat altered in the cooking process, wine retains the grapes' essential characteristics, including fruitiness, acidity, moisture, and color. Each of these elements contributes to the final dish. The fruit adds flavor and sugar; the acidity adds liveliness, while cutting the heaviness of fats and oils; the liquid creates a gentle cooking environment and helps to deglaze the pan; and the color in red wine can add a rich tone to otherwise pale ingredients.

The quality of the wine you use for cooking directly affects the final outcome: higher-quality wines tend to create more favorable results than the "cooking wines" sold in your local supermarket. If I have any drinking wine left over from a meal (not a frequent event), I like to save it for cooking. When stored correctly, by removing excess air from the bottle with a special wine capper and then keeping it in a cool, dark place, leftover wine is suitable for cooking for up to two weeks.

The term *wine* most commonly refers to the juice of grapes that has been fermented. In the course of the filtering and aging process, the juice acquires a complexity and layering of flavors that makes it an exciting and versatile ingredient with which to cook. The juice of fresh-picked grapes should not be overlooked, however, for it provides a marvelous braising liquid that won't overly sweeten a dish. I prefer to use wine grapes if possible, but any juice variety works nicely.

Each time I visit the vineyards and talk with farmers and winemakers, it reinforces the idea that what grows together goes together, a simple philosophy that is a cornerstone of Pacific Northwest cuisine.

Today, as I travel back and forth between the ocean and the city, I pass through the hills of Yamhill County's burgeoning wine country. If I have the luxury of time, I wander off the now-busy highway onto the serene back roads of the valley, where small vineyards, hidden in the protective folds of the rolling hillsides, are tended by winemakers with a contagious enthusiasm and pioneering spirit.

Chardonnay-Poached Halibut with Warm Potato-Caper Salad and Gamay Noir Vinaigrette — SERVES 4 AS AN ENTRÉE

WARM POTATO-CAPER SALAD

4 russet potatoes, peeled

1 tablespoon salt

1 cup Gamay Noir

1 red onion, minced

2 teaspoons capers, drained

1 teaspoon Dijon mustard

1 teaspoon chopped fresh basil

1 cup olive oil

$^1/4$ cup fresh orange juice

1 teaspoon red wine vinegar

1 teaspoon freshly ground
  black pepper

3 cups water

2 cups Chardonnay

1 carrot, peeled and chopped

1 yellow onion, chopped

1 rib celery, chopped

1 leek (white part only), washed
  and chopped

1 bay leaf

$^1/2$ bunch parsley sprigs

1 tablespoon fennel seeds, cracked
  (page 224)

1 teaspoon peppercorns, cracked
  (page 224)

1 teaspoon coriander seeds, cracked
  (page 224)

4 halibut fillets (4 to 5 ounces each)

Poaching is one of the more conventional methods for cooking with wine. The key to this technique is to simmer the poaching liquid for 20 to 30 minutes before adding the fish, poultry, or meat. This allows the flavor of the liquid to develop fully before the poaching process begins.

This recipe for Chardonnay-poached halibut includes a potato salad made with a red wine vinaigrette for a flavor contrast. Any thick fillet of fish works nicely in this dish, including salmon, cod, or any other firm, flaky fish.

To make the potato-caper salad: In a large pot, cover the potatoes with water. Add 1 $^1/2$ teaspoons of the salt, bring the water to a boil, reduce heat, and simmer for 20 to 25 minutes, or until just fork tender. Drain well and let cool. Slice $^1/4$ inch thick; set aside.

In a small saucepan, bring the Gamay Noir to a simmer. Cook over medium heat to reduce to $^1/4$ cup; set aside.

In a large bowl, combine the onion, capers, mustard, and basil. Whisk in the oil, orange juice, vinegar, reduced wine, the remaining 1 $^1/2$ teaspoons salt, and the pepper. Add the potatoes and gently toss. Cover and let the flavors blend for 2 hours.

Meanwhile, make the poaching liquid: In a large pot, combine the water, Chardonnay, carrot, onion, celery, leek, bay leaf, parsley stems, fennel seeds, peppercorns, and coriander seeds. Bring to a boil, reduce heat, and simmer for 20 minutes. Let cool slightly. Strain, discarding the vegetables.

To poach the halibut: Put the poaching liquid in a large nonreactive skillet. Bring to a simmer. Carefully add the halibut and poach for 12 to 15 minutes, or until it flakes easily and is opaque throughout. Remove from the poaching liquid and drain thoroughly.

To serve, portion the potato salad onto plates. Place the poached halibut on top of the salad.

Braised Shoulder of Lamb with Pinot Noir, Raisins, and Carrot Purée — SERVES 4 AS AN ENTRÉE

Braising is a particularly effective technique for tenderizing tough cuts of meat. When braising meats with wine, it is important to add the wine to the pan after the meat has been browned and removed from the pan. Then reduce the wine slowly until it is almost dry. If you reduce the wine too quickly, it can become highly acidic and undesirable. Periodically, I like to add a little dried fruit to increase the sugar content and counterbalance the acid. Most dried fruits work well, including cherries, Black Mission figs, plums, or raisins, as demonstrated in this recipe.

This preparation works well with a rolled and tied shoulder of lamb or lamb shanks. The carrot purée adds flavor and color and can be made while the lamb is braising.

~~~~~~~~~~~~~~~~~~~~~~~~~~~

To braise the lamb: Preheat the oven to 350°. In an ovenproof pan at least 4 inches deep and large enough to hold the lamb, heat the olive oil over medium heat. Brown the lamb roast on all sides. Remove from the pan and drain off the fat. Add the wine and simmer for 4 to 5 minutes, stirring to scrape up the browned bits from the pan bottom. Stir in the garlic, rosemary, onions, carrots, 1/2 cup of the raisins, the salt, and pepper. Return the roast to the pan and add the stock. Braise, uncovered, in the oven for about 1 1/2 hours, or until an instant-read thermometer inserted in the center of the roast registers 145°. The top of the lamb will caramelize as it cooks.

While the lamb is braising, make the carrot purée: In a shallow casserole dish, arrange the carrots; set aside. In a small saucepan, melt the butter. Stir in the curry and cook for 3 to 4 minutes to allow the flavor to bloom. Blend in the stock, salt, and pepper. Pour over the carrots. Bake for about 45 minutes, or until tender. Let cool. In a food processor, purée the carrots. Stir in the orange zest and juice. The purée should be smooth and slightly stiff in texture. Adjust the consistency if necessary by adding more juice. Set aside and keep warm.

To finish the lamb: Remove the lamb from the braising liquid. Strain the liquid, discarding the vegetables. Pour the sauce into a small saucepan. Add the remaining 1/2 cup raisins and heat through. Slice the lamb 1/2 inch thick.

To serve, place several lamb slices on each plate and spoon the sauce over the lamb. Add a spoonful of the carrot purée.

2 tablespoons olive oil

2- to 3-pound lamb shoulder roast, boned, tied, and seasoned with salt and pepper

1 1/2 cups Pinot Noir

8 to 10 cloves garlic, chopped

4 to 5 sprigs rosemary

2 onions, thinly sliced

2 carrots, peeled and chopped

1 cup raisins

2 teaspoons salt

1 teaspoon freshly ground black pepper

2 1/2 cups chicken stock (page 221)

CARROT PURÉE

1 pound carrots, peeled and cut into 1-inch pieces

2 tablespoons unsalted butter

1 teaspoon curry powder

1 cup vegetable stock (page 222) or chicken stock (page 221)

1 teaspoon salt

1/2 teaspoon ground white pepper

2 teaspoons grated orange zest

2 tablespoons fresh orange juice

Grilled Lamb Chops with Pinot Noir–Braised Red Onions, Black Pepper, and Sage — SERVES 4 AS AN ENTRÉE

Braising also works well for firm vegetables such as onions and root vegetables. The following recipe combines lamb chops and onions braised in red wine and aromatics. I like to use a tender cut of meat that can be grilled, baked, or roasted to counterbalance the robust flavor of the onions. A little currant or berry jam added to the onion braising liquid creates a nice sauce for the chops.

At Wildwood, we're fortunate to have access, through our friends at "Your Kitchen Garden Farm" to the relatively uncommon red torpedo onion—a mild, sweet onion that takes its name from its projectilelike shape. It's well worth hunting down this variety at your local farmer's market, since its flavor marries nicely with the braising liquid.

To make the lamb marinade: In a small bowl, mix the garlic, sage, oil, and pepper. Rub this mixture onto the lamb chops. Place the chops on a plate, cover, and refrigerate for 2 to 24 hours. Remove the chops from the refrigerator 1 hour before cooking to allow them to come to room temperature.

To make the braised onions: Preheat the oven to 350°. In a medium skillet, combine the wine, thyme, fennel seeds, pepper, and salt. Simmer for 5 minutes. Blend in the butter. Put the onions in a medium baking dish. Pour the wine sauce over the onions. Braise, uncovered, in the oven for about 45 minutes, or until tender, turning them twice during the braising time. Remove the onions from the braising liquid and keep warm. Remove the thyme sprigs, if using, from the liquid. Blend the jelly into the liquid and keep warm.

To cook the lamb: Preheat a broiler or gas grill, or light a fire in a charcoal grill. Broil or grill the chops for 4 to 5 minutes on each side for medium-rare.

To serve, place 1 chop and 1 onion half on each plate. Spoon on the sauce and serve.

LAMB MARINADE

6 cloves garlic, minced

2 tablespoons coarsely chopped fresh sage

2 tablespoons olive oil

2 teaspoons coarsely ground black pepper

4 lamb chops, 3 inches thick

PINOT NOIR–BRAISED ONIONS

2 cups Pinot Noir

4 to 5 sprigs thyme, or 1 teaspoon dried thyme

2 teaspoons fennel seeds

1 teaspoon coarsely ground black pepper

1/2 teaspoon salt

2 tablespoons unsalted butter

2 red torpedo onions or large red onions, cut in half lengthwise (leave stem end intact to hold onion together during cooking)

2 tablespoons currant or blackberry jelly

Chicken Legs Braised in Pinot Noir and Blackberries, with Fennel Purée — SERVES 4 AS AN ENTRÉE

4 chicken quarters (leg and thigh
   sections)

1 teaspoon salt

1/2 teaspoon freshly ground
   black pepper

2 tablespoons olive oil

1 cup Pinot Noir

6 sprigs thyme

2 yellow onions, chopped into
   1-inch pieces

2 carrots, peeled and cut into
   1-inch pieces

2 bay leaves

2 cinnamon sticks

2 teaspoons fennel seeds

2 cups fresh or frozen unsweetened
   blackberries

1 small bulb fennel, trimmed and
   chopped into 1-inch pieces

1 to 1 1/2 cups chicken stock
   (page 221)

FENNEL PURÉE

1 pound Yukon Gold potatoes,
   peeled and cut into quarters

2 teaspoons salt

2 bulbs fennel, trimmed and
   chopped, including stems and
   greens (reserve some of greens
   for garnish)

1/4 cup Chardonnay

2 tablespoons anise-flavored liqueur,
   such as Pernod, Sambuca, or
   Ricard, or chicken stock and
   1/2 teaspoon anise extract

1 tablespoon fennel seeds, crushed
   (page 224)

1 cup heavy cream

1 teaspoon freshly ground
   black pepper

Though not as tough as their game counterparts, chicken legs are ideal for braising since their relatively mild flavor provides the perfect backdrop for a complex sauce made from the braising liquid. In this recipe, fennel seeds, blackberries, and Pinot Noir play the assertive role in the braising sauce, while an earthy fennel purée, spiked with anise liqueur, provides the finishing touch.

To make the chicken: Preheat the oven to 375°. Season the chicken with the salt and pepper. In a heavy ovenproof skillet large enough to hold all the chicken in a single layer, heat the oil over medium-high heat. Brown the chicken well on both sides, about 6 to 7 minutes per side. Remove the chicken from the pan and drain off the excess fat. Add the wine and simmer, stirring to scrape up the browned bits from the bottom of the pan; do not let the wine boil. Stir in the thyme, onions, carrots, bay leaves, cinnamon sticks, fennel seeds, 1 cup of the blackberries, and the fennel bulb. Add the chicken and enough chicken stock to fill the pan halfway; the chicken should not be submerged. Bring to a boil. Place the hot pan in the oven and braise for 45 minutes, or until the chicken is tender.

While the chicken is braising, make the fennel purée: Place the potatoes in a large saucepan, cover with water, and add 1 teaspoon of the salt. Bring to a boil and cook for about 20 minutes, or until the potatoes are fork tender.

While the potatoes are cooking, make the fennel. In a 8-cup saucepan, combine the chopped fennel, Chardonnay, anise liqueur or stock and extract, and fennel seeds. Bring to a boil, reduce heat, and simmer until the liquid evaporates. Add the cream and cook over low heat for about 20 minutes, or until the fennel is tender. Purée the fennel mixture in a food processor until smooth.

Drain the potatoes well and force through a ricer or food mill while hot. Stir in the fennel purée. Season with the remaining 1 teaspoon salt and the pepper. Set aside and keep warm.

To finish the dish: Remove the chicken from the pan and keep warm. Taste the sauce and adjust the seasoning. Remove the bay leaves and thyme sprigs. Just before serving, add the remaining 1 cup of blackberries.

To serve, place a chicken quarter on each plate. Add a spoonful of fennel purée and spoon the sauce over the top.

Salmon Steaks Braised in Grape Juice with Whipped Red Potatoes and Horseradish — SERVES 4 AS AN ENTRÉE

This recipe features an unusual combination: salmon and white grape juice. During the autumn months at Wildwood, we acquire fresh wine grape juice from Pinot Noir, Pinot Gris, or any available variety of grapes that a winemaker can supply. Salmon pairs well with this fresh grape juice, as the natural sugars from the juice complement the rich texture of the fish. Fresh wine grape juice is rarely available, so I recommend substituting a white grape juice that is not overly sweet. Salmon steaks on the bone with the skin intact are ideal for this preparation, for the bone adds that extra little bit of flavor to the sauce and the fish. A touch of horseradish added to the whipped red potatoes contrasts with the sweetness of the grapes.

To make the whipped potatoes: In a medium saucepan, cover the potatoes with water. Add 1 teaspoon of the salt and bring the water to a boil. Reduce heat and simmer for 20 to 25 minutes, or until fork tender. Drain and let stand for 5 minutes.

In a small pan, heat the milk and butter until just steaming. In a bowl, using an electric mixer, mash the potatoes on medium speed. Season with the remaining 1 1/2 teaspoons salt and the pepper. Gradually add the hot milk mixture, whipping the potatoes until light and fluffy. Fold in the horseradish and chives. Set aside and keep warm.

To make the salmon: Preheat the oven to 350°. In an ovenproof skillet large enough to hold the salmon, heat the oil over medium heat. Season the salmon with the salt and pepper. Add the salmon and brown for 3 minutes on each side. Remove from the pan and set aside.

Wipe out the pan and add the grape juice, wine, onion, grapes, and fennel seeds. Bring to a simmer. Return the salmon to the pan and braise in the oven for about 20 minutes for steaks and 10 minutes for fillets, or until the salmon flakes easily and is opaque throughout. Remove the salmon from the skillet and keep warm. Return the pan to the stove top and bring the sauce to a simmer over medium heat. Stir in the parsley, butter, and lemon juice. Cook for 1 minute.

To serve, portion the whipped potatoes onto each plate. Place a salmon steak or fillet on the potatoes and spoon on the sauce.

WHIPPED RED POTATOES

1 pound unpeeled Red Bliss or Yukon Gold potatoes, halved

2 1/2 teaspoons salt

1 cup milk

1 tablespoon unsalted butter

3/4 teaspoon freshly ground black pepper

1 tablespoon prepared horseradish

1 tablespoon minced fresh chives

2 tablespoons olive oil

4 salmon steaks (8 to 10 ounces each) or fillets (6 to 8 ounces each)

1 1/2 teaspoons salt

1 teaspoon freshly ground black pepper

2 1/2 cups white grape juice

1/4 cup Chardonnay

1 small red onion, cut vertically into thin crescents

1 cup Thompson or other seedless green grapes

1 teaspoon fennel seeds, crushed (page 224)

1/4 cup minced fresh flat-leaf parsley

2 tablespoons unsalted butter

2 tablespoons fresh lemon juice

Pinot Noir–Glazed Squab
with Roasted Summer Vegetables — SERVES 4 AS AN ENTRÉE

1 cup olive oil

2 tablespoons Dijon mustard

1 tablespoon honey

1 cup Pinot Noir

4 squabs or Cornish game hens, halved and back bone removed

2 yellow summer squashes, sliced 1 inch thick

2 zucchini, sliced 1 inch thick

2 red bell peppers, seeded, deribbed, and chopped into 1-inch pieces

1 pound white mushrooms, wiped clean and stemmed

1 red onion, halved lengthwise and sliced lengthwise into thin strips

1 tablespoon minced fresh sage

1 tablespoon minced fresh rosemary

2 teaspoons salt

1 1/2 teaspoons freshly ground black pepper

Reducing wine down to a concentrate creates a wonderful basting liquid that adds intensity and color to many meat and fish dishes. I often add a little sugar or honey to balance out the high acidity, then fold in some butter to create body, allowing the liquid to act as a glaze. Red wine and squab (or any red-fleshed fowl such as guinea fowl or duck) is a nice combination for this technique.

In a small bowl, whisk together the oil, mustard, and honey; set aside. In a small saucepan, cook the wine over medium heat to reduce to 1/4 cup; let cool. Gradually whisk the reduced wine into the oil mixture. Use 2 self-sealing plastic bags and pour one quarter of the marinade into each bag. Add the squabs or Cornish game hens, turning to coat. Refrigerate for at least 2 hours or overnight. Remove the fowl from the refrigerator 1 hour before cooking to allow them to come to room temperature.

Preheat the oven to 425°. In a large bowl, toss the squash, zucchini, bell peppers, mushrooms, onion, sage, and rosemary with the remaining marinade and let stand for 15 minutes. Pour into a jelly roll pan or the bottom of a broiler pan and season with salt and pepper. Roast in the oven for 15 minutes, stirring twice. Remove from the oven and set aside.

Reduce the oven temperature to 375°. Spray a jelly-roll pan with vegetable-oil cooking spray. Remove the squabs or Cornish game hens from the marinade and discard the marinade. Place the squabs or hens, skin-side up, on the pan. Roast in the oven for about 25 minutes, or until the juices run clear when the thighs are pierced with a knife. Cover loosely with aluminum foil and let stand for 5 minutes. Return the vegetables to their pan and place in the oven to roast for an additional 5 minutes.

To serve, portion the vegetables onto plates and place the squabs or Cornish game hen halves on top.

Pinot Noir Barbecue Sauce

Vinegar is a common ingredient in barbecue sauce and gives it a little acidic kick. I've found that red wine, used in conjunction with the vinegar, maintains that punch, but lends additional color, complexity, and a little fruitiness. This barbecue sauce is slightly thick and chunky, making it ideal for basting or simply spooning on top of a grilled, roasted, or sautéed piece of fish, poultry, or meat.

In a heavy sauté pan or skillet, heat the oil over medium heat. Add the onion, garlic, and $1/4$ teaspoon of the salt. Reduce heat to low and sauté for 5 minutes, being careful not to brown. Add the wine and simmer for 5 minutes to reduce the wine slightly. Stir in the tomatoes and cook for an additional 5 minutes. Blend in the molasses, brown sugar, vinegar, honey, cumin, fennel, cinnamon, bay leaf, star anise, cayenne, and the remaining $1 1/4$ teaspoons salt. Simmer for 20 minutes. Remove the cinnamon stick, bay leaf, and star anise. Stir in the parsley. Adjust the salt and cayenne to taste.

Leave the sauce chunky to use as a sauce over meat, fish, or poultry. Purée the sauce (add more wine as needed) to use as a barbecue sauce or a marinade.

1 tablespoon olive oil

1 yellow onion, thinly sliced

2 cloves garlic, minced

$1 1/2$ teaspoons salt

1 cup Pinot Noir

8 Roma (plum) tomatoes, peeled, seeded, and chopped

2 tablespoons molasses

1 tablespoon packed brown sugar

1 tablespoon red wine vinegar

1 tablespoon honey

1 teaspoon ground cumin

1 teaspoon fennel seeds

1 cinnamon stick, or $1/4$ teaspoon ground cinnamon

1 bay leaf

1 star anise pod

$1/4$ teaspoon cayenne pepper

1 tablespoon chopped fresh flat-leaf parsley

Riesling-Marinated Chicken with Bacon-Wrapped Onions — SERVES 4 AS AN ENTRÉE

6 cloves garlic, chopped

4 sprigs thyme

1 cup late-harvest Riesling

1 yellow onion, chopped

5 tablespoons extra-virgin olive oil

4 bone-in chicken breast halves, skinned

2 tablespoons balsamic vinegar

4 teaspoons red wine vinegar

2 teaspoons minced fresh sage

1 teaspoon Dijon mustard

2 teaspoons salt

2 teaspoons freshly ground black pepper

1 red onion, cut into 4 wedges with root end intact (to make it easier to roast)

4 slices bacon, halved lengthwise

8 ounces butternut squash, seeded and cut into 8 pieces

1 Granny Smith apple, cored and quartered

If you drive through the wine country in the fall, after the main grape harvest is over and crush has begun, you may see a few grapes still hanging from the autumn vines. These late-season varieties, which include Riesling and Gewürztraminer, are left on the vine to develop the higher sugar content needed for sweeter and fruitier wines.

The Riesling marinade in this recipe adds liveliness and fruitiness to the roasted chicken breast. The bacon wrapped around the onions creates a nice contrast to the sweetness of the wine.

~~~~~~

In a large self-sealing plastic bag, combine the garlic, thyme, wine, onion, and 2 tablespoons of the oil. Add the chicken, seal, and refrigerate overnight, turning occasionally.

Preheat the oven to 375°. In a small bowl, combine the vinegars, the sage, mustard, 1/2 teaspoon of the salt, and 1/2 teaspoon of the pepper. Whisk in 2 tablespoons of the oil. Gently toss with the red onion wedges. Place the onion wedges, squash, and apple on a jelly-roll pan. Brush with the remaining 1 tablespoon oil and season with 1/2 teaspoon of the salt and 1/2 teaspoon of the pepper. Roast in the oven for 30 minutes, or until the squash and apple are tender and the onions are browned around the edges. Let cool.

Increase the oven temperature to 425°. Wrap the bacon around the onion wedges and secure with a toothpick. Remove the chicken from the marinade and discard the marinade. Season with the remaining 1 teaspoon salt and 1 teaspoon of pepper. Place in an oiled baking pan and roast for 30 minutes. During the last 10 minutes of roasting, return the squash and apple to the oven. At the same time, transfer the bacon-wrapped onions to a separate small pan and place in the oven. (If the bacon isn't crisp and brown after 10 minutes, leave the onions in the oven for an additional 5 minutes.)

To serve, place the onion, squash, and apple pieces on a platter and top with the roasted chicken.

Chicken Breasts Baked with Late-Harvest Riesling
Spiced Apples, Cabbage, and Parsnips — SERVES 4 AS AN ENTRÉE

The flavors created by the natural sugars of a late-harvest Riesling are often compared to those of apples and pears. These characteristics are showcased in this chicken breast dish.

~~~~~~

Preheat the oven to 375°. In a large skillet, heat the olive oil over medium-high heat. Season the chicken with 1 teaspoon of the salt and $1/2$ teaspoon of the pepper. Brown the chicken for 3 to 4 minutes on each side. Remove the chicken from the pan. Add the wine and simmer for 5 minutes, stirring to scrape up the browned bits from the bottom of the pan. Add the stock and sage. Simmer for 5 minutes and set aside.

In a 9-by-13-inch baking dish, arrange, in single layers, the apples, parsnips, cabbage, and red onion. Season the apples and vegetables with the remaining 1 teaspoon salt, 1 teaspoon pepper, and the caraway seeds. Place the browned chicken on top of the apples and vegetables. Bring the wine and chicken stock mixture to a boil and carefully pour over the chicken. Place in the oven and braise for 35 to 40 minutes, or until the chicken is opaque throughout and the apples and vegetables are tender.

Remove the chicken, apples, and vegetables from the pan; set aside and keep warm. Pour the pan liquid into a small saucepan and boil to reduce by one-half. Stir in the butter.

To serve, portion the apples, vegetables, and chicken onto plates. Spoon the sauce over the chicken.

2 tablespoons olive oil

4 boneless, skinless chicken breast halves

$1^1/2$ teaspoons salt

$1^1/2$ teaspoons freshly ground black pepper

$1^1/2$ cups late-harvest Riesling

3 cups chicken stock (page 221)

2 tablespoons chopped fresh sage

2 Golden Delicious apples, peeled, cored, and cut into quarters

2 parsnips, peeled and thinly sliced into rounds

1 small head green cabbage, cored and cut into 8 wedges

$1/2$ red onion, thinly sliced

1 tablespoon caraway seeds

2 tablespoons unsalted butter

Roasted Pork Loin with Gewürztraminer-Apricot Compote and Vegetable Barley — SERVES 4 AS AN ENTRÉE

GEWÜRZTRAMINER-APRICOT COMPOTE

1 cup Gewürztraminer

1 cup apple cider

1 cinnamon stick

1 whole vanilla bean, split and scraped, or 2 teaspoons vanilla extract

8 ounces dried apricot halves

One 4-rib pork loin roast (about 2 1/2 to 3 pounds), chine bone removed

1 1/2 teaspoons salt

1 1/2 teaspoons freshly ground black pepper

1 tablespoon vegetable oil

1 teaspoon unsalted butter

VEGETABLE BARLEY

2 tablespoons unsalted butter

2 carrots, peeled and cut into 1/4-inch dice

2 ribs celery, peeled and cut into 1/4-inch cubes

1 small yellow onion, minced

4 1/2 cups chicken stock (page 221), warmed

1 1/2 cups pearl barley

1 teaspoon chopped fresh thyme

1 teaspoon salt

1 teaspoon freshly ground black pepper

Wilted spinach (page 122)

Oregon Gewürztraminer grapes create a wine that pairs well with stone fruits, such as peaches, nectarines, and apricots—especially if the wine is a late-harvest variety, which has a higher sugar content. When reduced through cooking, Gewürztraminer is transformed into a semisweet liquid that provides a wonderful base for stone-fruit compotes, as with the apricot compote in this recipe.

At Wildwood, we buy our pork products from the Carlton Packing Company, based in the town of Yamhill in the heart of Oregon wine country. So if you find that the components of this dish—the pork, wine, apricots, and barley—have a particular affinity for each other, it's because the foods are grown and raised in the same earth, thus observing the rule that what grows together goes together.

To make the compote: In a medium saucepan, combine the wine, apple cider, cinnamon stick, and vanilla bean and scrapings. (If using vanilla extract, wait to add until the syrup is removed from the heat.) Bring to a boil, reduce heat, and add the apricots. Simmer for 20 minutes, or until a syrup consistency is achieved. Remove from heat. Set aside and keep warm. This mixture can be made 1 day ahead and reheated.

To make the pork: Preheat the oven to 350°. Season the pork with 1 teaspoon of the salt and 1 teaspoon of the pepper. In a large skillet, heat the oil over medium-high heat. Brown the pork on all sides. Place on a rack in a roasting pan and roast in the oven for about 45 minutes, or until an instant-read thermometer inserted in the center of the pork registers 145°.

While the pork loin is roasting, prepare the barley: In a 4-quart saucepan, melt 1 tablespoon of the butter over medium heat. Add the carrots, celery, and onion. Cook, stirring occasionally, for 5 minutes, or until tender, being careful not to brown. Remove the vegetables from the pan. Add 3 cups of the stock and stir in the barley. Bring to a boil, cover, and reduce heat to a simmer. Cook the barley for 40 to 45 minutes, or until tender, adding the remaining stock in small batches as the barley absorbs it. Mix in the vegetables and heat through. Stir in the remaining 1 tablespoon butter, the thyme, salt, and pepper.

To finish the dish: Remove the pork loin from the oven, cover loosely with aluminum foil, and let stand for 15 minutes.

To serve, cut the pork loin into 4 portions. Distribute the barley onto plates and top each portion with spinach and a slice of pork. Spoon on the apricot compote.

Roasted Pork Tenderloin with Smoky Bacon, Lentils, and Merlot Vinaigrette — SERVES 4 AS AN ENTRÉE

10 tablespoons olive oil

1 small bulb fennel, trimmed and finely chopped

1 small yellow onion, finely chopped

1 small carrot, peeled and finely chopped

1 rib celery, finely chopped

1 cup green French lentils or brown lentils, rinsed

2 1/2 cups water

2 teaspoons salt

2 teaspoons freshly ground black pepper

4 slices smoky bacon, cut into 1/4-inch strips

1 1/2 cups Merlot

3 tablespoons red wine vinegar

2 pork tenderloins (about 1 pound each), trimmed of excess fat and seasoned with salt and freshly ground black pepper

Pork tenderloin is the leanest cut of pork you'll find and also the quickest to cook. It doesn't have the more robust flavor of the loin, shoulder, or leg, but this recipe makes up for it with the accompanying bacon and lentil mixture. The wine in the vinaigrette adds a deep red color and a fruity accent.

To prepare the lentils: In a medium skillet, heat 2 tablespoons of the olive oil over medium heat. Add the fennel, onion, carrot, and celery. Sauté for 5 minutes, or until the onion is soft but not browned. Add the lentils, stirring to coat with the oil. Mix in the water, 1 1/2 teaspoons of the salt, and 1 1/2 teaspoons of the pepper. Bring to a boil, reduce heat to simmer, partially cover, and cook for about 40 minutes, or until the lentils are tender and the liquid is absorbed.

In a skillet, cook the bacon until crisp. Drain on paper towels and set aside.

Preheat the oven to 400°. In a medium saucepan, cook the wine over medium-low heat to reduce to 1/4 cup. Remove from heat and whisk in 6 tablespoons of the olive oil, the vinegar, and the remaining 1/2 teaspoon salt and 1/2 teaspoon pepper. Pour the vinaigrette over the lentils and mix in the bacon. Taste and adjust the seasoning; set aside and keep warm.

In a large ovenproof skillet, heat the remaining 2 tablespoons olive oil. Place the pork in a hot skillet and brown well on all sides. Place the skillet in the oven and roast for 10 to 15 minutes, or until an instant-read thermometer inserted in the center of the meat registers 145°. Remove from the oven, cover loosely with aluminum foil, and let rest for 5 minutes. Cut the pork into 1/4-inch-thick slices.

To serve, portion the marinated lentils onto each plate and top with 4 or 5 slices of pork.

THE LOWER COLUMBIA
RIVER REGION

8. THE LOWER COLUMBIA RIVER REGION: GAME AND FOWL COOKERY

*J*ust outside the town of Clatskanie, near the banks of the Columbia River, you'll find one of the best game and fowl farms in Oregon. Columbia River Farms spreads out over sixty acres and is the breeding ground for rabbits, quail, squabs, partridges, geese, and chickens.

The farm is located forty miles from the mouth of the Columbia River. Lined with poplar trees and low-growing vegetation, it is an ideal game farm, with its mild climate and spacious grounds.

Game and fowl have always been among Wildwood's most popular menu items, and we find ourselves experimenting with new preparations and pairings throughout the seasons. An exciting characteristic of game and fowl is the natural richness of the meats, which lends itself to robust additions such as cooked fruit sauces, balsamic vinegar marinades, braised cabbages, glazed root vegetables, and the smokiness of wood-fire roasting.

For our restaurant menu, I lean toward farm-raised game, which has the milder flavor preferred by most modern palates. Most of the recipes in this chapter were created with the milder meats that we use in the restaurant in mind. However, wild meat, which is often described as "gamey," offers a robust flavor that should not be overlooked and can be substituted in any of the preparations that follow.

Game flavors tend to reflect the natural foods supplied by the forests, streams, and fields where the animals live. I have eaten venison raised on a small farm on the central Oregon coast that had an almost sweet and berrylike flavor due to the surrounding wild huckleberries and mountain blackberries. I have also prepared venison raised in the eastern part of the state and found it to have grassy undertones due to the natural ground cover of the high desert. Game and fowl flavors tend to hit their peak in the fall, after a long summer diet of fruits and forest vegetation. All of these factors are important clues when considering how to prepare them.

The beauty of these recipes is their interchangeability: What works for duck will also work for quail or venison. Many of the recipes can also be altered according to the season and the ingredients available in your local market. If you mix and match these recipes, keep in mind the rule of thumb that darker-fleshed game and fowl tend to have a more robust flavor than lighter-fleshed counterparts, such as rabbit, partridge, and pheasant.

Duck Breast with Mushroom Spaetzle
and Red Wine–Braised Cabbage — SERVES 4 AS AN ENTRÉE

MUSHROOM SPAETZLE

1/2 cup milk

2 tablespoons ground dried
  mushrooms (use a spice mill)

1 cup flour

1 large egg, beaten

2 tablespoons minced mixed fresh
  thyme, flat-leaf parsley, and chives

1 teaspoon salt

1/2 teaspoon ground white pepper

2 whole cloves

1 teaspoon fennel seeds

1 teaspoon juniper berries

4 tablespoons unsalted butter

1 small red onion, halved vertically
  and cut into crescents

1 small head red cabbage, cored and
  thinly sliced

2 1/2 teaspoons salt

2 1/2 teaspoons freshly ground
  black pepper

1/2 cup Merlot

1/2 cup apple cider

4 boneless duck breasts, trimmed
  of excess fat

Spaetzle is a classic Austrian noodle. The batter is passed through a perforated pan into boiling water to produce the noodles, which are then cooked in hot butter until golden brown and crispy. By introducing vegetable purées or ground spices into the mix, you can transform this somewhat uneventful white noodle into an innovative starch. This recipe adds dried mushrooms to the spaetzle dough and is a great duck accompaniment.

To make the spaetzle dough: In a small saucepan, heat the milk over low heat just until it simmers. Remove from heat, stir in the ground mushrooms, and let stand for 15 minutes. In a large bowl, combine the milk mixture, flour, egg, herbs, salt, and pepper. Mix the batter until smooth, cover, and refrigerate for 1 hour.

To cook the spaetzle: Bring a large pot of salted water to a rolling boil. Place a colander or perforated pan over (not touching) the boiling water. Pour the batter into the colander or pan. Using a rubber spatula or your hand, quickly press the batter though the holes into the boiling water. Once all of the batter has been forced though the holes, remove the colander or pan. Stir the spaetzle and cook for 1 minute. Drain well and toss with a little olive oil; set aside.

To make the cabbage: In a spice mill, grind the cloves, fennel, and juniper; set aside.

In a 4-quart pot, melt 2 tablespoons of the butter over medium heat. Add the onion and sauté for 3 minutes, or until translucent. Mix in the cabbage, 1 teaspoon of the salt, and 1 teaspoon of the pepper and cook until the cabbage begins to wilt. Stir in the wine, cider, and spices. Cover and cook, stirring frequently, for 25 to 30 minutes, or until the cabbage is soft to the bite.

To prepare the duck: Heat 2 heavy sauté pans or skillets over high heat. Season the duck with 1 teaspoon of the salt and 1 teaspoon of the pepper and add to the pans, skin-side down. Cook for 4 to 5 minutes, using the rendered fat to baste the meat. Reduce heat and cook the duck for 10 to 12 minutes, or until the skin is crisp. Turn over the breasts and cook for 1 minute. Remove from heat, cover, and let stand for 5 minutes.

To finish the spaetzle: Using a 10-inch nonstick skillet, melt the remaining 2 tablespoons butter over medium-high heat. Add the spaetzle, season with the remaining 1/2 teaspoon each salt and pepper, and cook until brown and crispy.

To serve, portion the braised cabbage and spaetzle onto each plate. Thinly slice each duck breast and place on top.

Cory's Applesauce

Applesauce is one of my favorite toppings for pork chops or roasted game birds. Over the years, I've tried many different kinds of apples when making this sauce and tend to prefer the tart and firm varieties. However, this recipe leaves a lot of room for experimentation. The final flavor and consistency will vary depending on the type of apples you choose, so have fun with it.

The sauce starts with a base that includes apple juice, orange juice concentrate, aromatics, and sugar. The chopped apples are added and cooked quickly to make an applesauce that is light in color and fresh in flavor.

2 cups apple juice

1/4 cup undiluted orange juice concentrate

3 whole cloves

2 tablespoons sugar

2 star anise pods

1 cinnamon stick

1/4 teaspoon fennel seeds

3 large Golden Delicious, Braeburn, or McIntosh apples, peeled, cored, and chopped

1/2 teaspoon vanilla extract

In a medium saucepan, combine the apple juice, orange juice concentrate, cloves, sugar, star anise, cinnamon, and fennel. Bring to a boil, reduce heat, and simmer for about 20 minutes to reduce the liquid by half. Strain the liquid to remove the spices.

Return the liquid to the pan and add the apples. Simmer for 15 minutes, or until the apples are tender. Remove from the heat and stir in the vanilla extract. Let cool. In a food processor, process the apples until they are smooth. Serve warm, or let cool and store in a covered container in the refrigerator.

Red Wine–Braised Duck Legs with Sour Cherries, Parsnip Purée, and Balsamic Roasted Pears — SERVES 4 AS AN ENTRÉE

DUCK LEGS

1 tablespoon olive oil

8 duck legs (thighs attached), trimmed of excess fat

1 teaspoon salt

1 teaspoon freshly ground black pepper

1 cup Pinot Noir

10 cloves garlic, split

1 cup dried cherries, raisins, prunes, or apricots

6 to 8 sprigs thyme

4 cups chicken stock (page 221)

PARSNIP PURÉE

1 pound (about 4) parsnips, peeled and cut into 1-inch pieces

2 cups chicken stock

1 tablespoon unsalted butter

1/2 teaspoon salt

1/2 teaspoon fresh lemon juice

Dash of cayenne pepper

Dash of ground nutmeg

BALSAMIC ROASTED PEARS

2 firm, ripe pears, such as Bosc

1 tablespoon balsamic vinegar

2 teaspoons olive oil

1 teaspoon minced fresh thyme

1/2 teaspoon salt

1/2 teaspoon freshly ground black pepper

One of my favorite preparations for duck legs is to braise them in a good duck or chicken stock with red wine. The following recipe has become a favorite Sunday supper dish on our restaurant menu. If you prefer, you can prepare the legs 1 day in advance and leave them in the braising liquid overnight in the refrigerator. Soaking the legs overnight allows them to absorb the aromatics of the flavorful broth, thus enhancing the flavor of the meat. Degrease the liquid the next day, and heat the legs in the liquid while baking the parsnips. Serve this dish with wilted spinach or chard (page 122).

To prepare the duck legs: Preheat the oven to 350°. Using a large ovenproof skillet, heat the oil over high heat. Season the duck with salt and pepper and place, skin-side down, in a single layer in the pan. Cook the legs until the skin is golden brown. Turn the legs over and cook for 5 additional minutes. Remove the legs from the pan, discarding the fat.

In the same pan, cook the wine over medium heat, stirring with a wooden spoon to scrape up the browned bits on the bottom of the pan. Cook to reduce the wine by one-half. Add the garlic, 1/2 cup of the dried fruits, and the thyme. Place the duck legs on top of the fruit and herbs. Add the stock and bring to a simmer. Place the pan in the oven and braise for 2 hours, or until the meat begins to separate from the bone.

Meanwhile, to make the parsnip purée: Put the parsnips in a 4-cup baking dish. Heat the stock and butter; pour over the parsnips. Cover with aluminum foil and bake in the oven, along with the duck, for 40 minutes, or until tender. Let cool slightly. Using a slotted spoon, transfer the parsnips to a food processor. Add the salt, lemon juice, cayenne, nutmeg, and pan juices as needed and purée. Set aside and keep warm.

To make the pears: Spray a baking sheet with vegetable-oil cooking spray. Cut each pear in half, removing the core. Toss with the balsamic vinegar, oil, thyme, salt, and pepper. Arrange the pears on the prepared pan and roast in the oven, along with the duck, for 25 to 30 minutes, or until golden brown. Set aside.

When the duck is done, remove it from the pan and keep warm. Spoon off the excess fat, strain the pan juices, return the juices to the pan, and cook to reduce the pan juices slightly. Add the remaining dried fruit.

To serve, portion the parsnip purée onto each plate. Top with 2 duck legs and 1 pear half. Spoon on the fruit sauce and serve.

Quail with Grilled Walla Walla Onions, Cherries, and Wilted Arugula — SERVES 4 AS AN ENTRÉE

1/4 cup olive oil

2 tablespoons balsamic vinegar

1 teaspoon chopped fresh thyme

2 teaspoons salt

1 1/4 teaspoon freshly ground black pepper

4 boneless quail or boneless, skinless chicken thighs

2 large Walla Walla onions, cut into 1/2-inch-thick slices, kept intact

2 tablespoons grapeseed or olive oil

8 cups (8 ounces) arugula or mixed baby greens

8 ounces fresh sweet cherries, pitted and halved, or 4 ounces dried cherries, cranberries, chopped figs, or apricots

1/4 cup shaved Parmesan cheese

Quail is perhaps the easiest game bird to prepare, due in part to its small size. The bird has very little fat compared to duck and is best when broiled, grilled, or pan-roasted.

This recipe calls for Walla Walla onions, but any sweet onion variety will work, including Maui, Vidalia, and Texas Sweet. The sweetness of the onion, the tartness of the cherries, and the slight bitterness of the arugula will have your palate dancing.

To prepare the vinaigrette: In a small bowl, whisk together the olive oil, vinegar, thyme, 1/2 teaspoon of the salt, and 1/4 teaspoon of the pepper. Put the quail or chicken in a self-sealing plastic bag and add 3 tablespoons of the vinaigrette. Seal the bag and rotate to coat the poultry; refrigerate for 1 hour.

To prepare the onions: Preheat the broiler. Place the onion slices on a jelly-roll pan lined with aluminum foil. Brush them with 1 tablespoon of the grapeseed or olive oil and season with 3/4 teaspoon of the salt and 1/2 teaspoon of the pepper. Broil 4 inches from the heat source until brown and softened, 8 to 10 minutes. Transfer the onions to a plate and cover with plastic wrap, allowing them to steam in their own juices. Leave the broiler on.

To cook the quail or chicken: Remove it from the vinaigrette and season it with the remaining 3/4 teaspoon salt and 1/2 teaspoon pepper. In a large skillet, heat the remaining 1 tablespoon grapeseed or olive oil over medium-high heat. Brown the poultry evenly on all sides. Transfer to a broiler pan and broil 4 inches from the heat source, turning once, for 5 to 10 minutes, or until the juices run clear when the meat is pierced with a knife; set aside and keep warm.

To prepare the salad: Toss the greens, cherries, and warm onions with the remaining vinaigrette. Portion onto plates and top with the warm quail or chicken. Garnish with shaved cheese and serve.

Warm Quail Salad with Apple, Hazelnuts, and Oregon Blue Cheese — SERVES 4 AS AN APPETIZER

Oregon blue cheese is produced by the Rogue River Creamery, located in the southern portion of the state. While the Rogue River blue may not be as creamy as its American and European counterparts, it's perfect in salad preparations. Pair it with quail, apples, pears, and cracked hazelnuts for a hearty appetizer that celebrates the bounty of the autumn harvest in the Pacific Northwest.

4 tablespoons olive oil

2 tablespoons balsamic vinegar

2 shallots, minced

2 teaspoons water

1 tablespoon undiluted orange juice concentrate

1^1/$_2$ teaspoons salt

1^1/$_4$ teaspoons freshly ground black pepper

4 boneless quail or boneless, skinless chicken breasts or thighs

10 cups (10 ounces) mixed baby greens

1 unpeeled pippin apple, cored and thinly sliced

^{1}/$_4$ cup golden raisins

^{1}/$_4$ cup hazelnuts, toasted, skinned, and coarsely chopped (page 224)

4 ounces Oregon blue cheese or other blue cheese, crumbled (about 1 cup)

To prepare the dressing: In a small bowl, whisk together 3 tablespoons of the oil, the vinegar, shallots, water, orange juice concentrate, ^{1}/$_2$ teaspoon of the salt, and ^{1}/$_4$ teaspoon of the pepper; set aside.

To prepare the quail or chicken: Preheat the broiler. In a large skillet, heat the remaining 1 tablespoon oil over medium-high heat. Season the quail or chicken with the remaining 1 teaspoon each salt and pepper. Place the quail or chicken in the skillet and brown evenly on all sides. Transfer to a broiler pan and broil 4 inches from the heat source, turning once, for 5 to 10 minutes, or until the juices run clear when the meat is pierced with a knife; set aside and keep warm.

To prepare the salad, in a large salad bowl, combine the greens, apple, raisins, hazelnuts, and blue cheese. Add the dressing and toss.

To serve, portion the salad onto 4 plates. Top with the warm quail or chicken.

Squab with Bacon, Figs, Warm Spinach, and Goat Cheese Salad — SERVES 4 AS AN ENTRÉE

Much like quail, squab is wonderful in salad preparations. The meat is tender and stays moist even when not roasted on the bone. I recommend cooking squab medium-rare; if cooked much longer, it can take on an undesirable liver flavor and become gray and tough.

To prepare the squabs or hens: Preheat the oven to 375°. Season the birds with 1 teaspoon of the salt and 1 teaspoon of the pepper. In a large skillet, heat 2 tablespoons of the oil over medium-high heat. Place the squabs or hens in the skillet, skin-side down, and brown well. Turn and brown the other side. Put in a roasting pan and roast in the oven for 15 to 20 minutes, or until the juices run clear when the thighs are pierced with a knife; set aside and keep warm.

Place the spinach and figs in a large salad bowl; set aside.

In a large skillet, cook the bacon over medium heat, stirring frequently, until it just begins to brown. Add the shallots and cook for 1 to 2 minutes, or until translucent. Remove from heat and stir in the remaining 2 tablespoons oil, the vinegar, and mustard. Pour the hot dressing over the spinach and figs and season with the remaining 1 teaspoon salt and 1 teaspoon pepper. Toss quickly to wilt the spinach.

To serve, portion the wilted salad onto 4 plates and top with one leg and breast of cooked squab or Cornish game hen. Garnish with the goat cheese.

2 squabs or Cornish game hens, breasts boned with wing bones intact, and legs separated with thighs intact

2 teaspoons salt

2 teaspoons freshly ground black pepper

4 tablespoons olive oil

1 large bunch spinach, stemmed, washed, and dried

8 fresh or dried figs, sliced into wedges

4 slices smoky bacon, cut into 1-inch strips

3 shallots, thinly sliced

2 tablespoons balsamic vinegar

2 teaspoons Dijon mustard

2 1/2 ounces (1/2 cup) fresh white goat cheese, crumbled

Roasted Squab with Sautéed Raspberries and Sweet Garlic Cloves — SERVES 4 AS AN ENTRÉE

4 whole squab or Cornish game hens

2 tablespoons balsamic vinegar

1 1/2 teaspoons salt

1 1/2 teaspoons freshly ground
    black pepper

24 cloves garlic, peeled

1/2 cup water

3 tablespoons unsalted butter

2 tablespoons honey

5 to 6 sprigs thyme

2 shallots, minced

2 cups fresh raspberries, blackberries,
    or blueberries

2 tablespoons red wine vinegar

1 bunch (about 8 ounces) escarole or
    other bitter greens

Squab's dark-red flesh offers a full flavor that is comparable to red meat and can stand up to the most exotic preparations. Squab is often sold frozen but can be ordered fresh by mail or from specialty butcher shops.

In the summer months, when the berries in Oregon are at their peak and bursting with extraordinary flavor, I like to sauté them in butter with a splash of red wine vinegar. The result is a wonderful, tangy sauce that will enliven any game or fowl dish.

To prepare the squab or game hens: Preheat the oven to 375°. Rub the birds with the balsamic vinegar and season with 1 teaspoon of the salt and 1 teaspoon of the pepper. Place on a rack in a roasting pan. Roast in the oven for 25 to 30 minutes, or until the juices run clear when the birds are pierced in the thigh with a knife. Remove from the oven, cover loosely with aluminum foil, and let stand for 10 minutes. Carve the breast and legs off the bone.

To prepare the garlic: Blanch the cloves twice in boiling water. Rinse under water after each blanching. In a heavy small sauté pan or skillet, combine the water, 1 tablespoon of the butter, the honey, and thyme. Bring to a simmer and add the garlic. Cook until the garlic begins to caramelize and turn golden brown. Continue cooking to reduce the liquid until almost dry. Remove the thyme; set the garlic aside and keep warm.

To prepare the raspberries: In a small sauté pan or skillet, melt 1 tablespoon of the butter over medium heat. Sauté the shallots for 1 minute. Add the berries and cook for 3 to 4 minutes, or until they release their juices. Stir in the vinegar and simmer for an additional 4 to 5 minutes, or until the berries become sauce consistency. Set aside and keep warm.

To prepare the escarole or greens: In a large skillet, melt the remaining 1 tablespoon butter over medium heat. Add the greens, season with the remaining 1/2 teaspoon salt and 1/2 teaspoon pepper, and cook until wilted.

To serve, portion the greens onto 4 plates. Spoon on the raspberry sauce. Top each plate of greens with 2 breasts and 2 legs. Spoon the raspberry sauce and 6 cloves of caramelized garlic over the squabs and onto each plate.

Roasted Pheasant with Cauliflower Purée and Cabbage Cooked with Apple and Grain Mustard

SERVES 4 AS AN ENTRÉE

When roasting pheasant or partridge, leaving the breast on the bone and pan-roasting the legs separately ensures moist breast meat. The legs tend to have a higher fat content and can withstand a longer roasting period without becoming overly dry.

To prepare the cauliflower purée: Preheat the oven to 350°. Arrange the cauliflower and potatoes in a 9-by-13-inch baking pan. In a small saucepan, bring the stock, butter, and salt and pepper to a boil. Pour over the vegetables and cover with aluminum foil. Bake in the oven for about 45 minutes, or until the vegetables are very tender. Let cool slightly. Purée through a food mill or ricer (a food processor will make the potatoes too starchy). In a small saucepan, bring the cream just to a simmer; remove from heat. Slowly add the cream to the purée to the desired consistency (the mixture should be thick). Season to taste with salt, pepper, and nutmeg. Leave the oven on.

To prepare the pheasants: Cut each pheasant into 4 pieces: 2 breasts and 2 legs with thigh sections attached. Rub the pieces with 1 tablespoon of the oil and season with the salt and pepper. In a large skillet, heat 1 tablespoon of the oil over medium heat. Brown the leg sections on all sides. Place the leg sections in the roasting pan and roast in the oven for 10 minutes. In the same skillet, heat the remaining 1 tablespoon oil over medium heat. Brown the breasts on all sides. Put in a roasting pan with the leg sections and roast for an additional 25 to 30 minutes, or until the meat is firm to the touch and the juices run clear when a leg is pierced with a knife. Cover loosely with aluminum foil and keep warm.

To prepare the chicken, if using: Rub with the oil and season with salt and pepper. Roast whole for 45 to 65 minutes, or until the juices run clear when a thigh is pierced with a knife, or an instant-read thermometer inserted in a thigh registers 175°. Cut the chicken into serving pieces and keep warm.

To prepare the cabbage: In a 10-inch skillet, cook the bacon over medium heat until crisp. Using a slotted spoon, transfer the bacon to paper towels to drain. Pour out the bacon drippings, reserving 2 tablespoons. Return the reserved bacon drippings to the skillet. Heat over medium heat and add the onion, salt, and pepper. Cook until the onion is soft, 4 to 5 minutes. Add the cabbage, cider, vinegar, and mustard; cook for about 8 minutes to wilt the cabbage. Add the apple, cover, and cook over low heat for 5 minutes, or until the apple is tender. Taste and adjust the seasoning. Add the sage and cooked bacon.

To serve, portion the cabbage and the cauliflower purée onto 4 plates. Top each serving with a pheasant breast and leg section or a roasted chicken piece.

CAULIFLOWER PURÉE

1 head cauliflower, cut into small florets

2 Yukon Gold potatoes, peeled and cut into 1-inch pieces

1 1/4 cups chicken stock (page 221)

2 teaspoons unsalted butter

1 teaspoon salt

1 teaspoon freshly ground black pepper

1/4 cup heavy cream

Dash of ground nutmeg

2 pheasants (about 1 1/2 pounds each), or one 3- to 4-pound roasting chicken

3 tablespoons olive oil

1 teaspoon salt

1 teaspoon freshly ground black pepper

CABBAGE

4 ounces bacon, cut into 1/4-inch strips

1 small white onion, thinly sliced

1 teaspoon salt

1 teaspoon freshly ground black pepper

1/2 head Savoy cabbage, thinly sliced

1/3 cup apple cider or juice

2 tablespoons apple cider vinegar

2 teaspoons whole-grain mustard

1 Gravenstein, Granny Smith, or McIntosh apple, peeled, cored, and chopped into 1/2-inch pieces

1 teaspoon julienned fresh sage

Roasted Partridge with Creamed Brussels Sprouts, Walnuts, and Bacon — SERVES 4 AS AN ENTRÉE

MARINADE

2 bay leaves, crumbled

1 orange, chopped into 1-inch pieces

1 yellow onion, chopped into
  1-inch pieces

1 clove garlic, coarsely chopped

1 tablespoon chopped fresh
  rosemary

1 tablespoon fresh thyme leaves

1 teaspoon coarsely ground
  black pepper

4 partridges or Cornish game hens

2 teaspoons salt

2 teaspoons freshly ground
  black pepper

2 cups water

5 slices bacon, cut into 1/4-inch slices

1 pound Brussels sprouts

3/4 cup heavy cream

2 teaspoons fresh lemon juice

1/2 cup chopped walnuts, toasted
  (page 224)

Partridge and pheasant are often only available fresh in late fall. Partridge is a little sweeter and moister than pheasant, and tends to have a more pronounced flavor. Pheasant is the leaner of the two, and becomes dry if not roasted on the bone.

When preparing either partridge or pheasant, I find that marinating the meat overnight enhances its natural flavor and makes for a more tender bird.

~~~~~~

To prepare the marinade: In a medium bowl, combine the marinade ingredients. Coat the birds, inside and out, with the marinade and refrigerate for at least 2 hours, but preferably 24.

To prepare the birds: Preheat the oven to 325°. Wipe the excess marinade off the birds. Season the birds with 1 teaspoon of the salt and 1 teaspoon of the pepper. Put in a roasting pan and roast in the oven for 45 to 65 minutes, or until the breasts are firm and the juices run clear when the thighs are pierced with a knife. Cover loosely with aluminum foil and let rest for 10 to 15 minutes. Split in half; set aside and keep warm.

Meanwhile, prepare the Brussels sprouts: In a 4-cup saucepan, bring the water to a boil and blanch the bacon pieces for 1 minute. (This removes some of the excess fat from the bacon so the cream sauce will not be greasy.) Drain the bacon and dry on paper towels for 10 minutes. Thinly slice the Brussels sprouts into circles. Heat a 10-inch skillet over medium heat and cook the bacon until it begins to brown. Add the sliced Brussels sprouts and the remaining 1 teaspoon salt and 1 teaspoon pepper. Stir and cook for 2 to 3 minutes, or until the Brussels sprouts turn bright green. Add the cream and cook until thick, 5 to 8 minutes. Mix in the lemon juice and walnuts.

To serve, spoon a portion of the creamed Brussels sprouts onto each plate and top with 2 partridges or Cornish game hen halves.

Split Roasted Rabbit with Sautéed Greens and Balsamic Butter — SERVES 4 AS AN ENTRÉE

Rabbit is a first-rate game meat with virtually no fat that may be cooked in a variety of ways at any time of the year.

You can purchase rabbit whole or in parts. The primary cuts are the hindquarters, or back legs; the forequarters, or front legs; the saddle with the two loins on the bone; or the boned loin. Culinary logic suggests handling each of the cuts separately, as they each benefit from a different cooking technique. The legs are best if slow-roasted in the oven, the loin does nicely in a quick sauté, and the forequarters do well braised with stock, wine, and appropriate aromatics.

Sometimes I like to toss culinary logic aside, however, and simply split the rabbit in half and roast it in the oven. As it cooks, I baste it with a balsamic vinegar butter and serve it on a bed of garlic mashed potatoes with sautéed escarole or other bitter greens.

To prepare the butter: In a medium saucepan, simmer the balsamic vinegar over low heat to reduce to about 1/4 cup; let cool. In a medium bowl, combine the butter, shallots, rosemary, fennel, salt, pepper, and reduced vinegar. Mix, blending well; set aside. (This can be made ahead and frozen for up to 1 month.)

To make the rabbit: Preheat the oven to 450°. Season the rabbit with salt and pepper. Rub with 2 tablespoons of the balsamic butter. Put in a roasting pan and roast, basting the rabbit every 5 minutes with the balsamic butter, for 20 to 25 minutes, or until the meat is firm. Remove from the oven and let cool slightly. Cover loosely with aluminum foil.

To sauté the greens: In a large skillet, melt the butter over medium–high heat. Add the greens, stir, and cook until wilted. Season with salt and pepper.

To serve, spoon a portion of the garlic mashed potatoes onto the center of each plate. Top with a portion of greens and half a rabbit.

BALSAMIC BUTTER

1 cup balsamic vinegar

4 tablespoons unsalted butter, at room temperature

3 shallots, minced

1 teaspoon minced fresh rosemary

1 teaspoon fennel seeds, toasted and cracked (see page 224)

1 teaspoon salt

1 teaspoon freshly ground black pepper

2 whole rabbits, each split in half lengthwise

2 teaspoons salt

2 teaspoons freshly ground black pepper

SAUTÉED GREENS

1 tablespoon unsalted butter

1 bunch escarole, spinach, or chard, stemmed, washed, and dried

1/2 teaspoon salt

1/2 teaspoon freshly ground black pepper

Garlic mashed potatoes (page 121)

Barbecued Rabbit Wings — SERVES 4 AS AN APPETIZER

BARBECUE SAUCE

3 ounces slab bacon, chopped into
   $^1/_2$-inch pieces

1 yellow onion, chopped into
   $^1/_2$-inch pieces

2 teaspoons salt

$^1/_2$ cup chopped red bell pepper
   ($^1/_2$-inch pieces)

$^1/_2$ cup chopped green bell pepper
   ($^1/_2$-inch pieces)

1 jalapeño chile, minced (leave
   seeds and membrane intact if
   you like heat)

2 cloves garlic, minced

3 tomatoes, chopped (include juice)

$^1/_2$ cup red wine vinegar

$^1/_4$ cup molasses

2 tablespoons packed brown sugar

3 black peppercorns

1 bay leaf

$^1/_4$ teaspoon cayenne pepper

10 sprigs cilantro, chopped

16 rabbit forequarters

Butchers often have a large supply of rabbit forequarters, also called "wings," because this portion of rabbit is outsold by the more popular cuts, such as the leg and loin of rabbit. This next recipe makes a great finger food and includes Wildwood's popular barbecue sauce. Try it with Wildwood Coleslaw (page 25). Chicken wings may be substituted for the rabbit in this dish.

To make the barbecue sauce: In a heavy 2-quart saucepan, cook the bacon, onion, and salt over medium heat for 5 minutes, or until the bacon begins to brown. Stir in the bell peppers, jalapeño, and garlic; continue to cook for 5 minutes. Reduce heat to low, add the tomatoes, vinegar, molasses, brown sugar, peppercorns, bay leaf, and cayenne and simmer, stirring occasionally, for 30 to 40 minutes, or until a thick consistency is achieved. Remove the bay leaf and add the cilantro. Let cool. Blend the mixture in a food processor. Taste and adjust the seasoning. Reserve $^1/_2$ cup of the barbecue sauce; cover and refrigerate the reserved sauce.

Put the rabbit in a large pan and pour over the remaining barbecue sauce. Cover, refrigerate, and marinate overnight.

To grill the rabbit: Light a fire in a charcoal or gas grill. Drain the rabbit well and discard the sauce. Using indirect heat (see note below), grill the rabbit for 15 to 20 minutes, turning often and basting with the reserved sauce. The rabbit is done when the meat is easily separated from the bone. Or, roast the rabbit in a roasting pan in a preheated 350° oven for 25 to 30 minutes, basting occasionally with the reserved sauce.

CHEF'S NOTE: To grill the rabbit using indirect heat, pile hot coals around the edge of a grill and cook the rabbit in the center of the grill. On a gas grill, use the lowest setting or, on a dual grill, turn one side on and grill on the opposite side with the cover closed.

Rabbit Legs Braised with Tomatoes, Green Olives, and Capers — SERVES 4 AS AN ENTRÉE

Rabbit tends to have the mildest flavor of the game meats, so it can be paired with stronger flavors, such as garlic, capers, olives, and tomatoes. The leg meat stands up to these flavors and absorbs their pungent quality very well. If you purchase the loin, it can also be served in this dish by searing it on top of the stove after the legs are removed from the oven.

Preheat the oven to 350°. In a 12-inch ovenproof skillet, heat the olive oil over medium-high heat. Brown the rabbit legs on all sides. Remove the rabbit from the pan. Add the onion, bell pepper, garlic, jalapeño, and 1 teaspoon of the salt. Cook over medium-low heat, stirring occasionally, for 5 minutes, or until the onion is tender. Stir in the wine and tomatoes; cook for 3 additional minutes, or until the liquid comes to a simmer. Blend in the stock, olives, rosemary sprig, capers, the remaining 1 teaspoon salt, and 1 teaspoon pepper. Add the rabbit legs. Bring to a simmer. Place in the oven and braise for 1 hour. Remove the pan from the oven. Transfer the rabbit to a platter and keep warm. Remove the rosemary sprig and add the zucchini, submerging it in the braising liquid. Let stand for 5 minutes.

To serve, place a leg section in each of 4 large shallow bowls. Ladle on the sauce with the zucchini and garnish with parsley.

2 tablespoons olive oil

4 rabbit leg sections (with thighs), seasoned with salt and pepper

1 yellow onion, thinly sliced

1 red bell pepper, seeded, deribbed, and chopped into $^1/_2$-inch pieces

16 cloves garlic

1 jalapeño chile, seeded and minced

2 teaspoons salt

1 cup Chardonnay

8 vine-ripened tomatoes, halved, or 4 cups canned whole tomatoes, drained

2 cups chicken stock (page 221)

$^1/_2$ cup pitted picholine or other small green olives

1 sprig rosemary

$^1/_4$ cup capers, drained

2 teaspoons freshly ground black pepper

1 green or yellow zucchini, cut into $^1/_4$-inch slices

2 tablespoons chopped fresh flat-leaf parsley for garnish

Leg of Venison with Cider-Baked Apples, Red Chard, and Cranberry Sauce — SERVES 4 AS AN ENTRÉE

VENISON

1 teaspoon black peppercorns

1 teaspoon juniper berries

1 teaspoon fennel seeds

1 teaspoon dried or fresh thyme
  leaves

4 tablespoons olive oil

1 1/2 pounds (2 to 3 pieces) venison
  leg meat, trimmed (see note below)

CRANBERRY SAUCE

1 cinnamon stick, snapped in half

2 teaspoons fennel seeds

2 teaspoons whole cloves

2 teaspoons black peppercorns

2 teaspoons juniper berries

3 cups (12 ounces) fresh cranberries

3/4 cup Pinot Noir

1/2 cup balsamic vinegar

1/3 cup sugar

1/3 cup undiluted orange juice
  concentrate

Venison is rarely found in retail stores and usually must be ordered by mail or from a wholesale meat company. It comes in standard cuts, similar to those for lamb, veal, or beef. The leg is one of my favorite cuts because it offers great flavor with little waste. Any tender cut of venison, such as the loin, leg, or saddle, may be used in the following recipes.

Part of the current popularity of game and fowl is the natural leanness of the meat. Because it lacks fat, the meat does not have a built-in basting method to help keep it moist during cooking. For this reason, it is particularly important that game and fowl not be over-cooked. This is certainly the case with venison, as even the most tender or carefully braised pieces can become dry if not handled carefully. Medium-rare to rare is the most desirable degree of doneness.

I like to use a marinade that enhances the flavor of venison without overpowering it. A few hours before cooking, I rub the meat with a mixture of equal parts freshly ground black pepper, juniper berries, and fennel seeds mixed with a little dried thyme and olive oil.

To prepare the venison: In a spice grinder or food processor, grind the pepper-corns, juniper berries, fennel seeds, and thyme together. Mix with 2 tablespoons of the olive oil and rub on the venison. Cover and let stand in the refrigerator for 4 to 12 hours. Remove the venison from the refrigerator 1 hour before cooking to come to room temperature.

To make the cranberry sauce: In a food processor or spice grinder, grind the cin-namon, fennel seeds, cloves, peppercorns, and juniper berries together. Place in a cheesecloth square and tie closed with a string.

In a heavy medium saucepan, combine the cranberries, wine, vinegar, sugar, and orange juice concentrate. Add the spice bundle and bring the liquid to a boil. Reduce heat to a simmer and cook for 25 to 30 minutes, or until the cranberries are very soft. Remove the spice bundle, pour the sauce into a bowl, and let cool. Use now, or cover and refrigerate for up to 3 days. Bring to room temperature before serving.

While the cranberry sauce cools, make the baked apples: Preheat the oven to 325°. In a medium saucepan, cook the cider, vinegar, star anise, cinnamon, cloves, allspice, and butter for 5 minutes. Place the apples, cut-side down, in a baking pan. Pour the cider mixture over the apples. Bake for 15 to 20 minutes, or until semisoft; set aside and keep warm, or reheat just before serving.

To make the venison: Preheat the oven to 350°. In a large skillet, heat the remaining 2 tablespoons oil and brown the venison on all sides. Place on a rack in a roasting pan and roast in the oven for 15 minutes for medium-rare. For medium-done, roast 6 to 7 minutes longer. Remove the venison from the oven, cover loosely with aluminum foil, and let stand for 5 minutes before slicing.

To make the chard: In a large skillet, melt the butter over medium heat. Add the chard and apple cider and sauté for 5 minutes, stirring occasionally. Season with salt and pepper.

To serve, portion the chard onto 4 plates and top with an apple half. Place 4 to 5 slices of venison on each plate and spoon on the cranberry sauce.

CHEF'S NOTE: The venison leg pieces will all be different, so ask your butcher for the top and bottom round pieces. These cuts are lean and do not have excessive sinew that must be removed. Lamb can be used in this recipe in place of venison.

CIDER-BAKED APPLES

2 cups apple cider

1/4 cup apple cider vinegar

4 star anise pods (optional)

2 cinnamon sticks

2 whole cloves

1/4 teaspoon ground allspice

2 tablespoons unsalted butter

2 Braeburn, Jonathan, Gala, or Red Delicious apples, cored and halved lengthwise

CHARD

1 tablespoon unsalted butter

1 bunch firm red or white chard, stemmed

2 tablespoons apple cider (or cider residue from baked apples)

1/2 teaspoon salt

1/2 teaspoon freshly ground black pepper

Roasted Leg of Venison with Summer Berry Vinaigrette and Corn Pudding — SERVES 6 AS AN ENTRÉE

SUMMER BERRY VINAIGRETTE

1/3 cup olive oil

2 tablespoons red wine vinegar

1 tablespoon balsamic vinegar

1 teaspoon fennel seeds, toasted and ground (page 224)

1 teaspoon chopped fresh thyme

1/2 vanilla bean, split and scraped, or 1/2 teaspoon vanilla extract

1/2 teaspoon salt

1/4 teaspoon freshly ground black pepper

2 cups fresh blackberries, raspberries, huckleberries, or blueberries

VENISON

1 1/2 pounds boneless venison leg, trimmed of any excess sinew or skin

1 teaspoon salt

1 teaspoon freshly ground black pepper

2 tablespoons vegetable oil

SPINACH

1 tablespoon unsalted butter

8 ounces spinach, stemmed, washed, and dried

1/2 teaspoon salt

1/4 teaspoon freshly ground black pepper

Corn Pudding (opposite)

Corn and luscious, late-summer berries, such as blueberries and blackberries, cross seasons in August in the Pacific Northwest. These two components may not be a common fruit-vegetable pairing, yet they offer a contrast of textures and colors that complement roasted venison surprisingly well. The summer berry vinaigrette can be used in an array of game, poultry, or pork dishes as a refreshing alternative to cream- or stock-based sauces.

To make the vinaigrette: In a medium bowl, combine the oil, vinegars, fennel, thyme, vanilla bean and scrapings or extract, salt, and pepper. Add the berries and toss to coat with the vinaigrette. Let stand at room temperature for 1 to 2 hours, or cover and refrigerate overnight. Remove the vanilla bean, if using.

To prepare the venison: Preheat the oven to 350°. Season the venison with the salt and pepper. In a 12-inch skillet, heat the oil over medium heat and brown the venison on all sides. Place on a rack in a roasting pan and roast in the oven for 15 to 20 minutes, or until an instant-read thermometer inserted in the thickest part of the meat registers 135°. Cover loosely with aluminum foil and let stand for 5 minutes; slice thinly.

To prepare the spinach: In a large skillet, melt the butter. Add the spinach and sauté for 3 to 5 minutes, stirring until wilted. Season with salt and pepper.

To serve, spoon equal portions of the pudding onto each plate. Place a portion of spinach onto each plate and arrange 4 or 5 slices of venison on the spinach. Spoon some of the berry vinaigrette over the venison.

Corn Pudding — SERVES 6

Corn pudding has been in the Wildwood dessert repertoire since we opened in 1994. During the baking process, the cornmeal and flour separate, giving the pudding a creamy, layered texture that has won over more than a few of our guests through the years! When preparing this dish, do not allow the pudding to sit for longer than 45 minutes after removing it from the oven, as it can become dry and bready. The pudding can be prepared even when fresh corn is not available since canned kernels are a fine substitute.

Preheat the oven to 350°. Butter a 9-by-13-inch baking pan. In a small skillet, fry the bacon over medium heat until crisp. Transfer the bacon and 1/4 cup of the drippings to a large bowl. If needed, add melted butter to make 1/4 cup. Add the milk, eggs, sugar, and vinegar to the bacon drippings, beating until smooth.

Sift the flour, baking powder, salt, cayenne, and baking soda together into a medium bowl. Stir in the cornmeal. Add the dry ingredients to the liquid ingredients, whisking until smooth.

The batter will be thin. Stir in the green onions and corn. Pour the batter into the prepared pan. Pour the cream into the center without stirring. Place the pan in a larger baking pan. Fill the larger pan with hot water to reach halfway up the side of the spoon bread pan. Bake for about 1 1/4 hours, or until the spoon bread moves just a bit when the pan is gently shaken. Remove from the oven and water; let stand for 15 to 20 minutes before serving.

4 slices smoky bacon, cut crosswise into 1/4-inch strips

Melted butter if needed

3 cups milk

3 large eggs, beaten

2 tablespoons sugar

1 teaspoon white wine vinegar

1 1/2 cups flour

1 1/2 teaspoons baking powder

1 teaspoon salt

1/2 to 1 teaspoon cayenne pepper

3/4 teaspoon baking soda

1 cup yellow cornmeal

1/4 cup thinly sliced green onions

1/4 cup fresh corn kernels

1 1/2 cups heavy cream

THE WILLAMETTE VALLEY

9. THE WILLAMETTE VALLEY: SUMMER'S BOUNTY OF BERRIES

*L*ong before the days when I shook oyster trays in Yaquina Bay or washed dishes in my family's restaurant, I spent early-summer mornings picking strawberries in the lush Willamette Valley near my family's home in West Linn, a small town that at the time seemed worlds away from the bustle of busy Portland. Berry picking seems to be a rite of passage in this agricultural area, where you are paid by the flat, not by the hour. You can eat as many berries as you want in the process, and although time spent grazing cut into my earning potential, I found the fresh berries too good to resist. Many a morning went by that I gobbled up the ticket money I had hoped to earn for the afternoon movie in town.

Willamette Valley strawberries have a color, purity, sweetness, and aroma that are unmatched by any other strawberries I have eaten. The burst of flavor from a perfectly ripe organic berry is difficult to duplicate, and many of the scientifically engineered varieties designed to pack and travel well fall far short of my now-lofty expectations. When I'm on the hunt for berries, I visit the local farmer's markets with the hope that maybe one of those baskets in one of those stalls will allow me to reexperience the flavor I so strongly remember from my childhood.

When strawberries reach a deep red color and are perfectly ripe, they are desserts in themselves. For this reason, I like to keep the preparation simple and let the strawberries do all the work. One easy, yet decadent, way to enjoy summer-ripe strawberries is to toss them whole with fruit brandy (such as cherry, plum, apple, or pear) and then evenly coat them with a little sugar. The result is comparable to indulging in fine European chocolates, for it is a sin to consume more than one without stopping to savor the experience of the flavor on your palate.

My great-grandmother Elizabeth was married to my great-grandfather Louis Charles for almost fifty years and out-lived him by another twenty. She adored fruit, and her backyard was a cornucopia of flavors in the summer. On visits to her home in Portland, I'd always be drawn to the Concord grapes that grew alongside the house. I plucked the ripe morsels and marveled at the sensation of the skins popping in my mouth. When I wasn't harvesting grapes, I was perched in a tree, relishing the flavor of the Italian blue plums that melted in my mouth like spoonfuls of honey.

From a very early age, I shared Elizabeth's passion for fruit and couldn't resist plucking everything in sight. At the age of four, I wandered off from our rural home to follow a trail of juicy blackberries that started in our garden. Before I knew it, I was stuck in brambles with no way out. When my family finally discovered me in the thorny bushes, my body was covered with scratches and my face was smeared with tears and berry juice. I've paid the price for thieving from prickly blackberry bushes many times since then, but the flavor still seems worth the scrapes and scratches. When my berry bucket is full, I head inside to make blackberry cobbler with cornmeal-biscuit topping.

Years later, after I had begun my career as a chef, I had the pleasure of sorting through Elizabeth's recipe file. Her affinity for sweets was unmistakable, for almost every recipe in the box had something to do with dessert. Interspersed among the recipe cards were letters from friends sharing favorite dishes, and a note from Betty Crocker, the well-known fictional character, thanking my grandmother for her interest in Gold Medal flour.

When the heat of those early-summer afternoons reached its peak, my brother, sister, and I often sought refuge in the thick shade of the hazelnut trees that grew near our home. At the time, I knew nothing of the heritage of those trees, which I now know date back to the 1850s. Today, thick groves of hazelnut trees are abundant in the valley, and the round, sweet nuts have become synonymous with the Pacific Northwest.

My childhood in the rural Willamette Valley gave me an early appreciation for flavors from the source. The surrounding fields and orchards offered us a variety of fresh produce with a robust and pure flavor that is hard to find in today's world of mass production.

Many of the farms are gone now, driven out by a freeway development that eventually forced us to leave our home. As I've watched the agricultural base drop over the last thirty years, I have made a commitment to support local growers by buying their produce and shopping at farmer's markets. I have come to know many of these farmers and am heartened by the pride they have in their product. If I am going to recapture the pure flavors of my youth, it will be through these people, who have not lost sight of the bounty that dedication and attention to detail can reap through careful tending of the soil.

Elizabeth Wachsmuth, c. 1906.

Strawberry-Citrus Shortcake — SERVES 8

SUGARED STRAWBERRIES WITH GRAND MARNIER

8 cups fresh strawberries, stemmed and sliced

$1/4$ to $1/3$ cup sugar, depending on sweetness of berries

3 tablespoons fresh orange juice

3 tablespoons Triple Sec, Grand Marnier, or orange juice

SHORTCAKES

$2^1/2$ cups flour

$2^1/2$ teaspoons baking powder

$1/2$ cup yellow cornmeal

$2/3$ cup sugar

1 teaspoon salt

$1^1/2$ cups heavy cream

4 teaspoons grated lemon zest

4 teaspoons grated orange zest

4 tablespoons unsalted butter, melted

Sugar for coating (about $1/3$ cup)

Whipped cream (page 223)

Strawberry shortcake is a classic dessert that is easy to make and is sure to satisfy any summer sweet tooth. The key to a good shortcake (other than starting with great strawberries!) is the biscuits themselves, which are best when taken warm from the oven and immediately split open to receive the strawberry compote. I've added a citrus twist to this recipe, both in the shortcakes and in the berries. If you prefer your shortcake without lemon and orange, just omit them and prepare the rest of the recipe as shown.

To prepare the strawberries: In a large bowl, combine all the ingredients. Marinate for 30 minutes to 2 hours.

To make the shortcake: Preheat the oven to 350°. In a medium bowl, combine the flour, baking powder, cornmeal, sugar, and salt. Stir in the cream, lemon zest, and orange zest until just combined. Turn the dough out onto a floured board. Form into a ball and knead 8 to 12 times, or until the ball holds its shape. Cut the dough into 8 equal portions and roll into balls. Roll the dough in the melted butter, then the sugar. Place on a greased baking sheet and bake for 20 to 25 minutes, or until lightly browned and cooked through. Let cool slightly on a wire rack.

Cut each shortcake in half. Top the bottom halves with fruit and whipped cream. Place the top halves on top and serve.

Strawberry-Buttermilk Ice Cream ⟶ MAKES ABOUT 2 QUARTS

No remembrance of strawberries past would be complete without mention of my father's ice cream. The process of making it was an ordeal well worth the undertaking, as the brilliant berries, warm from the sun, were transformed into a cool and soothing sweetness. Long before the days of the electric ice-cream maker, my brother, sister, and I would take turns cranking the dasher in anticipation of the rich blend of strawberries, buttermilk, and vanilla. Fortunately, technology has made things a little easier today, so that you can enjoy the fruits without all the labor.

~~~~~~

To make the purée: In a medium saucepan, combine all the ingredients and bring to a boil. Reduce heat and simmer for 7 to 9 minutes, or until the purée begins to thicken, skimming the surface as scum comes to the top. Remove from heat and let cool. In a blender, purée the mixture in 2 batches. If desired, strain through a fine-meshed sieve to remove the seeds. Let cool.

To make the base: In a heavy 4-quart saucepan, whisk together 1 1/2 cups of the heavy cream, the buttermilk, sugar, and egg yolks. Cook over low heat, whisking constantly, for 12 to 15 minutes, or until the custard coats a metal spoon without running off. Remove from heat and let cool. In a small bowl, whisk together the remaining 3/4 cup heavy cream, the sour cream, and salt. Stir into the custard. Pour the mixture into a large bowl and set it in a bowl of ice to cool. Blend in the strawberry purée.

Freeze the mixture in an ice-cream maker according to the manufacturer's directions.

**SWEETENED
STRAWBERRY PURÉE**

6 cups fresh strawberries, stemmed

3/4 cup sugar

1 teaspoon vanilla extract

1 to 2 tablespoons fresh lemon juice

ICE CREAM BASE

2 1/4 cups heavy cream

1 1/2 cups buttermilk

1 1/2 cups sugar

6 large egg yolks

3/4 cup sour cream

1/8 teaspoon salt

Blackberry Cobbler
with Cornmeal-Biscuit Topping — SERVES 9

FILLING

1 1/2 **cups packed brown sugar**

3 **tablespoons cornstarch**

1/8 **teaspoon salt**

1/4 **cup water**

6 **cups ripe blackberries**

2 **teaspoons vanilla extract**

CORNMEAL TOPPING

1 1/2 **cups flour**

3/4 **cup fine white cornmeal**

1/4 **cup plus 3 tablespoons
granulated sugar**

1 **tablespoon baking powder**

1/2 **teaspoon salt**

1 1/3 **cups heavy cream**

3 **tablespoons packed brown sugar**

3 **tablespoons unsalted butter,
melted**

When this dessert appears on the Wildwood menu, it is always the most popular. It tempts you right from the start, with its thick, pitch-dark berry juice bubbling up around the topping.

Preheat the oven to 325°. Spray a 9-inch square baking dish with vegetable-oil cooking spray.

To make the filling: In a medium saucepan, blend the brown sugar, cornstarch, and salt. Stir in the water and 3 cups of the blackberries. Cook over medium heat, stirring, until thick and clear. Stir in the vanilla and let cool slightly. Pour the cooked mixture and the remaining 3 cups fresh berries into the bottom of the dish; set aside.

To prepare the topping: In a medium bowl, combine the flour, cornmeal, 1/4 cup granulated sugar, baking powder, and salt. Add the cream and mix until the dough comes together. Turn out onto a floured board and knead 8 to 12 times, or until smooth. Cut the dough into 9 portions and roll into balls. Combine the brown sugar and the 3 tablespoons granulated sugar. Dip each ball in the butter, then the sugar. Place the balls on top of the fruit. Bake for 30 to 35 minutes, or until the mixture is bubbling and the topping is lightly browned and cooked through. Let cool slightly and serve.

Brown Butter Chess Tart with Blackberries — SERVES 12

Combining sweet blackberries and tart lemons creates a delightful explosion of flavor, as in this chess tart. Browned butter adds a nuttiness to the cornmeal tart shell, which is offset by the slightly acidic bite of the cider vinegar batter and the addition of fresh berries on top of the tart.

Preheat the oven to 350°. In a heavy saucepan, melt the butter over medium heat and cook until the butter turns from light to dark brown. Remove from the heat and stir in the vanilla bean and scrapings or vanilla extract. Pour the mixture through a fine-meshed sieve; set aside.

Using an electric mixer on medium speed, beat the eggs and granulated sugar together. With the mixer running, drizzle in the brown butter. Add the cornmeal, vinegar, and salt and mix until smooth. Pour into the tart shell. Bake for about 30 minutes, or until the top is golden brown and the filling has set. Let cool on a wire rack.

Remove the tart from the pan and place on a serving platter. Just before serving, arrange the berries on the tart in concentric circles and dust with confectioners' sugar. Slice and serve.

$^1/_2$ cup (1 stick) unsalted butter

$^1/_2$ vanilla bean, split and scraped, or 2 teaspoons vanilla extract

3 large eggs

1 cup granulated sugar

$^1/_4$ cup yellow cornmeal

1 tablespoon cider vinegar

$^1/_2$ teaspoon salt

1 partially baked 12-inch tart crust in a false-bottom tart pan (page 223)

4 cups fresh blackberries, hulled strawberries, blueberries, or raspberries

Confectioners' sugar for dusting

Great-Grandmother Elizabeth's Blackberry Roly-Poly with Sliced-Lemon Sauce — SERVES 8

2 cups flour

2 teaspoons baking powder

$1/2$ teaspoon salt

4 tablespoons chilled unsalted butter, plus 2 tablespoons butter, melted

$3/4$ cup milk

$1^1/2$ cups fresh ripe blackberries

6 tablespoons sugar

SLICED-LEMON SAUCE

$1/2$ cup sugar

2 tablespoons cornstarch

$1/4$ teaspoon salt

$1^1/2$ cups water

$1/3$ cup fresh lemon juice

1 vanilla bean, split and scraped, or 1 teaspoon vanilla extract

3 tablespoons unsalted butter

1 to 2 lemons, preferably Meyer lemons, peeled, halved lengthwise, seeded, and cut into paper-thin crosswise slices on a mandoline or by hand

One of the recipes in Elizabeth's box had a name that intrigued me. The words roly-poly, written in her elegant hand, jumped out at me like a secret that had been kept hidden inside the box for too long.

Preheat the oven to 350°. Lightly butter two 12-inch loaf pans. Sift the flour, baking powder, and salt together into a medium bowl. Using a pastry blender or 2 knives, cut in the 4 tablespoons cold butter until the mixture resembles crumbs. Add the milk and mix with a fork until the dough comes together. Turn out onto a floured board and knead 4 or 5 times, or until smooth. Cut the dough in half. On a floured board, roll out half of the dough into a rectangle 8 inches wide and $1/4$ inch thick. Brush with half of the melted butter. Top with $3/4$ cup of the blackberries and sprinkle with 3 tablespoons of the sugar. Roll up jelly-roll style, forming an 8-inch-long roll. Place, seam-side down, in one of the prepared pans. Repeat the process, using the remaining half of the dough and filling. Bake in the pans for 35 to 40 minutes, or until the crust is firm and beginning to brown.

While the roly-poly is cooking, make the sauce: In a medium saucepan, blend together the sugar, cornstarch, and salt. Stir in the water, lemon juice, and vanilla bean and scrapings until smooth. (If using vanilla extract, wait to add until the syrup is removed from the heat.) Cook over medium heat, stirring, for 5 minutes, or until the mixture is thick and clear. Remove from heat and add the butter and continue to stir until melted and blended. Let cool slightly and stir in the lemon slices. Take out the vanilla bean, if using.

Remove the roly-poly from the oven and let cool in the pans for 10 minutes. Turn out onto a wire rack. Cut into 2-inch slices and serve with lemon sauce.

CHEF'S NOTE: The lemon sauce will keep for 3 to 4 days but is best served the day it is made. It will thicken when refrigerated; simply stir to loosen the sauce.

Vanilla Bean Crème Brûlée
with Summer Berries — SERVES 8

2 cups heavy cream

1/4 cup milk

1 vanilla bean, split and scraped,
  or 2 teaspoons vanilla extract

4 large egg yolks

1/2 cup granulated sugar

1/8 teaspoon salt

1/4 to 1/3 cup superfine sugar

2 cups fresh blueberries, raspberries,
  blackberries, or sliced hulled
  strawberries

CHEF'S NOTE: You can also use a small butane blowtorch, available in kitchenware shops, to caramelize the topping.

With so many berry varieties available in the summer, it's only natural to mix and match them. Many berries, including raspberries, blackberries, boysenberries, and blueberries, are alike in their water content and their reaction to baking and cooking. Such similarities make it easy to interchange or blend berries in many dishes.

Crème brûlée is one example of a traditional dessert that benefits from a seasonal fruit garnish. The name means "burnt cream" and refers to the melted sugar topping. When you take your spoon to the custard, the topping cracks like glass, exposing a creamy vanilla custard. A few fresh organic berries on top add a little touch of summer. The custard base may be made 2 days before baking; the custards should be baked and refrigerated for at least 4 hours before topping.

If using the vanilla bean, combine the cream, milk, and vanilla bean and scrapings in a heavy medium saucepan, stirring to blend. Heat over low heat until the milk just begins to steam. Remove from heat and let steep for 1 hour. Remove the vanilla bean and reheat once again until steaming. Set aside.

If using the vanilla extract, combine the cream and milk as directed and heat until steam rises. Remove from heat.

In a small bowl, whisk together the egg yolks, granulated sugar, and salt. Whisk a small amount of hot cream into the eggs. Whisk the egg mixture into the cream. Strain through a fine-meshed sieve into a bowl. Set the bowl in a bowl of ice for 30 minutes to cool, stirring occasionally. Stir in the vanilla extract, if using. (Cover and refrigerate for up to 2 days, if desired.)

Pour into eight 4- or 6-ounce flameproof ramekins, leaving room at the top to accommodate the berries. Place the filled ramekins in 2 baking pans and fill each pan with hot water to reach halfway up the sides of the ramekins. Place in a cold oven and bake at 325° for 35 to 50 minutes, or until the middle of the custards quake just a bit and the custards are not quite set. Remove the ramekins from the pan and let cool completely. Refrigerate for at least 4 hours, or up to 12 hours.

Sprinkle each custard with 2 to 3 teaspoons superfine sugar. Place the ramekins 2 inches from the heat source for 2 minutes, or until the sugar has melted and caramelized. Let cool a few minutes before serving.

Just before serving, top each brûlée with 1/4 cup fresh berries.

Gratin of Summer Berries with Poured Brûlée ⟶ SERVES 6

This recipe departs from the traditional method for preparing crème brûlée. The custard is cooked first, then poured over berries and set in the refrigerator to cool before being sprinkled with sugar and broiled to caramelize the topping. The combination of creamy cooked custard and uncooked fresh berries creates a delightful contrast.

If using the vanilla bean, warm the cream in a small saucepan over low heat just until it begins to steam. Watch carefully, as it can boil over quickly. Add the vanilla bean and scrapings and salt. Remove from heat and let steep for 30 minutes. Remove the vanilla bean and reheat once again until steaming. Set aside.

If using the vanilla extract, heat the cream until steaming, as directed. Remove from heat and set aside.

Slice any large berries. Place $^1/_2$ cup fruit in each of six 6-ounce flameproof gratin dishes. Set aside.

In a double boiler, whisk the egg yolks and granulated sugar together over simmering water; make sure that the water does not touch the bottom of the upper pan. Whisk the mixture constantly until it is thick and lemon colored and forms a slowly dissolving ribbon on the surface when the whisk is raised from the pan. Remove the top pan of the double boiler from heat. Slowly pour a small amount of the warm cream into the egg mixture, whisking constantly. Then gradually whisk in the remaining cream. Return to heat. Bring the water in the lower pan almost to a simmer and cook the custard, stirring occasionally, for 40 to 45 minutes, or until thick enough to coat a metal spoon without running off. Stir in the vanilla extract, if using. Pour the custard over the fruit in the dishes. Cover and refrigerate for at least 4 hours or overnight.

Preheat the broiler. Sprinkle each custard evenly with 2 to 3 teaspoons superfine sugar. Place the ramekins 2 inches from the heat source for 2 minutes, or until the sugar has melted and caramelized. Let cool for a few minutes before serving.

$1^1/_2$ **cups heavy cream**

$^1/_2$ **vanilla bean, split and scraped, or 1 teaspoon vanilla extract**

$^1/_8$ **teaspoon salt**

3 cups mixed berries or sliced pitted stone fruit such as apricots, peeled peaches, or nectarines

8 large egg yolks

$^1/_4$ **cup granulated sugar**

$^1/_4$ **to** $^1/_3$ **cup superfine sugar**

Buttermilk Spice Cake with Last Year's Berries Sauce — SERVES 8

1³/4 cups flour

1 teaspoon ground cinnamon

³/4 teaspoon salt

¹/2 teaspoon baking powder

¹/4 teaspoon baking soda

¹/4 teaspoon ground allspice

¹/4 teaspoon ground cloves

¹/4 teaspoon ground ginger

¹/8 teaspoon freshly ground black pepper

¹/2 cup (1 stick) butter, at room temperature

²/3 cup packed dark brown sugar

¹/3 cup granulated sugar

1 large egg

1 egg yolk

1 teaspoon vanilla extract

¹/2 cup buttermilk

LAST YEAR'S BERRY SAUCE

4 cups (1 pound) frozen unsweetened blueberries, raspberries, or blackberries

1 cup Pinot Noir

¹/2 cup sugar

¹/4 cup undiluted orange juice concentrate

1 vanilla bean, split and scraped, or 2 teaspoons vanilla extract

2 tablespoons honey

Confectioners' sugar for dusting

It does wonders for your soul to eat blueberries in the midst of a gray, wet Northwest winter. So before the berry season slips away with the coming of fall, I make sure to stash a supply in the freezer to satisfy my midwinter cravings. Fortunately, most berry varieties freeze well and can be used with great success all year round.

One of my favorite blueberry treats is warm buttermilk spice cake topped with a sauce made from last year's berries.

Preheat the oven to 325°. Spray an 8-inch square cake pan with vegetable-oil cooking spray. Line the bottom of the pan with a round of parchment paper or waxed paper.

Sift the flour, cinnamon, salt, baking powder, baking soda, allspice, cloves, ginger, and pepper together into a medium bowl; set aside.

In a mixer bowl, with the mixer on high speed, beat the butter and sugars together until light and fluffy. Add the egg and egg yolk, beating until creamy. On low speed, alternately blend in the dry ingredients and buttermilk in small batches.

Pour the batter into the prepared pan and tap the pan to settle the batter. Bake for 45 to 50 minutes, or until the cake is golden brown and a toothpick inserted in the center of the cake comes out clean.

While the cake is baking, prepare the sauce: In an 8-cup stainless-steel pan, combine the blueberries, wine, sugar, orange juice concentrate, and vanilla bean and scrapings. (If using vanilla extract, add it later.) Bring to a boil, reduce heat, and simmer for 20 minutes, stirring occasionally. Remove from heat and stir in the honey; let cool. Remove the vanilla bean, if using, or stir in the vanilla extract.

Let the cake cool in the pan for 10 minutes, then turn out onto a wire rack. Let cool for 30 minutes before cutting into wedges. Place a wedge on a dessert plate and spoon berries over the top. Dust with confectioners' sugar and serve.

CHEF'S NOTE: The berry sauce can be made 1 day ahead, covered, and stored in the refrigerator.

Blueberry-Lemon Buckle with Whipped Cream — SERVES 12

Blueberries are the most enduring fruit of the berry family. They ripen in the early summer and, with their seemingly indestructible tight blue skins, can last into the hot, dry days of August.

Lemon cake batter poured and baked over blueberries makes a wonderfully textured fruit buckle. The blueberries stay plump and pop in your mouth amid the soft and moist lemon cake. Most buckle recipes call for fresh fruit to be folded into a simple cake batter. I prefer too much of a good thing and put a layer of fruit on the bottom as well.

~~~~~~~~~~~~~~~~~~~~

Preheat the oven to 350°. Lightly butter a 9-by-13-inch baking dish.

To make the filling: In a medium saucepan, blend the sugar and cornstarch. Stir in the water and blueberries. Cook over medium heat until the berries release their juices and the mixture is thick and clear, about 20 minutes. Stir in the butter. Pour the blueberries into the prepared dish.

To make the batter: In a small saucepan, heat the lemon juice over medium heat. Simmer until the juice is reduced to $^1/_4$ cup and appears syrupy; set aside.

In a medium bowl, stir together the flour, baking powder, salt, and lemon zest; set aside.

In a mixer bowl, with the mixer on high speed, cream the butter and sugar until light and fluffy. With the mixer running, add the eggs, one at a time, beating until creamy. On low speed, blend in the dry ingredients, vanilla, and reduced lemon juice. Fold the blueberries into the batter. Pour over the blueberry mixture in the baking dish and spread evenly to the sides of the pan. Sprinkle with almonds, if desired. Bake for 35 minutes, or until a toothpick inserted in the center comes out clean. Let cool slightly and spoon onto dessert plates. Top each serving with a dollop of whipped cream and serve.

FILLING

$^2/_3$ cup sugar

3 tablespoons cornstarch

2 tablespoons water

6 cups fresh blueberries

2 tablespoons unsalted butter

CAKE BATTER

$^1/_2$ cup fresh lemon juice

$1^1/_2$ cups flour

$2^1/_2$ teaspoons baking powder

$^3/_4$ teaspoon salt

Grated zest of 2 lemons

1 cup (2 sticks) plus 2 tablespoons butter, at room temperature

1 cup plus 2 tablespoons sugar

5 large eggs

$1^1/_2$ teaspoons vanilla extract

2 cups fresh blueberries

TOPPING

$^1/_2$ cup sliced almonds (optional)

Whipped cream (page 223)

Arborio Rice Pudding with Dried Blueberries — SERVES 6

4 3/4 cups milk, or as needed

1/3 cup granulated sugar

1/2 teaspoon salt

1/2 vanilla bean, split and scraped, or 2 teaspoons vanilla extract

2/3 cup Arborio rice

1 large egg, beaten

3 tablespoons mascarpone cheese or cream cheese

4 teaspoons grated lemon zest

1/2 teaspoon ground mace (optional)

1/2 cup dried cranberries, cherries, strawberries, or blueberries

Fresh blueberries or blackberries

Confectioners' sugar for dusting

Rice pudding has been a favorite dessert of mine since childhood, and I still order it every time I see it on a restaurant menu. Variations to the recipe seem as numerous as the varieties of rice from which this popular dessert is made. At Wildwood, we use the Italian Arborio rice, which is commonly used in risotto. This variety offers a creamy texture and makes a rich and delicious dessert when you add a little cream and mascarpone cheese. Fresh fruit tends to make the pudding watery, so I prefer to use dried fruit instead. Fresh berries are sprinkled over the finished pudding just before serving.

If using the vanilla bean, in a heavy 3-quart pan, combine 4 cups of the milk, the granulated sugar, salt, and vanilla bean and scrapings. Warm over low heat just until it begins to steam; let steep for 15 minutes. Remove the vanilla bean.

If using the vanilla extract, skip the steeping step and proceed with the instructions, waiting to add the extract until later.

Stir in the rice. Cook, stirring occasionally, over medium heat for 15 to 20 minutes, or until the rice is tender. Whisk a small portion of rice into the egg. Mix the egg mixture into the rice and cook for an additional 2 minutes. Stir in the remaining 3/4 cup milk, the cheese, lemon zest, and mace, if desired. Remove from heat and let cool slightly. Fold in the dried fruit and add the vanilla extract, if using. Add additional milk if the mixture is too thick.

To serve, portion 6 servings out into small bowls and chill for 4 hours or overnight. Serve at room temperature, topped with fresh fruit and dusted with confectioners' sugar.

Blueberry-Sour Cream Tart   SERVES 8

Jennifer Welshhons, the pastry chef at Wildwood, prepares an old family recipe that has found a timeless place in our restaurant repertoire. For this simple tart, blueberries are baked with a sour cream custard, and fresh blueberries and whipped cream are used as a garnish just before serving.

To make the tart shell: In a medium bowl, combine the flour, sugar, and salt. Using a pastry blender or 2 knives, cut in the butter until the mixture resembles crumbs. Using a fork, mix in the cream, 1 tablespoon at a time, until the mixture comes together. Form into a ball, cover with a tea towel, and let rest for 15 minutes. On a floured board, roll out the pastry to fit a 12-inch round false-bottom tart pan. Tuck the pastry into the pan, pressing into the bottom and sides of the pan. Trim off the extra dough at the top of the pan. Refrigerate for 15 minutes. Preheat oven to 350°. Bake for 10 minutes, or until lightly browned. Remove from the oven and let cool, leaving the oven on.

To make the filling: Pour the blueberries into the cooled crust. In a medium bowl, whisk together the sour cream, sugar, flour, egg, lemon zest, lemon juice, and salt. Pour over the blueberries. Bake for 35 to 40 minutes, or until a toothpick inserted in the custard comes out clean. Remove from the oven and let cool. Remove the tart from the pan and place on a serving platter.

Serve with whipped cream and additional fresh blueberries.

TART SHELL

1 cup flour

2 teaspoons sugar

1/4 teaspoon salt

3 tablespoons chilled unsalted butter

1/4 cup plus 2 tablespoons heavy cream

FILLING

3 cups blueberries

1 cup sour cream

3/4 cup sugar

2 1/2 tablespoons flour

1 egg, beaten

1 tablespoon grated lemon zest

2 teaspoons fresh lemon juice

1/4 teaspoon salt

Whipped cream (page 223) and additional fresh blueberries for garnish

Raspberry Sorbet — SERVES 8

2 cups sugar

2 cups water

4 cups fresh raspberries

1/4 cup framboise, raspberry liqueur, or apple juice

1/2 teaspoon fresh lemon juice

1/8 teaspoon salt

Raspberries are perhaps the most delicate members of the berry family, both in structure and flavor. In Oregon we are fortunate to have two raspberry seasons. After the early summer bounty, the berry mysteriously reappears in late August and early September for an encore. The best of seasons also blesses us with the golden raspberry for about two weeks in July.

The color of this sorbet is bold, as is the flavor. You can substitute any type of berry.

In a heavy 3-quart saucepan, combine the sugar and water. Bring to a boil, reduce heat, and simmer for 5 minutes. Add the raspberries and simmer for 5 additional minutes. Let cool.

Force the raspberry mixture through a fine-meshed sieve; discard the seeds. Add the framboise (or liqueur or juice), lemon juice, and salt. Let cool completely.

Freeze in an ice-cream maker according to the manufacturer's directions.

Currant-Hazelnut Cookies — MAKES 3 DOZEN COOKIES

These cookies, a Wildwood favorite, are a great accompaniment to crème brûlée. Make a double batch of dough and freeze half of it for when guests appear unexpectedly on a Sunday afternoon.

Preheat the oven to 375°. Sift the flour, baking powder, and salt together into a medium bowl; set aside.

In a mixer bowl, with the mixer on high speed, cream the butter and sugar together until light and fluffy. Add the egg, vanilla extract, and anise extract, beating until creamy. On low speed, mix in the dry ingredients until just blended. Stir in the hazelnuts and currants.

Drop heaping teaspoonfuls of dough 1 inch apart on a greased baking sheet. Bake for 12 to 15 minutes, or until golden brown. Let cool on wire racks, then serve.

1³/4 cups flour

1¹/2 teaspoons baking powder

¹/4 teaspoon salt

¹/2 cup (1 stick) unsalted butter, at room temperature

1 cup sugar

1 large egg

1 teaspoon vanilla extract

1 teaspoon anise extract

1 cup hazelnuts, toasted, skinned, and coarsely chopped (page 224)

¹/2 cup dried currants or golden raisins, soaked in hot water for 10 minutes and drained

Three-Chocolate Hazelnut Tart   — SERVES 8

I have used hazelnuts often in this book, but no selection of hazelnut recipes would be complete without some calling for chocolate. This decadent treat blends not one, but three different types of chocolate: milk, bittersweet, and white.

~~~~~~

To make the pastry: In a food processor, combine the flour, confectioners' sugar, cocoa, salt, and baking soda. Pulse 4 times to blend. Add the butter chunks and pulse until the mixture resembles coarse crumbs. Add the ice water and pulse until the dough comes together. Remove the dough from the processor and form into a 6-inch disk. Wrap in plastic wrap and refrigerate for 20 minutes.

On parchment paper or waxed paper, roll out the dough into a 14-inch round. Dust the surface of the dough with the cocoa. Spray a 12-inch false-bottom tart pan with vegetable-oil cooking spray. Fit the dough into the pan, paper side up. Peel off the paper and press the dough carefully into the pan up to the top of the sides. Refrigerate for 15 minutes.

Preheat the oven to 350°. Cut a piece of aluminum foil large enough to cover the tart pan and spray it with vegetable-oil cooking spray. Place the foil on the tart pan, sprayed-side down, fitting over the dough and tucked down around the pastry. Weigh the foil down with pie weights or dried beans. Bake for 15 to 20 minutes, or until a toothpick inserted in the dough comes out clean. Remove the tart crust from the oven, leaving the oven on, and let cool for 20 minutes.

To make the filling: In a blender or food processor, combine the eggs, corn syrup, butter, vanilla, and salt. Blend until smooth; set aside.

Evenly sprinkle the hazelnuts and chocolates over the crust. Pour the egg mixture over the nuts and chocolates. Bake for 30 to 35 minutes, or until the filling is slightly puffed and set. Remove from the oven and let cool. Remove the tart from the pan and place on a serving platter. Cut into wedges and serve.

CHOCOLATE PASTRY

$1^1/_2$ cups flour

$^2/_3$ cup sifted confectioners' sugar

$^1/_2$ cup unsweetened cocoa powder

$^1/_2$ teaspoon salt

$^1/_4$ teaspoon baking soda

$^3/_4$ cup ($1^1/_2$ sticks) chilled unsalted butter, cut into 1-inch pieces

2 tablespoons plus 2 teaspoons ice water

Unsweetened cocoa powder for dusting

FILLING

4 large eggs, at room temperature

$1^1/_4$ cups light corn syrup

$^1/_2$ cup unsalted butter, melted

$1^1/_2$ teaspoons vanilla extract

$^1/_4$ teaspoon salt

$1^1/_2$ cups hazelnuts, toasted and skinned (page 224)

$^1/_2$ cup chopped white chocolate (3 ounces)

$^1/_2$ cup chopped milk chocolate (3 ounces)

$^1/_2$ cup chopped bittersweet chocolate (3 ounces)

Warm Chocolate-Hazelnut Fudge Pudding Cake

8 ounces semisweet chocolate, coarsely chopped

1/2 cup (1 stick) unsalted butter, at room temperature

1 cup granulated sugar

6 large egg yolks

1 cup hazelnuts, toasted, skinned, and coarsely chopped (page 224)

8 large egg whites

Confectioners' sugar for dusting

Whipped cream (page 223) for serving

Warm, soft-centered chocolate desserts are irresistible, and the hazelnut flavor makes this one even more delectable. This cake will slowly collapse as it cools and should be served with a light sprinkling of confectioners' sugar while still warm.

Preheat the oven to 350°. Butter a 10-inch ring mold or eight 5-ounce ramekins. In a double boiler over barely simmering water, melt the chocolate, stirring frequently until smooth. Set aside to cool.

With an electric mixer, beat the butter on medium speed until light and creamy. Add the granulated sugar and beat until light and fluffy. Beat in the egg yolks, one at a time, mixing well after each addition. Stir in the cooled chocolate and hazelnuts; set aside.

Using clean beaters and a large bowl, beat the egg whites until stiff, glossy peaks form. Stir one-quarter of the egg whites into the chocolate mixture. Gently fold the remaining whites into the mixture. Pour the batter into the prepared mold or ramekins. Cover the mold or ramekins with a large sheet of buttered aluminum foil, buttered side down. Place the mold or ramekins in a large baking pan. Add hot water to the pan to reach halfway up the side of the ring mold or ramekins. Bake for 35 to 45 minutes if using the mold, or 25 to 30 minutes if using the ramekins, or until the edges of the cake are almost firm to the touch and the center is still slightly moist. It is important that the cake does not overbake and become dry, so watch carefully. Carefully remove the mold or ramekins from the water. Let cool for several minutes on a wire rack.

To serve, spoon the warm cake from the mold onto plates or leave in ramekins, dust with confectioners' sugar, and top with a dollop of whipped cream.

Opposite: Fall comes to the Portland Farmer's Market.

THE HOOD RIVER VALLEY

10. THE HOOD RIVER VALLEY: ORCHARDS IN THE SHADOW OF MOUNT HOOD

*N*estled between Mount Hood and the majestic Columbia River is a valley unlike any other in the world. The ten-thousand-acre Hood River Valley is like a natural science experiment that has produced magical results. Its mineral-rich blend of volcanic and alluvial soils, coupled with the dueling climates of the western Cascades and the arid eastern desert, have created a fruit grower's and fruit lover's paradise.

A drive through the valley's famous Fruit Loop reveals a rolling landscape of orchards and produce stands. As you make your way south, apple, peach, pear, apricot, and cherry trees line the roads like sentries for the mighty mountain that looms ahead. The mood of the valley is constantly changing from the colorful energy of the spring bloom to the fiery colors of fall harvest. The constant transition allows you to discover something new with every visit.

Perhaps the most popular time to visit the valley is during the apple harvest. Stop at any one of the myriad produce stands and you'll find stacks and stacks of crates holding a seemingly endless variety of apples. The shiny red Empires, bright green and firm Granny Smiths, red and green streaked McIntoshes, and yellow and red Galas are a far cry from the waxy red apple we found in our school lunch bags. The difference in texture, flavor, sweetness, and coarseness is amazing and inspires me to create dishes that work with each of their characteristics.

The transition from summer to fall marks the arrival of one of my favorite fruits: the pear. Pears make up approximately three-quarters of the valley's fruit crop, and shipments from the region represent close to 30 percent of the country's winter pear supply.

The first crop to arrive is the Bartlett, which begins its harvest in mid-August. This variety has a relatively high water content that does not lend itself well to baking or poaching, but is wonderful on its own or as part of a purée.

In September and October, more pear varieties begin to emerge, including Bosc, Comice, Forelle, Anjou, Winter Nelis, and the small Seckel. As with many apple varieties, these pears are often picked before they are ripe and are stored for up to ten months. Because they can endure such long storage periods, apples and pears are the lone fresh fruit survivors of winter.

Lucinda Parker of Portland's Clear Creek Distillery shows off a bottle of their prized pear brandy.

As the days become cooler and winter begins to set in, I feel a bit of melancholy for the flavors of summer. The valley becomes quiet and the produce stands take a brief respite from the season's activities.

Perhaps my fondness for pears stems from childhood memories of the pear tree that stood at the school bus stop across the street from my home. On chilly fall mornings, my brother, sister, and I waited under that tree and would often pick an impromptu breakfast or launch an arsenal of overripe fruit at an unsuspecting sibling.

Today, I can see a similar tree in my neighbor's yard up the street. It's hard to resist the childhood temptation to hop the fence and help myself to the juicy fruits. I find that I consult that tree all summer as a kind of natural calendar: When it begins to drop its fruit, I know that winter isn't far around the bend.

Deep-Dish Apple Pie — SERVES 12

FILLING

4 tablespoons butter

1 3/4 cups granulated sugar

1/4 cup water

1 cup apple cider

3 tablespoons apple brandy or
   hard apple cider

1 tablespoon ground cinnamon

1 teaspoon salt

1/2 teaspoon ground allspice

1/2 teaspoon ground cloves

1/2 teaspoon ground mace
   or nutmeg

1/2 teaspoon freshly ground
   black pepper

12 Gala, pippin, or Granny Smith
   apples (about 4 1/2 pounds),
   peeled, cored, and thinly sliced

1/2 cup plus 1 tablespoon flour

STREUSEL

1/3 cup flour

3 tablespoons brown sugar

1/2 teaspoon salt

4 teaspoons unsalted butter,
   at room temperature

1 recipe Pastry Dough (page 223)

1 egg, beaten with 1 tablespoon
   water

Turbinado sugar or granulated sugar
   for sprinkling

When selecting apples for this pie, I recommend a firm green apple like the Gala, pippin, or Granny Smith. These varieties tend to have a tartness that offsets the sweetness of the added sugar, and their low water content helps them stay firm when cooking. Peeling the apples before adding them to the pie eliminates the slight bitterness of their skins and avoids a stringy texture when cooked. I also recommend cooking apples briefly before placing them in the pie dish—you'll be rewarded with a tall, easy-to-slice pie that has a thick consistency.

To make the filling: In a 12-inch skillet, melt the butter over medium heat. Stir in the sugar and water and cook until the sugar caramelizes to a medium amber color. Carefully add the apple cider and brandy or more cider, stirring to dissolve the caramel. Mix in the cinnamon, salt, allspice, cloves, mace or nutmeg, and pepper. Fold in half of the apple slices, stirring carefully to coat with the caramel sauce. Sprinkle the flour over the apples and mix with the apples and sauce; cook for 10 minutes. Stir in the remaining apples, coating with the sauce. Cook for about 8 to 10 minutes, or until the apples are just tender when pierced with the tip of a paring knife. Remove the pan from heat and pour the mixture onto parchment-paper-lined jelly-roll pans. Spread out to cool.

While the filling cools, make the streusel: In a small bowl, combine the flour, brown sugar, and salt. Using a pastry blender or two knives, cut in the butter to make coarse crumbs; set aside.

To assemble the pie: Preheat the oven to 425°. Butter a 2-inch-deep, 12-inch pie plate. On a lightly floured board, roll out one half of the pastry into a 16-inch round. Fit the pastry into the pie plate. Trim the pastry to extend 1 inch over the edge of the plate.

Sprinkle the streusel or cake crumbs over the bottom of the pastry. Add the apples, layering and piling them high in the center of the plate. (Precooked apples will not cook down as much as raw apples.)

Roll the remaining pastry into a 16-inch round. Fit the pastry over the apples and trim to extend 1 inch over the edge of the plate. Roll the two crusts together around the edge of the pie plate. Flute the edge of the crust. Cut vent holes in the crust. Brush the egg mixture over the crust. Sprinkle with sugar. Place the pie plate on a parchment-paper-lined pan. Bake for 10 minutes. Reduce the oven temperature to 350° and bake for 40 to 45 minutes, or until the crust is golden brown and the filling is bubbling. If the crust browns too quickly, shield it with aluminum foil. Let cool for 2 to 3 hours before serving.

Hood River Country Apple Tart — SERVES 12

If you have a creative flair, you'll have fun with this recipe. The tart is folded into a free-form shape and baked on a baking sheet, which gives it a more rustic appearance. Once again, I recommend using Gala, pippin, or Granny Smith apples because of their lower moisture content, tartness, and ability to maintain their shape when cooked for an extended amount of time.

To make the filling: In a 12-inch skillet, melt the butter over medium heat. Stir in 1 1/2 cups of the cream and the sugar. Simmer for about 40 minutes, or until the mixture just begins to caramelize. Stir in the mace or nutmeg, cinnamon, and salt. Add the remaining 1/2 cup cream and the apples, stirring to coat. Cook, stirring occasionally, for about 1 hour, or until the mixture is thick and the apples are tender when pierced with the tip of a paring knife. Stir in the almonds and brandy or cider. Spread the mixture on a parchment-paper-lined jelly-roll pan to cool.

Preheat the oven to 400°. On a floured surface, roll out the pastry into an 18-inch round. Transfer the pastry to a large pizza pan sprayed with vegetable-oil cooking spray. Mound the cooked apples in the center of the pastry, forming an 8-inch square. Fold over the sides, leaving a small opening in the center to form an imperfect square shape. Brush the dough with the remaining 2 tablespoons cream and sprinkle with sugar. Bake for about 40 minutes, or until golden brown. If the crust browns too quickly, shield it with aluminum foil. Let cool for 30 minutes on the baking pan. Cut into wedges and serve.

APPLE FILLING

3 tablespoons unsalted butter

2 cups heavy cream

1 1/2 to 2 cups sugar, depending on sweetness of apples

2 teaspoons ground mace or nutmeg

1 1/2 teaspoons ground cinnamon

1 teaspoon salt

12 Gala, pippin, or Granny Smith apples, peeled, cored, and thinly sliced

1 cup sliced almonds, lightly toasted (about 5 minutes)

3 tablespoons Calvados, apple brandy, or hard cider

1 recipe Pastry Dough (page 223)

2 tablespoons heavy cream

Turbinado sugar or granulated sugar for sprinkling

Apple-Apricot-Ginger Buckle — SERVES 12

If you've ever attended an apple-pie contest at a state fair, you may have been boggled by the number of "traditional" recipes entered. I'll throw my hat into the ring and offer yet another version of an American favorite: the apple buckle. A buckle consists of a cakelike batter with fruit folded into it. I like to add a layer of cooked fruit on the bottom. The primary twist in this recipe lies in the batter, which includes a little ginger and puffs up into a browned, yet semisoft crust. You can adapt the fruit filling to whatever is in season. Apples and dried apricots make a colorful flavor combination.

~~~~~~

To make the molasses mixture: In a tall 6-quart pan, bring the water and molasses to a boil. Remove from heat and stir in the baking soda. The mixture will foam up. Set aside to cool.

In a small saucepan, bring the apricots and 1 cup of the apple cider to a boil. Remove from heat and let the apricots plump for about 20 minutes.

Preheat the oven to 350°. Spray a 9-by-13-inch baking dish with vegetable oil cooking spray.

In a medium saucepan, blend the brown sugar and cornstarch. Stir in the remaining $^1/_2$ cup apple cider, the butter, cinnamon, salt, and cloves. Cook over medium heat until clear and thickened. Stir in all but $^1/_4$ cup of the plumped apricots. Stir in all but $^3/_4$ cup of the apples. Pour the mixture into the prepared dish; set aside.

To make the cake layer: Sift the flour, ginger, baking powder, cinnamon, cloves, allspice, pepper, and salt together into a medium bowl; set aside.

In a mixer bowl, using the mixer on high speed, cream the brown sugar and butter until light and fluffy. Add the egg, beating until creamy. On low speed, alternately blend in the dry ingredients and the molasses mixture. The batter will be thin. Stir in the reserved apricots and apples. Pour the cake batter over the fruit layer in the baking dish. Bake for 40 to 45 minutes, or until a toothpick inserted just into the cake layer comes out clean. Let cool slightly and serve with whipped cream.

MOLASSES MIXTURE

1$^1/_2$ cups water

1 cup dark molasses

1 teaspoon baking soda

1 cup (6-ounce package) dried apricots, julienned

1$^1/_2$ cups apple cider

$^3/_4$ cup packed brown sugar

1 tablespoon cornstarch

4 tablespoons unsalted butter

1$^1/_2$ teaspoons ground cinnamon

$^1/_4$ teaspoon salt

$^1/_8$ teaspoon ground cloves

8 Granny Smith, Braeburn, or pippin apples, peeled, cored, and chopped

CAKE LAYER

3$^1/_4$ cups flour

2 teaspoons ground ginger

1$^1/_2$ teaspoons baking powder

$^3/_4$ teaspoon ground cinnamon

$^1/_2$ teaspoon ground cloves

$^1/_2$ teaspoon ground allspice

$^1/_2$ teaspoon freshly ground black pepper

$^1/_2$ teaspoon salt

1 cup packed brown sugar

$^1/_2$ cup (1 stick) unsalted butter, at room temperature

1 large egg

Whipped cream for serving (see page 223)

Apple Cake with Pear Brandy–Caramel Sauce — SERVES 12

2 1/4 cups cake flour

1 teaspoon ground cinnamon

1 teaspoon baking soda

1/2 teaspoon salt

1/4 teaspoon ground cloves

1 1/4 cups packed brown sugar

1/2 cup (1 stick) butter, at room
  temperature

2 large eggs

1/2 cup applesauce

1 Granny Smith apple, peeled, cored,
  and coarsely chopped

1/2 cup chopped walnuts, toasted
  (see page 224)

PEAR BRANDY–CARAMEL
  SAUCE

1 cup apple cider

1/4 cup water

1 cup sugar

4 tablespoons unsalted butter,
  cut into pieces

3/4 cup heavy cream

1 tablespoon pear brandy or Calvados

Pinch of salt

With apples and pears sharing the same early autumn season, it seems only fitting that they be combined in a recipe. At Wildwood, a key component of this brandy-caramel sauce is a delightful pear brandy produced by Clear Creek Distillery, which is located just blocks from the restaurant. All of the pears used to make the brandy are from a farm that has been in distiller Steve McCarthy's family for over one hundred years. For a variation, replace this sauce with pear compote (page 207).

To make the cake: Preheat the oven to 350°. Grease a 12-inch bundt pan or a 14-inch tube pan. Sift the flour, cinnamon, soda, salt, and cloves together into a large bowl; set aside.

In a mixer bowl, using the mixer on medium speed, cream the brown sugar and butter together until light and fluffy. Add the eggs, beating until creamy. On low speed, alternately blend in the dry ingredients and the applesauce. Stir in the chopped apple and nuts.

Pour the batter into the prepared pan, and tap it to settle the batter. Bake for 35 to 40 minutes, or until a toothpick inserted in the center of the cake comes out clean. Let cool for 10 minutes. Turn out onto a rack to cool.

While the cake is baking, prepare the sauce: In a small pan, cook the cider over medium heat until it reaches a syruplike consistency and is reduced to 1/4 cup; set aside.

In a heavy medium saucepan, combine the water and sugar. Cook over medium-high heat, swirling the pan gently, until the sugar is dissolved and the syrup is clear; do not let the mixture boil. Increase heat to high, cover, and boil the syrup, without stirring, for 2 minutes. Uncover the saucepan and continue to boil the syrup until it begins to darken around the edges. Gently swirl the pan until the syrup turns a deep amber and just begins to smoke. Remove from heat and, with a wooden spoon, carefully beat in the butter until well blended. Stir in the cream until smooth. If the sauce becomes lumpy, return the pan to the stove and cook over low heat, stirring until smooth. Remove from heat and stir in the reduced apple cider, the brandy or more cider, and salt.

To serve, cut the cake into slices and top with the warm caramel sauce.

Clover Honey–Baked Apples with Raisins and Cinnamon — SERVES 6

One of the strongest food memories from my childhood is the smell of baking apples drifting from the kitchen on a drizzly fall day. Now, as then, the aroma evokes a feeling of simple comfort mixed with anticipation of the warm sweetness of the apple blended with cinnamon, cloves, nutmeg, and allspice. This next dish is well suited to apples with a high moisture content, such as Jonagold, Braeburn, and Gala; they soften nicely and produce a full-flavored juice that can be spooned back over the top of the apples when served. I use clover honey from the Pacific Northwest, but any variety will do.

In a medium saucepan, combine the apple cider, brown sugar, honey, cinnamon, salt, and pepper. Bring to a boil, reduce heat, and simmer for about 25 minutes or so, or until the mixture is syrupy and reduced to about 2 2/3 cups.

Preheat the oven to 350°. Put the apples, cut-side down, in a 12-inch baking pan. Distribute the raisins, apricots, cloves, star anise, and cinnamon sticks, if using, over the apples. Pour the hot syrup over the apples. Cover the pan with aluminum foil. Bake for 25 to 30 minutes, or until the apples are almost tender when pierced with the tip of a sharp knife. Remove from the oven, turn the apples over, and let the pan stand, covered, for 15 minutes.

Serve in small bowls with ice cream and gingersnaps.

3 1/2 cups apple cider

1/2 cup plus 2 tablespoons packed brown sugar

1/3 cup clover honey

1 teaspoon ground cinnamon

1/8 teaspoon salt

Pinch of freshly ground black pepper

6 unpeeled Jonagold, Braeburn, or Gala apples, halved and cored with a melon baller

1/2 cup golden raisins or currants

1/2 cup dried apricots, julienned

6 whole cloves

2 to 3 star anise pods

2 to 3 cinnamon sticks (optional)

Ice cream and gingersnaps for serving

Upside-Down Peach-Gingerbread Cake — SERVES 12

Although you can find fresh peaches in the market as early as June, they hit their prime in the valley in mid- to late July. Early Red Haven, Suncrest, Elberta, and Flamecrest are only a few of the names that you'll run across at local produce stands.

A peach is at its best when it is slightly firm and has a high sugar content. Peaches and other stone fruits are a popular base for many summer desserts, including upside-down cake. Here, peaches are combined with gingerbread batter to give this traditional recipe a nontraditional twist. Nectarines and plums make a nice substitute if fresh peaches are not available.

To make the molasses mixture: In a tall 6-quart pan, bring the water and molasses to a boil. Remove from heat and stir in the baking soda. The mixture will foam up. Let cool to room temperature.

While the molasses cools, prepare the baking pan: Preheat the oven to 350°. Grease the sides and bottom of a 9-by-13-inch baking pan. Line the bottom of the pan with parchment paper or waxed paper. Sprinkle the brown sugar evenly over the paper. Drizzle the butter over the brown sugar. Arrange the peach slices over the brown sugar; set aside.

To make the batter: Sift the flour, baking powder, ginger, salt, cinnamon, pepper, cloves, and allspice together into a large bowl; set aside.

In a mixer bowl, with the mixer on high speed, cream the brown sugar and butter until light and fluffy. Add the egg and beat until creamy. On low speed, alternately blend in the dry ingredients and the molasses mixture. The batter will be thin. Pour over the peaches. Bake for 40 to 45 minutes, or until a toothpick inserted just into the cake comes out clean. Let cool on a wire rack for 20 minutes. Turn out onto a serving platter. Cut into squares and top with whipped cream, if desired.

MOLASSES MIXTURE

1 1/2 cups water

1 cup dark molasses

1 teaspoon baking soda

1/2 cup packed brown sugar

2 tablespoons unsalted butter, melted

4 peaches, peeled, pitted, and sliced 1/4 inch thick

GINGERBREAD BATTER

3 1/4 cups flour

1 1/2 teaspoons baking powder

1 1/2 teaspoons ground ginger

1/2 teaspoon salt

1/2 teaspoon ground cinnamon

1/4 teaspoon ground black pepper

1/8 teaspoon ground cloves

1/8 teaspoon ground allspice

1 cup packed brown sugar

1/2 cup (1 stick) unsalted butter, at room temperature

1 large egg

Whipped cream (see page 223) for serving (optional)

Peaches Wrapped in Filo Dough with Walnuts, Cheese, and Cherry Sauce — SERVES 6

12 sheets frozen filo dough, thawed and covered with a damp cloth

$3/4$ cup ($1^1/2$ sticks) unsalted butter, melted

$3/4$ cup walnuts, toasted and finely chopped (page 224)

$3/4$ cup sugar

2 ripe peaches, peeled, pitted, and cut into thirds

$3/4$ cup orange marmalade

8 ounces fresh white goat cheese or Brie cheese, cut into 6 portions

Turbinado or granulated sugar for sprinkling

CHERRY SAUCE

2 cups pitted fresh sweet cherries, or 1 cup dried cherries

$1/2$ cup water

$1/4$ cup sugar

1 cinnamon stick

$1/4$ cup brandy, kirschwasser, or orange juice

1 teaspoon vanilla extract

Peaches wrapped in filo dough with marmalade, walnuts, and goat cheese are an unusual and robust combination. When wrapping fruit in filo dough, it is important to keep the filling fairly dry; too much liquid can make the dough limp and soggy. Select peaches that are firm yet ripe.

Preheat the oven to 350°. On a large wooden board, lay out 1 sheet of the filo dough (keep the remaining sheets of filo covered with the damp cloth so they will not dry out). Brush lightly with butter and sprinkle with 1 tablespoon of the walnuts and 1 tablespoon of the sugar. Repeat the process, layering 5 more filo sheets on top of the first layer. Using a sharp knife, cut the stack of filo lengthwise into 3 equal strips. On the bottom of each strip, place 1 peach third, 1 tablespoon marmalade, and 1 cheese portion. Roll each strip up jelly-roll style and place on a baking sheet lined with parchment paper. Repeat the process to make 3 more rolls. Sprinkle the tops of the rolls with sugar. Bake for 15 to 20 minutes, or until golden brown. Let cool on wire racks.

To make the sauce: In a medium stainless-steel saucepan, combine the cherries, water, sugar, and cinnamon stick. Bring to a boil, reduce heat, and simmer for about 25 minutes to reduce by half. Stir in the brandy or juice and simmer for 3 minutes. Remove from heat and stir in the vanilla extract. Let cool and remove the cinnamon stick.

To serve, spoon 2 tablespoons of the cherry sauce onto each plate and place a filo package on the sauce.

Peach-and-Hazelnut Cinnamon Rolls — MAKES 18 ROLLS

There is nothing quite like a sweet, juicy peach on a fresh summer morning. These peach and hazelnut cinnamon rolls are gobbled up each week at the restaurant's Sunday brunch and make a nice start to a lazy summer day. You will need to make the brioche dough the day before.

In a small bowl, stir together the brown sugar, cinnamon, nutmeg, salt, and nuts; set aside.

In a small bowl, blend the melted butter and the orange or lemon zest; set aside. On a floured surface, roll out the brioche dough into a 12-by-18-inch rectangle. Spoon the melted-butter mixture evenly over the surface of the dough. Distribute the peaches evenly over the surface of the dough, gently pressing them into the dough. Sprinkle with half of the nut mixture. Starting at one long side of the dough, roll up fairly tight, jelly-roll style. Place seam-side down on a baking sheet, cover, and refrigerate for 30 minutes.

Line a 12-by-17-inch jelly-roll pan with parchment paper or waxed paper. Distribute the remaining half of the nut mixture over the paper. Pour on the orange juice and dot with the butter pieces; set aside.

Remove the roll from the refrigerator, uncover, and cut into eighteen 1-inch slices. Place the slices, cut-side down, in the prepared jelly-roll pan. Cover with a lightly-floured tea towel and let rise at room temperature until almost doubled, about 60 minutes.

Preheat the oven to 375°. Uncover the pan and bake the rolls for 35 to 45 minutes, or until they are golden brown and the dough looks done when the center of a roll is separated with the tip of a knife. Remove from the oven and let cool for 5 to 10 minutes. Turn out and serve.

2 cups packed light brown sugar

1 tablespoon ground cinnamon

1 teaspoon ground nutmeg

1/2 teaspoon salt

1 cup hazelnuts, toasted and skinned, or pecans, toasted (page 224)

4 tablespoons unsalted butter, melted, plus 4 tablespoons butter, cut into small pieces

2 tablespoons coarsely grated orange or lemon zest

Brioche Dough (page 56), made through the first rise, covered and refrigerated overnight

3 to 4 peaches, peeled, pitted, and chopped

2/3 cup fresh orange juice

Peach and Bing Cherry Cobbler
with Snickerdoodle Topping — SERVES 8

PEACH PURÉE

1 cup chopped peeled peaches

2 tablespoons apple cider

2 tablespoons sugar

$1/2$ teaspoon vanilla extract

PEACH AND CHERRY FILLING

4 cups chopped unpeeled peaches
  (about 5 peaches)

2 cups sweet cherries, pitted,
  or $1^1/2$ cups fresh cranberries

3 tablespoons cornstarch

$1/2$ to $3/4$ cup packed light brown
  sugar, depending on sweetness
  of peaches

$1/4$ teaspoon salt

1 tablespoon unsalted butter,
  cut into small pieces

SNICKERDOODLE TOPPING

$3/4$ cup flour

$1/2$ teaspoon ground nutmeg

$1/4$ teaspoon baking soda

$1/4$ teaspoon salt

$1/2$ cup sugar

4 tablespoons unsalted butter,
  at room temperature

1 large egg

1 egg yolk

$1/2$ teaspoon vanilla extract

2 teaspoons granulated sugar

$1/4$ teaspoon ground cinnamon

For a brief period in midsummer, peaches and cherries are in season at the same time, a natural pairing that inspired this cobbler made with snickerdoodle cookie dough.

To make the purée: In a small saucepan, combine the peaches, cider, and sugar. Simmer for 10 to 15 minutes, or until the peaches are soft. Remove from heat and stir in the vanilla extract. Let cool. Purée in a food processor; strain and set aside. This may be made 1 day ahead and refrigerated.

To make the filling: In a large bowl, combine the peaches, cherries or cranberries, the peach purée, cornstarch, brown sugar, and salt, and mix well. Distribute the filling evenly into eight 5-ounce ramekins, or into a 10-inch cake pan. Top with the butter.

To make the topping: Preheat the oven to 350°. Sift the flour, nutmeg, baking soda, and salt together into a medium bowl; set aside. In a mixer bowl, with the mixer on medium speed, cream the sugar and butter together until light and fluffy. Add the egg, egg yolk, and vanilla, beating until creamy. On low speed, blend in the dry ingredients.

Use a tablespoon to drop the snickerdoodle batter on top of the fruit. In a small bowl, blend the sugar and cinnamon. Sprinkle on top of the batter. Bake for 30 to 35 minutes, or until the fruit is bubbling and the crust is lightly browned. Let cool slightly and then serve.

Apricot and Blueberry Crumble — SERVES 12

1 cup packed brown sugar

1¹/₂ tablespoons cornstarch

1 teaspoon salt

6 cups pitted and halved fresh
   apricots or sliced peaches
   (about 1 pound)

2 cups blueberries

2 teaspoons vanilla extract

TOPPING

2 cups rolled oats

1 cup flour

³/₄ cup packed brown sugar

2 teaspoons ground cinnamon

1 teaspoon salt

¹/₂ cup (1 stick) unsalted butter, cut
   into cubes, at room temperature

The apricot packs a lot of flavor into a small package. When apricots achieve perfect ripeness, they remain at their peak of flavor for about 24 hours, so you'll have to keep on your toes. This recipe pairs fresh apricots with summer blueberries, although any berry will do.

Preheat the oven to 325°. Spray a 9-by-13-inch baking dish with vegetable-oil cooking spray. In a small bowl, stir together the brown sugar, cornstarch, and salt; set aside.

In a large bowl, combine the fruits and vanilla. Add the dry ingredients, gently tossing to coat the fruit. Pour the fruit mixture into the prepared dish.

To make the topping: In a food processor, combine the oats, flour, brown sugar, cinnamon, and salt. Process to blend. Add the butter and process until coarse crumbs form. To prepare by hand, combine the dry ingredients in a large bowl. Add the butter cubes and cut in with a pastry blender or 2 knives until the mixture is crumbly.

Sprinkle the topping over the fruit. Bake for 35 to 40 minutes, or until the top is lightly browned and the fruit is bubbling. Let cool and serve.

Dried Apricot–Cranberry Pound Cake — SERVES 6

Dried apricots and other dried fruits provide a flavorful substitute for fresh fruit and can often prevent a dish from becoming too wet, as demonstrated in this recipe. The sweetness of the dried apricots is offset by the tartness of the cranberries. If fresh apricots are available, slice a few on top to create a nice contrast. This cake can also be used as a breakfast bread.

1 1/3 cups dried apricots

2/3 cup apple juice

5 large eggs

1 1/2 teaspoons vanilla extract

1 1/2 teaspoons grated lemon zest

3/4 cup (1 1/2 sticks) butter, at room temperature

1 1/3 cups granulated sugar

2 cups flour

1 1/2 cups fresh or frozen cranberries

Confectioners' sugar for dusting

In a small saucepan, combine the apricots and apple juice. Simmer until the liquid is absorbed and the apricots are soft, about 30 minutes. Let cool slightly. Transfer to a food processor and purée; set aside.

Preheat the oven to 325°. Generously grease a 10-cup bundt pan. In a medium bowl, whisk together the eggs, vanilla, and lemon zest; set aside.

In a mixer, beat the butter on high speed until creamy. Gradually beat in the sugar and beat until light and fluffy, 3 to 5 minutes. Gradually add the egg mixture, 1 tablespoon at a time, beating at high speed until light and fluffy, 3 to 4 minutes. On low speed, alternately blend in the flour and the apricot purée. Fold in the cranberries.

Pour the batter into the prepared pan and tap the pan to settle it. Bake for 45 to 50 minutes, or until a toothpick inserted in the center of the cake comes out clean. Let cool on a wire rack for 10 minutes. Unmold and let cool completely. Dust with confectioners' sugar. Slice and serve.

Brown Butter–Cherry Clafoutis — SERVES 6

4 tablespoons unsalted butter

$^1/_2$ vanilla bean, split and scraped, or 1 teaspoon vanilla extract

3 large eggs

1 cup milk

$^3/_4$ cup plus 1 tablespoon granulated sugar

$^1/_2$ cup flour

2 tablespoons brandy or orange juice

$^1/_4$ teaspoon salt

8 ounces Bing or other sweet cherries, pitted, or any kind of berry

Confectioners' sugar for dusting

Clafoutis is a rustic puddinglike dessert that originated in Limousin, in the center of France. It is traditionally prepared with cherries that are left unpitted. I am fond of the following recipe, which was developed by the first pastry chef at Wildwood and old childhood schoolmate of mine, Nancy Forrest Colwell. This recipe was part of our opening menu, and people still ask for it.

Preheat the oven to 350°. Butter an 8-inch round cake pan. In a small pan, melt the butter over medium heat and cook until golden brown. Add the vanilla bean and scrapings or extract and let cool. Remove the vanilla bean, if using.

In a medium bowl, whisk together the eggs, milk, $^3/_4$ cup sugar, flour, brandy or orange juice, salt, and cooled butter. Sprinkle the prepared pan with the 1 tablespoon sugar. Distribute the cherries or berries over the bottom of the pan. Pour the batter over the fruit. Bake for 30 to 40 minutes, or until puffed and lightly browned. Let cool slightly. Dust with confectioners' sugar and serve warm.

Warm Bartlett Pear Brown Betty — SERVES 8

When a tray of freshly baked brown betty is left unattended in the Wildwood kitchen, there's always a chance that one or two will mysteriously disappear—their aroma is simply too intoxicating to resist.

This betty incorporates a brioche bread topping and pear purée with a pear or other fruit-based brandy.

Preheat the oven to 250°. Place the bread cubes on a baking sheet and toast in the oven for 25 to 30 minutes, or until golden brown and crisp. Let cool and set aside.

In a medium saucepan, combine half of the quartered pears, the brown sugar, water, butter, brandy or cider, cinnamon, nutmeg, salt, and cloves. Cover and cook until the pears are very soft, about 20 minutes. Remove from heat and stir in the vanilla extract. Let cool. In a food processor, purée until smooth.

Preheat the oven to 350°. Spray an 8-cup deep baking dish or eight 6-ounce soufflé cups with vegetable-oil cooking spray. Cut the remaining quartered pears into 1/2-inch dice. You should have about 3 cups. In a large bowl, mix together the toasted bread cubes, cubed uncooked pears, and pear purée. Pour the pear mixture into the baking dish or soufflé cups. Bake for 45 to 55 minutes, or until lightly browned on top. Serve warm or at room temperature.

4 cups 1/2-inch-cubed bread (crust removed) such as Wildwood Brioche (page 56), challah, or egg bread

8 Bartlett pears, peeled, cored, and quartered

1 1/4 cups packed brown sugar

1 cup water

6 tablespoons unsalted butter, melted

3 tablespoons pear brandy, brandy, or hard apple cider

1/2 teaspoon ground cinnamon

1/4 teaspoon ground nutmeg

1/4 teaspoon salt

1/8 teaspoon ground cloves

1 teaspoon vanilla extract

Pear Compote — MAKES ABOUT 3 CUPS

Pears are a fickle fruit. A Comice or French butter pear purchased one day may become overly ripe the next; whereas in the case of a Bosc pear, you may spend the whole winter waiting for it to ripen! Softer pears, such as Comice or Bartlett, will yield a sauce that has a higher water content and may seem closer to a purée than a chunky sauce, while Boscs will stand up to longer cooking times and maintain a thick consistency.

Use this compote in place of the caramel sauce in the apple cake recipe on page 194, or as a topping for any type of rustic cake preparation, such as carrot cake or the warm walnut spice cake on page 209.

2 cups apple or pear cider

$1/4$ cup undiluted orange juice
concentrate

3 whole cloves

2 tablespoons sugar

2 star anise pods

1 cinnamon stick

$1/4$ teaspoon fennel seeds

3 firm ripe Bosc, Comice, or Bartlett
pears, peeled, cored, and chopped

$1/2$ teaspoon vanilla extract

In a medium saucepan, combine the cider, the orange juice concentrate, cloves, sugar, star anise, cinnamon, and fennel. Bring to a boil, reduce heat to a simmer, and cook to reduce the liquid by half. Mix in the pears and simmer for 20 minutes. The mixture will thicken as it cools. Remove from the heat and stir in the vanilla extract. Let cool completely. Use now, or cover and refrigerate. Bring to room temperature to serve.

Opposite: Rachel Showalter monitors the distilling of Clear Creek's pear and apple brandies.

The Hood River Valley: Orchards in the Shadow of Mount Hood • 207

Pear and Dried Cherry Turnovers

1 cup pear or apple cider

5 tablespoons cornstarch

1/2 cup packed brown sugar

3 tablespoons unsalted butter

1 tablespoon grated lemon zest

2 tablespoons fresh lemon juice

1/2 teaspoon salt

6 ripe Anjou, Bosc, or Bartlett pears,
   peeled, cored, and chopped

3/4 cup dried cherries

1 teaspoon vanilla extract

3 tablespoons water

3 large eggs

1 recipe Pastry Dough (page 223)

Turbinado or granulated sugar for
   sprinkling

Anjou pears are another versatile variety that can be enjoyed raw or cooked. They are harvested in late autumn and are often available throughout the winter and early spring. If you cannot find Anjous, substitute any firm pears for this Sunday brunch favorite.

In a small bowl, combine 1/2 cup of the cider and the cornstarch, stirring until smooth; set aside.

In a medium saucepan, combine the remaining 1/2 cup cider, the brown sugar, butter, lemon zest, lemon juice, and salt. Cook over medium heat, stirring to dissolve the sugar. Stir in the pears, cherries, and vanilla. Reduce heat and simmer for about 10 minutes, or until the pears are tender and the cherries are plump. Add the cider mixture and cook for another 5 minutes, or until the liquid is thick and clear. Pour into a bowl and let cool completely.

In a small bowl, whisk the water and eggs together to make an egg wash; set aside.

Preheat the oven to 350°. Grease a baking sheet or line with parchment paper. Divide the pastry into 4 portions, wrapping each of 3 portions in plastic wrap. On a floured surface, roll out the remaining portion into a rectangle 1/8 inch thick. Cut into 4-inch squares. Place about 2 tablespoons cooled fruit filling onto one-half of each pastry square. Brush the pastry edges with egg wash and fold over diagonally. Crimp the edges with the tines of a fork. Repeat the process until all the turnovers are prepared. Make a small slit in the top of each turnover. Brush the tops of the turnovers with the egg wash and sprinkle with sugar. Place on the prepared baking sheet. Bake for 15 minutes, or until lightly browned. Serve warm or at room temperature.

Maple Syrup–Poached Pears
with Warm Walnut Spice Cake — SERVES 8

Bosc pears are ideal for poaching, as they remain firm and can be cooked for an extended amount of time, allowing the flavors of the poaching liquid to be absorbed into the pears. The poached pears can be served as a dessert by themselves with a spoonful of whipped cream and some cookies.

To prepare the cake: Preheat the oven to 350°. Spray a 9-inch round cake pan with vegetable-oil cooking spray. Sift the flour, baking powder, baking soda, cinnamon, salt, allspice, pepper, and cloves together into a medium bowl. Stir in the ground walnuts; set aside.

In a mixer bowl, with the mixer on high speed, cream the brown and granulated sugars and butter together until light and fluffy. Add the egg and egg yolk; beat until creamy. On low speed, blend in the dry ingredients alternately with the milk. Stir in the vanilla and toasted walnuts. Using clean beaters, beat the egg white until stiff, glossy peaks form. Fold into the cake batter.

Pour the batter into the prepared pan. Tap the pan to remove air bubbles. Bake for 30 minutes, or until a toothpick inserted in the center of the cake comes out clean. Let cool in the pan 10 minutes.

While the cake is baking, prepare the pears: Cut a piece of parchment paper to fit just inside of a 12-inch skillet; set aside.

To prepare the pears: In a large skillet, combine the maple syrup, brown sugar, salt, cloves, cinnamon, butter, lemon juice, and pear brandy or apple cider. Bring to a boil. Reduce heat to a simmer. Carefully add the sliced pears, layering to submerge them in the liquid. Place the parchment paper over the pears and top with a smaller pan lid to keep the pears submerged. Cook the pears for 25 to 30 minutes, or until just tender when pierced with the tip of a paring knife (do not overcook). Drain the pears, reserving the liquid, and let cool.

Return the liquid to the pan and simmer to reduce by half, creating a syrupy sauce. Pour the sauce over the pears and let cool.

To serve, unmold the cake onto a wire rack. Place 3 pear quarters and a slice of warm walnut spice cake on each plate. Top with a dollop of whipped cream.

WALNUT SPICE CAKE

1 1/2 cups flour

1 teaspoon baking powder

1 teaspoon baking soda

1 teaspoon ground cinnamon

1/4 teaspoon salt

1/4 teaspoon ground allspice

1/4 teaspoon freshly ground
black pepper

1/8 teaspoon ground cloves

3/4 cup walnuts, ground

2/3 cup packed brown sugar

1/3 cup granulated sugar

1/2 cup (1 stick) unsalted butter,
at room temperature

1 large egg

1 large egg, separated

1 cup milk

1 teaspoon vanilla extract

1/2 cup chopped walnuts, toasted
(see page 224)

MAPLE SYRUP–
POACHED PEARS

3 cups maple syrup

1/2 cup packed brown sugar

1/2 teaspoon salt

4 whole cloves

2 cinnamon sticks

2 tablespoons unsalted butter

2 teaspoons fresh lemon juice

1/4 cup pear brandy or
hard apple cider

6 Bosc pears, halved, cored, and
quartered

Whipped cream (page 223)

JAMES BEARD'S
PASSION FOR OREGON

11. JAMES BEARD'S PASSION FOR OREGON: FAVORITE RECIPES FROM *Delights & Prejudices*

Overleaf: *James Beard and Mary Hamblet, c. 1975.*

Below: *The Beard mural near the entrance of Wildwood.*

I never met James Beard, but I remember standing in the kitchen of the Seasons Restaurant in the Bostonian Hotel on January 22, 1985, when I caught sight of his obituary on the cover of the *New York Times*. An era had passed, and my longtime dream of meeting the man who had so greatly influenced the culinary world had passed with it. As I read the article amid the bustle of the kitchen, I realized that meeting James Beard was not ultimately as important to me as having experienced his writings and sharing his passion for Oregon and the Pacific Northwest.

My connection with James Beard goes beyond an interest in cooking. To some degree, we had lived similar lives and shared some of the same influences from our Northwest upbringings. Beard grew up in his mother's hotel, where he was constantly exposed to her love for food. I grew up immersed in the history and traditions of my family's restaurant, where I formed an early appreciation for the unique qualities of the Pacific Northwest and its impeccable foods and natural resources. Beard spent his childhood summers crabbing and picking berries in the coastal town of Gearhart, Oregon. Years later, I would spend similar summers in the small town of Oysterville and areas around Yaquina Bay. Our parallel experiences evolved into a love for the region that kept drawing each of us home in the course of our careers.

In his book *Delights & Prejudices*, Beard explores the gastronomic riches of the Pacific Northwest. Family gatherings are mentioned often by Beard, and his memories paint images of summer days spent at the remote beach cabin in Gearhart gathering berries and assorted seafood. As he shares his memories of foods and feasts past, a basic philosophy begins to emerge: Bringing out the natural flavor of an ingredient is the key to good cooking. Beard even commented that one of the most satisfying foods was a baked potato, as long as it was cooked to perfection.

After Beard died, his ashes were sent to Mary Hamblet, Beard's dear friend. Although she and Beard had never talked about where his remains should rest, Mary knew there was only one option: to return his ashes to his beloved town of Gearhart by the sea. It seemed a fitting place to leave him, for he had left himself there at the end of *Delights & Prejudices*, watching the surf at sundown. So, after a lifetime of traveling the world, Beard returned to his native waters.

- ⋅ - ⋅ -

The loose format of Beard's recipes attests to his respect for the raw materials of cooking. A dash of this, a little of that, a sprinkling of another epitomizes a style of cuisine based on a spontaneous approach to ingredients at their peak of flavor. Such openness to improvisation, paired with an insatiable curiosity, can't help but inspire dishes that are interesting, fresh, and thoroughly enjoyable.

The following recipes, reprinted from *Delights & Prejudices*, preserve Beard's inimitable recipe-writing style, with minor adaptations on my part.

Grammie Hamblet's Deviled Crab

SERVES 8 AS AN APPETIZER OR LUNCH ENTRÉE

"Another thrill at the beach was Grammie Hamblet's deviled crab! I have maintained all my life that this is the best cooked crab I have ever known. It is made with crisp vegetables chopped fine, cracker crumbs and butter, and it is seasoned well and cooked just long enough to heat the crabmeat without turning it mushy. Served with a very brisk wine-a Muscadet or a Chablis—it is indescribably good, for there is the luscious flavor of the crabmeat in a crusty exterior. Grammie Hamblet deserved a seat in the gastronomic heaven for having thought that one up!"

—James Beard

Just inside the door of Wildwood hangs a glass mural tribute to James Beard that I commissioned for the restaurant's opening in 1994. The mural features three large and colorful pears among a collage of red bow ties, recipe titles, fish, shellfish, and other images connected with Beard. Soon after the opening, a woman dining at the restaurant was startled to find her mother's name in the mural. The inscription was "Grammie Hamblet's Deviled Crab," and because of it, I found myself face to face with Mary Hamblet, James Beard's lifelong friend. As I quickly learned, Grammie Hamblet was the family nickname for Mary's mother, Polly, who was a dear friend of James Beard's mother, Elizabeth.

After that chance meeting, I shared conversations with Mary on many occasions and inundated her with questions about times long past. I enjoyed getting to know her and am indebted to her for allowing me to finally "meet" James Beard through the stories and memories she so kindly shared with me.

—C.S.

Chop enough celery to make 1 cup. It must be cut finer than fine. Add 1 good-sized green pepper cut exceedingly fine, 1 cup of finely sliced green onions, $1/2$ cup of chopped parsley, 2 pounds of crabmeat (canned, rinsed, and picked through for cartilage), $2^1/2$ cups of coarsely crushed cracker crumbs, 1 teaspoon of salt, $1^1/2$ teaspoons of dry mustard, a healthy dash of Tabasco, $1/2$ cup of heavy cream, and 1 cup of melted butter. Toss the ingredients lightly and spoon them into a buttered baking dish. Top with additional crushed cracker crumbs and brush them with melted butter. Bake at 350° for 25 to 30 minutes, or until the crumbs are delicately browned. Serve the dish at once.

Our Beach Fricassee of Chicken

SERVES 8 AS AN ENTRÉE

James Beard brought a human element to cooking, as expressed in the names of his recipes. The title of this particular dish evokes images of summer days on the beach at Gearhart, Oregon. His personalized titles are a gentle reminder to us all that food is not just fuel for the body, but a sensual experience to be savored, both in the moment and in fond recollection of the sights, sounds, and smells of the place in which it was enjoyed.
—C. S.

"Sometimes Mother would come by a fine fowl, procured from the people who sold eggs, and this would make a rich fricassee....This dish could last for a couple of days if the weather was right; refrigeration at the beach was somewhat primitive."

—*James Beard*

Cut a large fowl (chicken) into serving pieces. If it is a very large one, make separate pieces of the thigh and the leg, cut the breast into 2 or 3 sections, and have the wings separate. The back and the ribs make 3 pieces, too.

You should have an extra package of back, necks, and gizzards to make a rich broth. In a large pot, combine 2 pounds of necks and gizzards with 2 quarts of water, 1 onion stuck with cloves, and salt. This should make a good, rich chicken broth, which has so many uses. We always seemed to have a great jar of it in the icebox or cooler.

Make a bed of the following vegetables, cut into matchlike sticks, on the bottom of the kettle in which you are to cook the chicken: 3 leeks (white part only), 2 carrots (peeled), 1 large onion, and 2 celery stalks. Several sprigs of parsley and 1 teaspoon of fresh thyme leaves should also be in the mixture. Arrange the chicken pieces on this and add 2 tablespoons of oil, $^1/4$ cup of white wine, and enough broth to cover the vegetables and touch the chicken pieces. Sprinkle with 1 teaspoon of salt and a little freshly ground black pepper. Cover the kettle tightly and simmer at 300° in the oven or atop the stove at medium heat until chicken is just tender—close to 2 hours.

About 30 minutes before the chicken has finished cooking, cook 2 cups of rice with 6 cups of chicken broth; bring the broth to a boil, add the rice, and bring to a boil again. Add salt to taste, cover the kettle, and put it on very low heat for 20 minutes. Test the chicken for doneness and make sure the rice has absorbed the broth.

Brown 2 tablespoons of flour in 3 tablespoons of butter; gradually stir in 2 cups of the rich chicken broth from the pan in which the chicken cooked, and continue stirring till the mixture is blended and thick. Cook for 2 minutes, add 1 cup of cream mixed with 3 egg yolks, and stir until the broth is thickened, but do not let boil. Taste the sauce for seasoning. Add some chopped parsley and serve with the chicken and rice. Sometimes we added tiny green olives to the sauce, which make a spectacular difference.

Poached Salmon with Egg and Parsley Sauce

"We had salmon during the entire season. Harry Hamblet and Peter Grants saw to that. The Grants were in the cannery business and commuted all summer between Gearhart and the plant in Astoria. About once a week they would ask if we wanted a fish, and that night a salmon would arrive, caught the same morning, sometimes sent along with a package of salmon cheeks, which the Hamblets and Beards preferred to almost anything else in the fish world because they were so tender, fat and flavorsome. The cheeks were easy to get in those days, for no one thought of cutting them out when the heads were removed. Nowadays they are as scarce as white caviar and nearly as expensive, if you can get them at all. We feasted on them sautéed in butter or occasionally grilled over the fire.

The rest of the salmon we poached, baked or cut into steaks to grill. The poached salmon was usually accompanied by an egg sauce or a parsley sauce."

—James Beard

This salmon recipe reminds me of my culinary apprentice days at the Benson Hotel, where I made many a classic sauce thickened with flour under the direction of chef Xavier Bauser. Chinook or king salmon from the Columbia River, near Astoria, was likely used in this recipe when it was prepared at the Beard family home in Gearhart, on the northern Oregon coast.

—C. S.

Choose a 4- to 5-pound piece of salmon from the center of the fish. Wrap it in cheesecloth with the ends of the material extending on either side of the fish for some distance so that you can raise it and lower it into the kettle. Prepare a court bouillon in a large kettle that will accommodate the fish. You will need 3 quarts of water, 1 cup of white wine, a dash of vinegar, an onion (cut in half) stuck with 2 cloves, a carrot (chopped), a sprig of parsley, 2 tablespoons of salt, and 2 or 3 slices of lemon. Bring the bouillon to a boil and boil it for 10 minutes. Reduce the heat and lower the salmon into the liquid. Poach it at a feeble ebullition (barely simmering) for about 6 minutes per pound, or until the fish flakes easily when tested with a toothpick or fork. Transfer the fish to a hot platter.

While the fish is cooking, melt 3 tablespoons of butter in a skillet, blend it with 4 tablespoons (1/4 cup) of flour, and cook for 2 or 3 minutes. Add 1 cup of the fish liquid and stir until the sauce is thickened. Season it to taste with salt and freshly ground pepper. Stir in 1 cup of heavy cream mixed with 2 egg yolks and stir until the mixture thickens slightly—do not let it boil! Fold in 1/2 cup of sliced hard-cooked eggs and 1/4 cup of chopped parsley. Correct the seasoning and serve the sauce with the fish, boiled potatoes, and a cucumber salad. Drink a brisk white wine—a Chablis or a Muscadet.

My Father's Favorite Pear Preserves — MAKES 8 JARS

This next recipe is the inspiration for the pears that are the focus of the mural in the Wildwood restaurant. Mary Hamblet has told me that Beard's father was not the cook his mother was, but always had an opinion about food and the preparation of it. This pear recipe was, as Beard remembers, a "favorite." In Delights & Prejudices, *Beard talks about the Hood River Valley and discusses the variety of pears that grow there. It is comforting to know that, many years later, pears are still thriving in the valley and taste as sweet and juicy as ever.*

—C.S.

"We used Winter Nelis or other firm pears for these preserves. The syrup would turn rather delicate pink and the pear slices remained firm and rather translucent, excellent with hot breads."

—James Beard

Prepare the syrup with 4 cups of water and 4 pounds of sugar, and boil it for 10 minutes. Add 4 pounds of peeled and sliced firm pears and cook them until they are translucent and the syrup has cooked down. Fill sterilized jars and add to each jar 1 or 2 cloves, a bit of cinnamon bark, and a small piece of fresh ginger. Seal the jars at once.

NOTE: The preserves should be placed in a large pan of boiling water and processed for 10 minutes. Carefully remove from the water and cool. Check lids for tightness.

Huckleberry Cake — SERVES 8

Here is the Hamblet family recipe for huckleberry cake, which I imagine was enjoyed at many of their summer gatherings with the Beards.

—C.S.

~~~~~~

In a mixer bowl, cream 1 cup of butter (at room temperature) and 1 cup of sugar together until the mixture is very light. Add 3 large eggs, one by one, beating after each addition. Beat in 1 cup of buttermilk.

Sift 2 cups of flour. Take $1/4$ cup of flour and mix it with 1 cup of huckleberries. In a medium bowl, combine the remaining $1 3/4$ cups of flour, 2 teaspoons of baking powder, and a pinch of salt. Stir the flour mixture into the wet mixture. Fold in 1 teaspoon of vanilla extract and the floured huckleberries. Pour the batter into a buttered and floured 8-inch square baking tin. Bake in a 375° oven for 35 to 45 minutes, or until the cake is nicely browned, or when a tester comes out clean.

Serve the cake warm, topped with whipped cream or ice cream and a few fresh huckleberries.

"Blue huckleberries were the most elusive of the wild berries. They usually grew in places difficult to reach, in the midst of a mountain wilderness. But once you found a patch you were in luck. No matter how they were prepared—in a deep-dish pie, which we had often, or in a strange English version of the clafouti, with a batter poured over the berries and baked, or in little dumplings, which were dropped into cooked huckleberries, or in the famous Hamblet huckleberry cake—they were fantastically good."

—James Beard

WILDWOOD PANTRY: BASIC RECIPES AND TECHNIQUES

The recipes and techniques in this section are referred to throughout this book. Some of the techniques are standard in most restaurant kitchens, while others, such as the technique for roasting garlic, are unconventional and specific to daily food preparations at Wildwood.

Above: *My great-grandmother Elizabeth, digging for razor clams in southwest Washington.*

Opposite: *Elizabeth (whose recipe for Blackberry Roly-Poly appears on page 172) at her stove, c. 1955.*

RECIPES

Chicken Stock

— MAKES ABOUT 8 CUPS

2 pounds chicken bones (4 to 5 chicken carcasses), or legs and thighs for a richer stock

8 cups water

1 cup dry white wine

3 carrots, peeled and chopped into 1-inch pieces

3 ribs celery, cut in half

2 yellow onions, coarsely chopped

1 small bunch parsley, thyme, basil, or tarragon sprigs

1 bay leaf

1 teaspoon crushed black peppercorns

In a large stockpot, combine the chicken bones or parts, water, and wine. If necessary, add more water to cover the bones. Bring to a boil, reduce heat to a simmer, and cook for about 30 minutes. Periodically skim off the foam and discard. Once most of the foaming action stops, add the carrots, celery, onions, herb stems, bay leaf, and peppercorns. Simmer the stock for an additional 40 minutes. Let cool and strain, pressing down on the vegetables with the back of a large spoon; discard the vegetables. Cover and refrigerate for up to 3 days or freeze for up to 3 months.

Fish Stock

— MAKES ABOUT 8 CUPS

2 pounds fish bones, preferably collar bones and pieces with some meat on them for extra flavor and/or fish heads with the gills removed

8 cups water

1 cup dry white wine

3 carrots, peeled and chopped into 1-inch pieces

3 ribs celery, halved

2 yellow onions, coarsely chopped

1 small bunch parsley, thyme, basil, or tarragon sprigs

1 bay leaf

1 teaspoon crushed black peppercorns

In a large stockpot, combine the fish bones, water, and wine. If necessary, add more water to cover the bones. Bring to a boil, reduce heat to a simmer, and cook for about 30 minutes. Periodically skim off the foam and discard. Once most of the foaming action stops, add the carrots, celery, onions, herb stems, bay leaf, and peppercorns. Simmer the stock for an additional 40 minutes. Let cool and strain, pressing down on the vegetables with the back of a large spoon; discard the vegetables. Cover and refrigerate for up to 3 days or freeze for up to 3 months.

Vegetable Stock

— MAKES ABOUT 4 CUPS

2 tablespoons unsalted butter

3 carrots, peeled and chopped into
    1-inch pieces

3 ribs celery, chopped

3 cloves garlic, chopped

2 yellow onions, coarsely chopped

1 bulb fennel, chopped, including stems
    and greens

1 leek (white part only), washed and
    chopped

1 teaspoon salt

4$^{1}/_{4}$ cups water

$^{1}/_{4}$ cup dry white wine

Parsley, thyme, basil, or tarragon sprigs

1 bay leaf

1 teaspoon crushed black peppercorns

In a large saucepan or skillet, melt the
butter over medium heat. Add the
carrots, celery, garlic, onions, fennel,
leek, salt, and $^{1}/_{4}$ cup of the water.
Reduce heat and cook the vegetables,
covered, for 30 minutes, stirring frequently and making sure they do not
color. Add more water if needed. Stir
in the remaining 4 cups water, the
wine, herb stems, bay leaf, and peppercorns. Simmer for 30 minutes.
Skim off the foam and discard.
Remove from heat and let stand for
30 minutes, allowing the cooked vegetables to release their natural juices.
Strain, pressing down on the vegetables with the back of a large spoon;
discard the vegetables. Let cool, cover,
and refrigerate for up to 3 days or
freeze for up to 2 months.

Court Bouillon

— MAKES 1 GALLON

*When cooking seafood in a court bouil-
lon, or flavored vegetable broth, you
want the food to absorb the flavor of the
broth without being overcooked. After
trying many methods over the years, I
have found this one to be the most successful. The key is to turn off the heat
when you add the fish or shellfish to the
simmering liquid.*

1 gallon water

4 carrots, peeled and chopped

3 ribs celery, peeled and chopped

2 unpeeled yellow onions, trimmed and
    chopped

2 unpeeled lemons, chopped

2 bay leaves

$^{1}/_{4}$ cup pickling spice, or 1 teaspoon
    allspice, 1 teaspoon berries, 1 teaspoon
    peppercorns, 1 teaspoon cloves,
    1 teaspoon fennel seeds, 1 teaspoon
    coriander seeds, and 1 teaspoon
    cinnamon sticks

2 tablespoons salt

In a large stockpot, combine all the
ingredients. Bring to a boil, reduce
heat, and simmer, uncovered, for 30
minutes. Let cool slightly. Strain the
bouillon through a sieve, pressing
down on the vegetables with the
back of a large spoon to extract all
the flavors.

Mushroom Stock

— MAKES ABOUT 6 CUPS

*This recipe combines fresh and dried
mushrooms for an intense flavor.*

1 tablespoon olive oil

4 yellow onions, thinly sliced

$^{1}/_{2}$ teaspoon salt

1 cup Pinot Noir

$^{1}/_{4}$ cup balsamic vinegar

6 cups water

1 bulb garlic, outer papery skin
    removed, quartered

3 sprigs thyme

1 teaspoon fennel seeds, cracked
    (page 224)

1 teaspoon black peppercorns, cracked
    (page 224)

2 bay leaves

2 pounds cremini or white mushrooms,
    wiped clean and chopped

2 ounces dried porcini, morel, or
    chanterelle mushrooms, or a mixture

In a heavy 4-quart saucepan, heat the
oil over medium heat. Add the onions
and salt. Cook for 5 minutes, reduce
heat to low, and cook the onions, stirring frequently, until they caramelize
to a coffee color, 20 to 25 minutes.
Stir in the wine and vinegar; simmer
until reduced by half, about 15 minutes. Add the water, garlic, thyme, fennel, peppercorns, and bay leaves.
Simmer for 20 minutes. Add the fresh
mushrooms and simmer for an additional 15 minutes. Strain the stock
through a fine-meshed sieve, pressing
the vegetables with the back of a large
spoon; discard the vegetables. Add the
dried mushrooms to the stock and let
steep while it cools. Cover and refrigerate overnight. Strain the stock,
reserving the mushrooms to use in
soups, stews, or sauces. Freeze 1-cup
portions of the stock to use in various
recipes.

Roasted Garlic Purée

— MAKES 1 CUP

Use this garlic purée in a variety of recipes or as a delicious spread for bread.

Preheat the oven to 350°. Take 4 or 5 large garlic bulbs and press down on them with your hand to loosen the cloves from the stem. Put the unpeeled cloves in a small pan. Season with salt and freshly ground black pepper and drizzle with a little olive oil. Toss to coat the garlic cloves. Add 1/4 inch water to the bottom of the pan and cover the pan with aluminum foil.

Bake in the oven for 45 minutes, or until the cloves are soft. Remove the baked cloves from the oven and force them through a food mill or a large-holed sieve using a firm rubber spatula or wooden spoon. Store in the refrigerator for up to 4 days.

Homemade Dried Bread Crumbs

Any type of bread will work for bread crumbs, though the quality and flavor of the bread will determine the quality and flavor of the crumbs. Stale bread is preferred because it is already dry. Be creative and select a variety of bread for crumbs such as corn, garlic, semolina, or rosemary.

To prepare homemade crumbs: Preheat the oven to 275°. Remove the crust from the bread and cut the bread into 2- to 3-inch pieces. Put the bread in a jelly-roll pan and cook in the oven for 30 to 40 minutes, or until dried out without coloring. If you prefer a toasted quality to the bread crumbs, let the bread brown slightly.

Put the bread in a food processor or blender and pulse the machine until the bread is broken down into small pieces. The coarse grade of crumbs produced by a processor will work fine for most recipes. If a very fine crumb is called for, force the crumbs through a fine-meshed sieve. If you do not have a food processor, place the bread in a plastic bag and pound with a meat mallet or crush with a rolling pin.

Pastry Dough

— MAKES ONE 12-INCH DEEP-DISH DOUBLE PIE CRUST OR 2 SINGLE 12-INCH PIE OR TART CRUSTS WITH ENOUGH DOUGH LEFT OVER FOR A LATTICE

3 cups flour

1 teaspoon salt

1/2 cup vegetable shortening

1/2 cup (1 stick) chilled unsalted butter

1/4 cup ice water

1 large egg

Sift the flour and salt together into a large bowl. Using a pastry blender or 2 knives, cut in the shortening and butter until the mixture resembles coarse meal. In a small bowl, beat together the water and egg. Mix into the flour mixture until the dough comes together. On a lightly floured surface, knead the pastry 3 times to blend. Cover with plastic wrap and let rest in the refrigerator for at least 30 minutes. This pastry will keep in the refrigerator for 5 days and can be frozen for up to 3 months.

PARTIALLY BAKED CRUST

Cut the pastry in half or thirds, as needed. Fit the pastry in a pie plate or false-bottom tart pan. Pierce the bottom of the pastry with a fork. Chill in the freezer for 30 minutes.

Preheat the oven to 400°. Place parchment paper over the crust and fill with pie weights or dried beans and partially bake in the oven for 12 minutes, or until the edges begin to brown. Remove the pie weights or beans and paper and proceed according to the recipe.

CHEF'S NOTE: For a sweet pastry crust, add 3 tablespoons sugar to the flour mixture.

Whipped Cream

— MAKES ABOUT 2 CUPS

1 cup cold heavy cream

1 teaspoon sugar or honey

1/4 teaspoon vanilla extract

Chill a large, deep bowl. Pour the cream into the bowl and add the sugar or honey and vanilla. Whip by hand with a whisk or with an electric mixer until soft peaks form. The finished consistency of the whipped cream should just hang from the edge of the whisk. This consistency is good for serving with any dessert or for use as a garnish. The whipped cream is best if used immediately, but it can be refrigerated for up to 4 hours.

Roasting Bell Peppers

The technique for roasting peppers varies, depending on how soft you want the peppers to be. For example, if you are using them in a salad, you want a firmer pepper. If the peppers will be puréed or used in a sauce, they should be softer.

Use either a gas burner or gas or electric broiler. Place a pepper directly over a high gas flame or under a preheated broiler and begin roasting. The skin will begin to blacken and blister. Keep turning the pepper to ensure that all sides are evenly roasted. Note that there is a lot of retained heat after the pepper is removed from the heat, so be careful not to overcook. If you want a firm pepper, immediately run it under cold water to stop the cooking process, and peel off the skin. For a softer and more full-flavored pepper, salt the outside of the pepper and place it in a paper bag. Close the bag and let the pepper cool for about 15 minutes, then peel. The salt will help the skin release from the pepper.

Once peppers are roasted, they can be marinated in oil with salt, ground pepper, and a sprig of thyme or rosemary. Cover and refrigerate for up to 1 week. Puréed peppers can be used in soups and sauces.

Peeling and Segmenting Citrus

Use this technique for oranges, lemons, grapefruits, or limes. Using a sharp boning knife or medium paring knife, cut off both ends of the fruit down to the flesh so the fruit can sit upright on the cutting board. Begin to peel down the side of the fruit, following its natural curve and cutting down to the flesh to reveal the bright interior color. Once all of the skin and white pith are removed, place the fruit in the palm of your hand. Place a bowl under your hand to catch the fruit juice. Carefully insert the knife on one side of the white line that indicates the membrane separating the segments of the fruit and cut down to the center of the fruit. Repeat the process on the other side of the fruit membrane. The segment will release from the fruit and drop into the bowl. Repeat the process, segmenting the entire piece of fruit. Each segment should have a bright color with no membrane on it. Squeeze the empty membranes over the bowl to save the juice.

Peeling and Chopping Garlic

Select bulbs of garlic with large cloves for easier peeling with the highest yields. Place the whole garlic bulb on the counter with the stem end face up. Place your hand on the top and press down hard, separating all the cloves. Pick out the individual cloves and discard the loose outer skin.

There are several ways to remove the skin from each clove. Kitchenware stores sell rubber tubular devices that work well. Another method is to soak the garlic in warm water for 10 minutes; the loosened skins can be easily removed with a paring knife. Or, trim off the ends of each clove, place the flat side of a knife on top of each clove, and lightly tap with your fist to loosen the skin; the skins can then be easily removed.

To chop large garlic cloves, slice the clove in half lengthwise using a French chef's knife. Turn and slice again. Cut the clove crosswise as you would an onion or finely chop. Another method is to smash the individual clove carefully with the side of the knife blade. Salt the cloves lightly and continue grinding the cloves with the side of the knife until a paste is created.

Toasting and Cracking Fennel, Cumin, or Coriander Seeds

Preheat the oven to 325°. Put the desired amount of seeds in a single layer on a jelly-roll pan. Toast in the oven for 10 minutes, or until they begin to darken in color, occasionally shaking the pan so the seeds will toast evenly. Remove the seeds from the oven and pour them onto a cool pan.

To crack the seeds, use a large knife. With the wide side of the blade, press down on the seeds. To grind, put them in a spice mill and grind to a powder.

Toasting Nuts

Preheat the oven to 325°. Place the nuts on a large jelly roll pan, spreading them out so they don't touch. Toast in the oven for 20 minutes, or until lightly browned, occasionally shaking the pan so the nuts toast evenly.

If toasting **hazelnuts**, remove the nuts from the oven and wrap them in a dish towel to steam and cool them. Once they have cooled a bit, roll the hazelnuts around in the towel to remove the skins. Transfer the hazelnuts to a colander with medium holes and roll them around with your hands to knock off the remainder of the skins. As the hazelnuts are skinned, remove them from the colander.

SOURCES AND RESOURCES OF THE PACIFIC NORTHWEST

The following sources have provided products to Wildwood since our opening in 1994. Many of these purveyors sell through mail order and will ship anywhere in North America, though the availability and freshness of ingredients will vary depending on the time of year. Should you be traveling in Oregon, I highly recommend dropping by the retail sales outlets that many of these purveyors have on site. Some, like the Clear Creek Distillery, even offer guided tours of their manufacturing operations. Do call in advance, though, since their hours can vary seasonally.

I've also included a number of commodity commissions in the list. These organizations are great resources for finding out where to purchase products, and for detailed information—in the form of pamphlets, Web sites, and magazines—on the specific foodstuffs they represent.

Bob's Red Mill Natural Foods, Inc.
5209 SE International Way
Milwaukie, OR 97222
(503) 654-3215
fax (503) 653-1339
www.bobsredmill.com
e-mail: lisa@bobsredmill.com

Pacific Northwest grains, flours, cereals, and related bread products.

Cascade Mushroom Company
223 SE 3rd Avenue
Portland, OR 97214
(503) 233-5881
fax (503) 233-6898

Wild and cultivated mushrooms.

Clear Creek Distillery
Steve McCarthy, proprietor
1430 NW 23rd Avenue
Portland, OR 97210
(503) 248-9470
fax (503) 248-0490
www.clearcreekdistillery.com
e-mail: steve@clearcreekdistillery.com

Spirits, eau de vies, and brandy made from Pacific Northwest fruit products.

Columbia Empire Farms
31461 Bell Road
Sherwood, OR 97140
(503) 554-9060
fax (503) 537-9693

Hazelnuts, berries, and honey. Products are available for purchase at all Your NorthWest locations (see below) or on the Web at www.yournw.com.

Gerard & Dominique Seafood
19726 144th Avenue NE #1
Woodinville, WA 98072
(425) 488-4766
fax (425) 488-9229
www.gdseafoods.com
e-mail: g-d_seafoods@msn.com

Smoked fish and shellfish.

Harry and David Company
2518 South Pacific Highway
Medford, OR 97501
(800) 345-5655
fax (800) 648-6640
www.harryanddavid.com
e-mail: comments@harryanddavid.com

Pears and apples from the Rogue River Valley.

Hazelnut Marketing Board
21595 A-Dolores Way NE
Aurora, OR 97002-9738
(503) 678-6823
fax (503) 678-6825
www.oregonhazelnuts.org

Juniper Grove Goat Cheese
Pierre Kolisch
2024 SW 58th Street
Redmond, OR 97756
(541) 923-8353

Farmstead goat cheeses from central Oregon.

Made in Oregon
921 SW Morrison Street
Portland, OR 97205
(800) 828-9673
(503) 273-8498
fax (503) 273-8313
www.madeinoregon.com

Cedar planks and merchandise manufactured in Oregon.

Meduri Farms
2453 Ridgeway Drive SE
Turner, OR 97392
(503) 362-5196
fax (503) 362-9104

Dried Oregon fruits. Wonderful strawberries and blueberries.

Nicky Game USA
223 SE 3rd Avenue
Portland, OR 97214
(503) 234-4263
fax (503) 234-8268
www.nickyusa.citysearch.com

Farm-raised game from the Pacific Northwest.

Northwest Pear Bureau
PO Box 22026
Milwaukie, OR 97269-2026
(503) 652-9720
fax (503) 652-9721
www.usapears.com
e-mail: info@usapears.com

Ocean Beauty Seafood
301 NW 3rd Avenue
PO Box 2706
Portland, OR 97208
(503) 224-1611
fax (503)241-8786

Retail fish and shellfish.

Olympia Oyster Company
1042 Bloomfield Road SE
Shelton, WA 98584
(360) 426-3354
fax (360) 427-0122

Olympia oysters.

Oregon Dungeness Crab Commission
964 Central Avenue
PO Box 1160
Coos Bay, OR 97420
(541) 267-5810
fax (541) 267-5772
www.ucinet.com/~dcrab/
e-mail: dcrab@ucinet.com

Oregon Raspberry, Blackberry, and
   Strawberry Commissions
712 NW 4th Street
Corvallis, OR 97330
(541) 758-4043
fax (541) 758-4553
Raspberry & Blackberry Commission:
   www.oregon-berries.com
Strawberry Commission:
   www.oregon-strawberries.org

Oregon Salmon Commission
PO Box 983
Lincoln City, OR 97367
(541) 994-2647
fax (541) 994-2647
e-mail: njf@class.orednet.org

Oregon Sweet Cherry Commission
PO Box 5506
Salem, OR 97304
(503) 585-7716
fax (503) 585-7733

Oregon Wine Advisory Board
1200 Naito Parkway, Suite 400
Portland, OR 97209
(503) 228-8336
fax (503) 228-8337
www.oregonwine.org
e-mail: owab@teleport.com

*Information on Oregon wines and
Oregon wine country.*

Pacific Seafood
15501 SE Piazza
PO Box 97
Clackamas, OR 97015
(503) 657-1101
fax (503) 655-8166
www.pacseafood.com

Retail fish and shellfish.

Rogue River Valley Creamery
311 North Front
Central Point, OR 97502
(541) 664-2233
fax (541) 664-0952

Oregon blue cheese.

Sweet Oregon Apple Company
6393 NW Cornelius Pass
Hillsboro, OR 97124
(503) 531-2501
fax (503) 531-4065

Numerous varieties of Oregon apple juices.

Taylor Shellfish Farms
Retail outlet
130 Lynch Road SE
Shelton, WA 98584
(360) 426-6178
fax (360) 427-0327
www.taylorshellfish.com
e-mail: taylor@olywa.net

Clams, oysters, and mussels.

Tillamook Creamery
4175 Highway 101 North
PO Box 313
Tillamook, OR 97141
(800) 542-7290
fax (503) 815-1305
www.tillamookcheese.com

*Oregon's largest creamery with a wide variety
of cow's milk cheeses.*

Walla Walla Onion Commission
29 East Sumach Street
Walla Walla, WA 99362
(509) 525-1031
fax (509) 522-2038
www.home.bmi.net/onions/
e-mail: onions@bmi.net

Your NorthWest, Dundee:
110 SW 7th St.
Dundee, OR 97115
(503) 554-8101

Your NorthWest, Portland:
Clackamas Town Center
12000 NE 82nd Ave.
Portland, OR 97266
(503) 653-1717

Your NorthWest, Tigard:
Washington Square Mall
9767 SW Washington Square Road
Tigard, OR 97223
(503) 598-8955

*A wide range of Pacific Northwest products,
including jams, berries, syrups, honey, and nuts
from Columbia Empire Farms.*

INDEX